Certificate in Corporate Finance

Corporate Finance Regulation

Edition 7, January 2016

This learning manual relates to syllabus
version 11.0 and will cover examinations from
11 April 2016 to 10 April 2017

APPROVED WORKBOOK

Welcome to the Chartered Institute for Securities & Investment's Corporate Finance Regulation study material.

This workbook has been written to prepare you for the Chartered Institute for Securities & Investment's Corporate Finance Regulation examination.

Published by:
Chartered Institute for Securities & Investment
© Chartered Institute for Securities & Investment 2016
8 Eastcheap
London
EC3M 1AE
Tel: +44 20 7645 0600
Fax: +44 20 7645 0601

Email: customersupport@cisi.org
www.cisi.org/qualifications

Author:
Stephen Holt, Chartered MCSI

Reviewers:
Jon Beckett, Chartered MCSI
Nick Harriss, Chartered FCSI

This is an educational manual only and the Chartered Institute for Securities & Investment accepts no responsibility for persons undertaking trading or investments in whatever form.

While every effort has been made to ensure its accuracy, no responsibility for loss occasioned to any person acting or refraining from action as a result of any material in this publication can be accepted by the publisher or authors.

A learning map, which contains the full syllabus, appears at the end of this manual. The syllabus can also be viewed on cisi.org and is also available by contacting the Customer Support Centre on +44 20 7645 0777. Please note that the examination is based upon the syllabus. Candidates are reminded to check the Candidate Updates area details (cisi.org/candidateupdate) on a regular basis for updates as a result of industry change(s) that could affect their examination.

The questions contained in this manual are designed as an aid to revision of different areas of the syllabus and to help you consolidate your learning chapter by chapter.

Learning manual version: 7.2 (January 2016)

Learning and Professional Development with the CISI

The Chartered Institute for Securities & Investment is the leading professional body for those who work in, or aspire to work in, the investment sector, and we are passionately committed to enhancing knowledge, skills and integrity – the three pillars of professionalism at the heart of our Chartered body.

CISI examinations are used extensively by firms to meet the requirements of government regulators. Besides the regulators in the UK, where the CISI head office is based, CISI examinations are recognised by a wide range of governments and their regulators, from Singapore to Dubai and the US. Around 50,000 examinations are taken each year, and it is compulsory for candidates to use CISI learning manuals to prepare for CISI examinations so that they have the best chance of success. Our learning manuals are normally revised every year by experts who themselves work in the industry and also by our Accredited Training Partners, who offer training and elearning to help prepare candidates for the examinations. Information for candidates is also posted on a special area of our website: cisi.org/candidateupdate.

This learning manual not only provides a thorough preparation for the examination it refers to, it is also a valuable desktop reference for practitioners, and studying from it counts towards your Continuing Professional Development (CPD). Mock examination papers, for most of our titles, will be made available on our website, as an additional revision tool.

CISI examination candidates are automatically registered, without additional charge, as student members for one year (should they not be members of the CISI already), and this enables you to use a vast range of online resources, including CISI TV, free of any additional charge. The CISI has more than 40,000 members, and nearly half of them have already completed relevant qualifications and transferred to a core membership grade. You will find more information about the next steps for this at the end of this manual.

With best wishes for your studies.

Lydia Romero, Global Director of Learning

It is estimated that this manual will require approximately 80 hours of study time.

What next?

See the back of this book for details of CISI membership.

Need more support to pass your exam?

See our section on Accredited Training Partners.

Want to leave feedback?

Please email your comments to learningresources@cisi.org

Chapter One
The Regulatory Environment in the UK

This syllabus area will provide approximately 20 of the 50 examination questions

1.   The Regulatory Infrastructure

1.1   The European Regulatory Landscape

Learning Objective

1.1.1   Understand the European context of financial services regulation (ie, the role of European institutions, in particular the European Securities and Markets Authority (ESMA), and regulations/directives)

A single market in financial services has long been an objective of the European Union (EU). In a single market, financial institutions authorised to provide financial services in one member state can provide the same services throughout the EU, competing on a level playing field within a consistent regulatory environment. Such a single market in financial services will: *'act as a catalyst for economic growth across all sectors of the economy, boost productivity and provide lower cost and better quality financial products for consumers, and enterprises'*.

In recent years, EU financial markets – and transactions across borders within the EU – have grown in size and improved in efficiency, because of the removal of barriers, greater competition promoted by global deregulation and the development of new technology.

However, the integration of financial markets in the EU has progressed much further and faster in wholesale than in retail financial services, with the latter still segmented largely on national lines. Moreover, while many barriers have been removed, those that remain appear more prominent now that the majority of EU countries share a single currency.

1.1.1   The European Union (EU) Regulatory Process

The main initiative for the development of the single market in financial services was the Financial Services Action Plan (FSAP) which was endorsed by the Lisbon European Council in March 2000. The FSAP consisted of a set of 42 measures intended to fill gaps and remove remaining barriers in order to provide a legal and regulatory environment that supported the integration of EU financial markets. Its specific objectives were to:

- create a single EU wholesale market
- achieve open and secure retail markets, and
- create state-of-the-art prudential rules and structures of supervision.

Some of the FSAP measures took the form of **EU directives**, which apply directly in all member states; these have to be transposed into the law of each member state. Of these, some replaced earlier directives (eg, on investment services), which were out of date, while others recast earlier proposals (eg, on takeover bids) which failed to gain acceptance. Some measures on the FSAP list (eg, on mutual funds) were already under negotiation when the FSAP was launched; others have been added to the list since it was launched.

An **EU regulation** is a legislative act of the EU that becomes immediately enforceable in law in all member states simultaneously. Regulations can be distinguished from directives, in that they do not need to be transposed into national law.

The normal procedure for introducing legislative measures (ie, regulations and directives) in the FSAP is that they are first proposed by the European Commission (EC) and then adopted by **co-decision**, under which the Council of Ministers of the Member States and the European Parliament both need to consider, amend and agree on the final content of each legislative proposal. Both regulations and directives have to be published in the official journal and come into force on a specified date. Member states are given a period (usually of 18 months) to implement directives, by transposing the provisions into their national law.

The main FSAP and FSAP-related measures are the following:

- Market Abuse Directive (MAD)
- Prospectus Directive
- Markets in Financial Instruments Directive (MiFID) (which replaced the Investment Services Directive (ISD) in 2007)
- Transparency Directive
- Takeover Directive
- Settlement Finality Directive
- Collateral Directive
- Fair Value Accounting Directive
- Accounting Modernisation Directive
- Company Law Directive
- Insurance Mediation Directive
- Distance Marketing Directive
- Pension Funds Directive
- E-Money Directive
- Electronic Commerce Directive
- Second (and subsequently the Third) Money Laundering Directive
- Financial Conglomerates Directive
- Capital Requirements Directive
- Taxation of Savings Income Directive
- Undertakings for the Collective Investment of Transferable Securities (UCITS)
- Packaged Retail and Insurance-based Investment Product (PRIIP)
- European Market Infrastructure Regulation (EMIR).

1.1.2 The EU Regulatory Bodies

At the start of the financial crisis in 2008, concern was expressed at EU level about the fact that, whilst financial institutions operated at an international level, their regulatory supervision operated at a national level and was uneven and unco-ordinated. The De Larosiere group was appointed to consider what action was needed, and concluded that there was a need for ensuring co-ordination between supervisors of the same cross-border institution, and for ensuring that co-ordinated decision-making could take place in emergency situations. In September 2010, the European Parliament voted through a new supervisory framework for financial regulation in Europe, which came into force in January 2011.

Firstly, the **European Systemic Risk Board (ESRB)** was established on 1 January 2011 and is the new body with responsibility for the macro-prudential oversight of the financial system within the EU.

The regulation of financial services across Europe is now overseen by three European Supervisory Authorities (ESAs). These are:

- The **European Securities and Markets Authority (ESMA)**
- The **European Banking Authority (EBA)**, and
- The **European Insurance and Occupational Pensions Authority (EIOPA)**.

Their role is to create a single EU rule book, by developing draft technical standards, to be adopted by the Commission as EU law, and issuing guidance and recommendations with which national supervisors (such as the Financial Conduct Authority (FCA)) and firms must make every attempt to comply. They also have the power to investigate situations where they believe that a national supervisory authority is failing to apply EU law, or appears to be in breach of EU law.

The ESAs work with the newly established European Systemic Risk Board (ESRB) to ensure financial stability and to strengthen and enhance the EU supervisory framework. They will improve co-ordination between national supervisory authorities, such as the FCA, and raise standards of national supervision across the EU.

European Securities and Markets Authority (ESMA)

The ESMA is an independent EU authority, which aims to safeguard the stability of the EU financial system by ensuring the integrity, transparency, efficiency and orderly functioning of securities markets, as well as enhancing investor protection. It fosters supervisory convergence amongst national securities regulators (such as the FCA) and across financial sectors, working closely with the other ESAs. ESMA took over the role of a predecessor body, the Committee of European Securities Regulators (CESR), but has additional powers including:

- the ability to draft technical standards that are legally binding in EU member states
- the ability to launch a fast-track procedure to ensure consistent application of EU law
- new powers in resolving disagreements between national authorities
- additional responsibilities for consumer protection (including the ability to prohibit financial products that threaten financial stability or the orderly functioning of financial markets for a period of three months)
- emergency powers
- participating in colleges of supervisors and on-site inspections
- monitoring systemic risk of cross-border financial institutions
- a new supervisory role (in particular for direct supervision of credit rating agencies)
- the ability to enter into administrative arrangements with supervisory authorities, international organisations and the administrations of third countries.

ESMA's work on securities legislation, and in particular its role within the Lamfalussy Process (described in Section 1.1.3), contributes to the development of a single rulebook in Europe. This serves two purposes:

1. it ensures the consistent treatment of investors across the EU, enabling an adequate level of protection of investors through effective regulation and supervision
2. it promotes equal conditions of competition for financial service providers.

As part of its role in standard setting and reducing the scope of regulatory arbitrage, ESMA strengthens international supervisory co-operation. Where requested in European law, ESMA undertakes the supervision of certain entities with pan-European reach. At present this is limited to the direct supervision of credit rating agencies.

Finally, ESMA also contributes to the financial stability of the EU, in the short-, medium- and long-term, through its contribution to the work of the ESRB, which identifies potential risks to the financial system and provides advice to diminish possible threats to the financial stability of the EU.

ESMA had an extension of its powers in 2013. Its objectives and priorities are based on three key elements:

New and revised legislation

The introduction of new, and the overhaul of existing, legislation will be a key challenge for ESMA. Continued revision of the Markets in Financial Instruments Directive (which will be superseded by a revised directive and a new regulation, MiFID 2 and MiFIR respectively), and of the revision of the Market Abuse Directive (a new regulation – MAR – and a new directive – MAD 2). These new legislative texts form part of the key deliverables initiated by the EU Institutions in response to the financial crisis.

Other key texts are also planned for:

- a new Credit Rating Agencies Regulation (CRA III)
- the revision of the Transparency Directive, and
- the Regulations on Venture Capital (VC) and Social Entrepreneurship Funds (SEFs).

CSD Regulation

In order to build a single rulebook for Europe, ESMA will develop technical standards, guidelines and advice. ESMA's focus goes beyond establishing new regulation though.

At the same time, ESMA will promote supervisory convergence. Since 2013, ESMA has been fully exercising all its powers to drive greater convergence of national supervisory activity and implementation of EU regulation on the ground.

Following several years of crisis, ESMA's work will aim to support the restoration of confidence in Europe's financial markets.

1.1.3 The Lamfalussy Process

Given the scale of the task involved in implementing the FSAP, the European Council of Finance Ministers (ECOFIN) decided in July 2000, as its top priority, to complete a single EU capital market by 2003.

The Lamfalussy process is designed to improve the quality and effectiveness of EU financial services legislation by:

- differentiating between framework legislation and technical implementing measures, so that changes in technology and market practice can readily be accommodated
- consulting market participants more fully as it is drawn up, and
- creating an EU network of national regulatory authorities to ensure consistent and equivalent transposition of legislation at Levels 1 and 2.

The Lamfalussy process for developing regulation in securities markets has four levels:

- **Level 1 – legislative acts** – framework legislation is proposed by the Commission and adopted by the Council and Parliament, generally under the ordinary legislative procedure, otherwise through the special legislative procedures. This legislation (directive or regulation) specifies in individual articles whether legislative power is delegated to the Commission to adopt Level 2 measures.
- **Level 2 – implementing measures** – secondary legislation is drafted and adopted by the Commission in line with the delegation of legislative competence in the Level 1 text. The Commission does so with the assistance of four specialist Level 2 committees of finance ministry experts. These are the European Banking Committee (EBC), the European Securities Committee (ESC), the European Insurance and Occupational Pensions Committee (EIOPC) and the European Financial Conglomerates Committee (EFCC). The Commission submits its draft measure to the relevant committee for discussion and an opinion.

The Commission will often seek advice from the relevant ESA on implementing measures, which it then uses as it sees fit.

- **Level 3 – facilitating convergence of regulatory practice** – The ESAs (EBA, ESMA and EIOPA) advise the Commission when they prepare detailed Level 2 requirements. This may include drafting binding technical standards in certain areas. Extensive consultation between the ESAs and providers/users of financial services takes place, where time permits. The ESAs are also empowered to adopt guidance, which is to be treated on a comply-or-explain basis by national supervisors. The ESAs are required to consult and undertake cost-benefit analysis on this **where appropriate**.
- **Level 4 – enforcement** – the Commission, as the guardian of the treaties, is responsible for ensuring that directives are properly transposed and that EU legal requirements are then applied, pursuing enforcement action where required. The Commission has tended to concentrate its resources on the first of these. The ESAs provide an additional resource and opportunity to investigate alleged breaches of EU law. In the event that a breach is ascertained, the ESA may recommend a course of action to the competent authority concerned. If the competent authority fails to respond, the matter may be escalated. This may lead to the Commission issuing a formal opinion and, if certain conditions are met, a decision addressed to an individual financial institution.

1.1.4 The Work of the Financial Conduct Authority (FCA)

From 1 April 2013, the Financial Conduct Authority (FCA) became the UK national regulator responsible for regulating conduct in retail and wholesale markets (including both exchange-operated markets and over-the-counter (OTC) dealing), supervising the trading infrastructure that supports those markets, and prudential regulation for those firms not prudentially regulated by the Prudential Regulation Authority (PRA). The FCA has continued the work of its predecessor, the Financial Services Authority (FSA), and actively engages with the EU and devotes significant resource to working with European institutions and its fellow EU regulators. It undertakes this approach because:

- deepening the single market in financial services has involved a comprehensive legislative programme which must then be implemented and applied in the UK, and
- the activities of internationally active firms require regulators to enhance their levels of co-operation and co-ordination if regulatory duplication is to be avoided and risks are to be better identified, prioritised and mitigated.

Since UK financial services regulation has to give effect to European law, active engagement with Europe is essential. Indeed, around 70% of the FCA's policymaking effort is driven by European initiatives, including the FSAP Regulations and Directives.

1.1.5 The FCA's Priorities for Work in the EU and the International Arena

The need for enhanced regulatory co-operation and co-ordination is particularly important in Europe because of the considerable level of integration in the wholesale market and because the European Community's single market legislation implies and requires high levels of co-operation and co-ordination. Within Europe, the regulator of a financial services group, the regulator of its subsidiaries and branches, and regulators in the countries where its customers are based each have areas of exclusive responsibility and control, as well as areas where their responsibilities overlap.

The result is that there are some areas where the home regulator delivers regulation, eg, in the areas of capital and depositor and investor compensation schemes; some areas where responsibility is shared, eg, liquidity; and some where the responsibility is mainly the host regulator's, eg, disclosure.

Enhanced regulatory co-operation is needed to ensure that regulators with their varying responsibilities are properly informed about relevant risks, that duplication of regulatory activities is avoided, that the oversight of internationally active firms is improved and that a consistent approach to common Community requirements is adopted.

The design of the FCA is framed in an EU and international context. This is particularly important given the growing influence of EU legislation and standards on UK policy-making and supervisory practices. In both consumer protection and securities and markets issues, the FCA aims to engage early and effectively in EU and international negotiations to influence the outcomes in ways that are consistent with its objectives and philosophy.

1.1.6 Better Regulation

The FCA views better regulation in the EU as a strategic priority. It is committed to better regulation principles in the UK context and is also committed to promoting these in the EU. By better regulation the FCA means:

- introducing new regulation only if there is a demonstrable market failure and where the cost of regulation can be shown to be less than that of allowing the market failure to persist; and integrating the economic assessment of the likely effects of legislative proposals into the policy-making process
- consulting at all stages in the introduction of new regulation
- always considering non-regulatory solutions such as competition or codes of conduct
- considering one-off regulatory interventions (such as thematic or catalytic work) rather than introducing new formal regulations, and
- subsequent evaluation.

Legislation is often not the best tool to use even if market failures can be shown to exist. This is because legislation may be:

- inflexible and difficult to amend or repeal if it fails to have the intended results
- subject to political special pleading, and
- disproportionate and costly to implement if firms have to update systems to comply with new requirements.

It therefore makes sense, if feasible, to tackle obstacles to the single market by considering first whether non-legislative action can better address market failures. In particular, there may well be a role for EU and national competition authorities to use their powers to attack anti-competitive practices, abuses of dominant positions or barriers to entry. In other areas, codes of conduct may have a useful role to play. Non-legislative approaches have recently been followed in the areas of clearing and settlement and enquiries into payments and business insurance.

European law takes priority over domestic law. Therefore, it is critical that European legislation does not undermine the FCA's ability to continue with its policy of moving to a more principles-based approach, if it is appropriate to do so. Regulatory experience has been that ever more detailed and prescriptive rules tend to be ineffective at preventing misconduct, do not allow for innovation and development in the market, and tend to encourage staff to comply with the letter of the rule but ignore what the rule is designed to achieve. In the FCA's view, it is important that high standards are viewed as everyone's business, with a particular emphasis on senior management responsibility.

Much European legislation is in the form of directives. These express the objective to be achieved, but leave member states to determine the manner and form, so that in essence they are principles-based. However, there has been a tendency for some directives to contain increasing levels of detail and it will be important to ensure that future legislation remains focused on objectives, is not excessively detailed, and does not prescribe ways in which directive objectives are to be met.

1.2 The Financial Services and Markets Act (FSMA) 2000

Learning Objective

1.1.2 Know the regulatory infrastructure generated by the Financial Services and Markets Act (FSMA) 2000 and the Financial Services Act 2012 and the status and relationship between Her Majesty's Treasury (HMT), the Bank of England (BoE), the Financial Policy Committee (FPC), the Prudential Regulation Authority (PRA) and the Financial Conduct Authority (FCA) and between the FCA and the Recognised Investment Exchanges (RIEs), Recognised Overseas Investment Exchanges (ROIEs), Designated Investment Exchanges (DIEs), Recognised Clearing Houses (RCHs), Designated Professional Bodies (DPBs), Regulated Markets and Multilateral Trading Facilities (MTFs)

The Financial Services and Markets Act (FSMA) 2000, which came into effect on 30 November 2001, introduced a new regime for the regulation of the financial services industry in the UK, replacing a number of self-regulatory organisations (SROs) with a single statutory regulator, the Financial Services Authority (FSA). The FSA had broad responsibility for both the **prudential** and the **conduct of business** regulation of firms within the financial services industry. The FSA shared responsibility with the Bank of England (BoE) and Her Majesty's Treasury (HMT) under a tripartite system of financial oversight. The failure of Northern Rock and the financial crisis starting in 2008, with the consequential perceived regulatory failings, signalled the start of the end of this system and the FSA subsequently introduced a more intrusive, outcomes-based approach to regulation, pending a more formal review of the regulatory system. In June 2010, the Chancellor of the Exchequer announced this review and the need for changes to the UK financial regulatory structure and how firms would be regulated going forward. The outcome of this review was the commencement of the Financial Services Act 2012 (effective 1 April 2013) which created three new bodies:

- The Financial Policy Committee (FPC).
- The Financial Conduct Authority (FCA).
- The Prudential Regulation Authority (PRA).

1.2.1 The Financial Policy Committee (FPC)

The BoE has the responsibility for financial stability, based on a statutory objective to protect and enhance the stability of the financial system of the UK. In support of this objective, the FPC is charged with identifying, monitoring and taking action to remove or reduce systemic risks. The FPC has the power to make recommendations and give directions to the PRA and the FCA on specific actions that should be taken in order to achieve the FPC's objectives. The BoE also has responsibility for the supervision of central counterparties and securities settlement systems, playing an increased role in co-ordinating financial sector resilience.

1.2.2 The Financial Conduct Authority (FCA)

The FCA is a separate institution and is responsible for ensuring that relevant markets function well, and for the conduct regulation of all financial services firms. It is also responsible for the prudential regulation of those financial services firms not supervised by the PRA, for example, asset managers.

Firms that are **dual-regulated**, such as banks, insurers and major investment firms are supervised by two independent groups for prudential and conduct matters. These groups work to different objectives and act separately with firms but co-ordinate internally to share information and data. The FCA has a single strategic objective *'to ensure that relevant markets function well'* and three operational objectives, which are to:

- secure an appropriate degree of protection for consumers
- protect and enhance the integrity of the UK financial system, and
- promote effective competition protecting the interests of consumers.

The FSMA (as amended by the Financial Services Act 2012) gives the FCA and the PRA certain duties and objectives in relation to their roles as financial services regulators and establishes the legal powers to enable them to fulfil their roles.

- Broadly, the FCA is responsible for ensuring that financial markets work well, so that consumers get a fair deal, whilst the focus of the PRA is on stability – the safety and soundness of deposit-taking firms, insurers and systemically important investment firms.
- The regulators' powers are over firms carrying on regulated activities, the exchanges that are used by many of those firms, and individuals carrying out particular functions for firms. In some cases, they also extend to those not currently authorised, for example, formerly authorised firms, or firms which ought to have had authorisation, but which have been doing business without it.
- The FCA and the PRA are funded entirely from fees paid by the firms which they regulate.
- The FCA is accountable to the government on how it carries out its functions, via HMT; the PRA is a unit of the BoE, which in turn is accountable to Parliament.

New Powers provided to the FCA under the Financial Services Act 2012

Temporary Product Intervention

The FCA stated (in its publication *Journey to the FCA*, published October 2012) that it will intervene earlier, than the previous regulator, and have a lower risk tolerance than the FSA in order to ensure an appropriate degree of consumer protection.

The Financial Services Act 2012 provides the FCA with temporary rules – for up to a period of 12-months, to prohibit or ban any product that it considers is causing, or will cause consumer protection problems.

The FCA's style of supervision means that it will intervene earlier in a product's lifespan and seek to address root causes or problems for consumers. Previous experience has taught the regulator that products designed for specific markets/consumers are routinely sold outside it. Therefore, the FCA will intervene directly by making product intervention rules to prevent harm to consumers – for example, by restricting the use of specified product features or the promotion of particular product types to some or all consumers.

The key to the FCA using the new powers is consumer protection.

The FCA has stated the instances when it feels that it will/could use the temporary product intervention rules. They are:

- Products being sold outside their target market or being inappropriately targeted.

- Products that would be acceptable but for the inclusion or exclusion of particular features.
- Products where there is a significant incentive for inappropriate or indiscriminate targeting of consumers.
- Markets where competitive pressure alone will not address concerns about a product, eg, where competition focuses on irrelevant features or exploits systemic consumer weaknesses such that market-based solutions will not address the problem.
- Products which may bring about significant detriment as result of being inappropriately targeted.
- In some particularly serious cases, a product may be considered inherently flawed, eg, a product that has such disadvantageous features that the majority of consumers, or specified types of consumer, are unlikely to benefit.

The FCA is subject to the wider EU legislative framework, and this has implications for firms which practise cross-border business. When a product provider is domiciled overseas, FCA rules do not apply to the development of potentially harmful products by such firms. However, if products from overseas providers are sold by intermediaries based in the UK, they are subject to regulatory action by the FCA.

Financial Promotions

The FCA is permitted to ban misleading financial promotions, meaning that financial promotions can be removed immediately from the market or prevented from being used in the first place without having to go through the lengthy enforcement process.

The use of this new power is determined by the specific promotion and not used against a firm as a whole. It can be used on its own or before the FCA takes enforcement action against a firm.

This new approach will work separately from existing disciplinary powers – which the FCA can and will use when firms fail to comply with the rules and their overall systems and approach are poor.

The FCA will give a direction to an authorised firm to remove its own financial promotion or one it approves on behalf of an unauthorised firm, setting out the reasons for banning it. The next step is for firms to make representations to the FCA if they think that it is making the wrong decision.

The FCA will decide whether to confirm, amend or revoke their direction. If it is confirmed, they will publish it – along with a copy of the promotion and the reasons behind their decision.

Enforcement/Disciplinary Action

The FCA is permitted to announce publicly that it has begun disciplinary action against a firm or individual. It can publish details of a warning notice proposing disciplinary action, to signal the start of formal enforcement proceedings. However, the FCA has to consult with the recipient of the warning notice before publishing the details.

FCA Duties and Objectives

The FCA has duties and objectives in relation to its role as regulator and, to enable the effective discharge of this, its power includes:

- **Authorisation** – the process of assessing applications from firms wishing to carry on regulated activities, and determining whether to permit them to do so.

- **Supervision** – the process of monitoring firms' activities, on an ongoing basis, to ensure that they continue to meet the FCA's authorisation requirements and that they comply with the Handbook rules and other obligations.
- **Discipline and sanctions** – to enable the FCA to enforce its rules, by punishing or limiting the activities of firms which fail to comply.
- **Enforcement** – the FCA's approach is to achieve credible deterrence in respect of the FSMA, using enforcement strategy as a tool to change behaviour in the industry. It focuses on cases which it thinks can make a real difference to consumers and markets.

These regulatory powers extend over firms carrying on regulated activities, the exchanges that are used by many of those firms, and individuals carrying out particular functions for firms. In some cases, they also extend to those not currently authorised, eg, formerly authorised firms, or firms which ought to have had authorisation but which have been doing business without it.

The FSMA requires the FCA to make rules in a number of areas. These rules, contained in the FCA Handbook, are discussed later in this workbook.

From the FCA 2015–16 Business Plan:

'As part of the new FCA strategy, we have shifted the emphasis of some of our work to be more markets-focused, looking broadly across the sectors we regulate. We will conduct competition market studies, looking at the operation of the markets we regulate, and deciding whether interventions are needed if those markets are not working in the interests of consumers.

We have ongoing work from 2014–15 that will continue or report back on later this year. We also have a programme of new market study and thematic work for 2015–16. In line with our new strategy and priorities, we will focus on delivering fewer, more in-depth pieces of work. We will provide updates on our programme during the course of the year, as we complete preliminary work and prioritise interventions.

In line with our key priorities for 2015–16, some of the significant work we plan includes our market study on investment banking and a thematic review of conflicts of interest in dark pools. We will also explore staff remuneration and incentives as well as debt collection practices, we plan a review of sales practices and how firms support consumers to make the right choices.'

1.2.3   The Prudential Regulation Authority (PRA)

The PRA is part of the BoE and responsible for the prudential regulation of banks, building societies and credit unions (collectively **deposit takers**), insurers and major investment firms. It shares the same regulatory processes as the FCA with regard to authorisation, supervision, enforcement and discipline, and makes rules for the firms that it regulates. As prudential regulator, the PRA promotes the safety and soundness of these firms, seeking to minimise the adverse effects that they can have on the stability of the UK financial system, and contributes to ensuring that insurance policyholders are appropriately protected. The PRA's objective to promote safety and soundness and the BoE's financial stability objective are complementary. The PRA, as part of the BoE, with close links to the FPC, allows the authorities to combine firm-specific supervision with work to protect and enhance the resilience of the financial system as a whole. The PRA co-operates closely with the rest of the BoE on the oversight of financial market infrastructure and works with the BoE's special resolution unit (SRU), which plans for and implements resolutions for failing UK banks and building societies on resolution and operational resilience. The PRA also co-operates closely with the FCA. The key principle underlying this co-operation is that each authority should focus on the key risks to its own objectives, while being aware of the potential for concerns of the other. The separate mandates of the PRA and FCA for prudential and for conduct regulation allows both regulators to apply more focus to their respective areas than under the former tripartite approach. Reflecting the international nature of the banking and insurance industries, the PRA has an active role with its counterparts globally and in the EU, assisting in developing and implementing prudential standards, and in supervising firms with international operations.

1.2.4 Her Majesty's Treasury (HMT)

HM Treasury, sometimes referred to as the Exchequer, or more informally the Treasury, is the department responsible for developing and executing the UK government's public finance policy and economic policies. HMT, to whom the FCA directly reports, is responsible for financial services in the UK. The FCA is accountable to HMT and through it to Parliament, although it is operationally independent of it.

Firstly, the Treasury appoints the FCA's board and chairman and has the power to dismiss members of the board.

Secondly, the FCA is required to submit a report to the Treasury at least once a year, detailing matters such as the way in which it has discharged its functions, the extent to which its statutory objectives have been met and any other matters the Treasury may direct. This report is accompanied by a report from the FCA's non-executive directors and is laid before Parliament.

Thirdly, the Treasury has the power to commission reviews and inquiries into aspects of the FCA's operations. Such reviews are conducted by an independent party, and are restricted to considering the economy, efficiency and effectiveness with which the FCA has used its resources in discharging its functions. Such inquiries may relate to specific, exceptional events occurring within the FCA's range of regulatory responsibilities.

1.2.5 The Bank of England (BoE)

The BoE performs all the functions of a central bank. The most important of these are maintaining price stability and supporting the economic policies of the Government, thus promoting economic growth. There are two main areas which are tackled by the BoE to ensure it carries out these functions efficiently:

- **Monetary stability.** Stable prices and confidence in the currency are the two main criteria for monetary stability. Stable prices are maintained by making sure price increases meet the Government's inflation target. The BoE aims to meet this target by adjusting the base interest rate which is decided by the Monetary Policy Committee (MPC). Maintaining financial stability involves protecting against threats to the whole financial system. Threats are detected by the BoE's surveillance and market intelligence functions. The threats are then dealt with through financial and other operations, both at home and abroad. In exceptional circumstances, the BoE may act as the lender of last resort by extending credit when no other institution will.
- **Financial stability** entails detecting and reducing threats to the financial system as a whole. It is in the area of financial stability that the FPC and the PRA operate.

In this respect and the relevance of financial stability, the PRA is responsible for promoting the safety and soundness of banks and other deposit-taking firms (building societies and credit unions), insurers and systemically important investment firms. The PRA works closely with the FPC at the BoE.

1.2.6 Recognised Investment Exchanges (RIEs) and Recognised Overseas Investment Exchanges (ROIEs)

Since a large proportion of trades in financial instruments are carried out through established investment exchanges, such as the London Stock Exchange (LSE), the FCA has the responsibility of recognising and supervising them. That said, the FSMA (OTC derivatives, central counterparties and trade repositories) (No. 2) regulations 2013, following FSA consultation, noted that recognised investment exchanges (RIEs) and recognised clearing houses (RCHs) have an exemption under Section 285 of the Act, permitting them to carry on certain activities which would otherwise require authorisation under Part 4A of the Act. This covers an exchange's business as an investment exchange and services designed to facilitate the provision of clearing services by another person, to reflect the extension of the S.166 power for the FCA to cover RIEs.

Any body corporate or unincorporated association, may apply to the FCA for an order declaring it to be an RIE. The FCA will seek to establish whether the applicant is fit and proper to operate as an exchange – including whether it has sufficient financial resources to carry out its activities properly. The applicant must be willing and able to share information with the FCA, and to promote and maintain high standards of integrity and fair dealing, including laying down rules for activities on the exchange. It must record, monitor and enforce compliance with these rules.

Once recognised, these exchanges are subject to supervision and oversight by the FCA. Being granted recognised status replaces the requirement to be an authorised person to conduct financial services business.

RIEs may be UK, or overseas-based; in the latter case, they are often referred to as recognised overseas investment exchanges (ROIEs).

At the time of writing, there are eight RIEs based in the UK, offering membership and access to their market to UK firms:

1. **London Stock Exchange PLC (LSE)** – this is the largest formal market for securities in the UK. It facilitates deals in shares, bonds and some derivatives (eg, those that take the form of covered warrants).
2. **LIFFE Administration and Management** – this is the largest derivatives exchange in the UK, trading a wide range of instruments, including equity futures and options and some commodity products.
3. **ICE Futures Europe (formerly known as the International Petroleum Exchange (IPE))** – this exchange is owned by a company listed on the New York Stock Exchange (NYSE), called InterContinental Exchange – hence ICE. It deals in futures for energy products, such as crude oil and gas, and also in such new instruments as carbon emission allowances.
4. **London Metal Exchange Ltd (LME)** – this exchange provides trading in a variety of futures and options on base metals and some plastics.
5. **ICAP Securities & Derivatives Exchange Ltd (ISDX) (formerly PLUS Stock Exchange)** – this market offers trading and listing facilities for small and mid-capitalisation companies.
6. **BATS Trading Ltd** – established in 2008 and previously an MTF, this exchange, authorised as of May 2013, is a low latency, low-cost alternative to exchange-traded equities and exchange-traded funds (ETFs) that are listed on primary exchanges, such as the LSE.
7. **CME Europe Ltd** – a London-based, FCA-supervised derivatives exchange. As a wholly-owned subsidiary of CME Group, CME Europe leverages the operations and expertise of the world's largest derivatives marketplace and is designed to meet evolving regional needs and trading practices.

8. **Euronext UK Markets Ltd** – a wholly-owned subsidiary of Intercontinental Exchange (NYSE: ICE), it operates Euronext's London market, the aim of which is to attract international issuers looking to list in the UK capital while enjoying access to Euronext's regulated, liquid and transparent markets.

ROIEs, in contrast, are based outside the UK, but carry on regulated activities within the UK (eg, by offering electronic trading facilities to members in this country) and to this extent are regulated and supervised by the FCA. They do not have physical UK operations (except for some support representation), so they are necessarily electronic marketplaces. At the time of writing, there were eight ROIEs. They include the National Association of Securities Dealers Automated Quotations (NASDAQ), established in the US, and the Australian Securities Exchange (ASX), established in Australia.

1.2.7 Designated Investment Exchanges (DIEs)

DIEs are, like ROIEs, overseas-based, but unlike ROIEs they do not offer membership and access to participants based in the UK and therefore need not be regulated directly by the FCA. Instead, the designated status indicates that the exchange is regulated and supervised to standards that the FCA believes meet certain criteria, in terms of protection for investors dealing on it. Examples of DIEs are the NYSE and the Minneapolis Grain Exchange. At the time of publication (January 2016) there are 30 DIEs.

1.2.8 Recognised Clearing Houses (RCHs)

In a similar fashion, clearing houses can be recognised to become RCHs. Clearing houses facilitate the clearing and, sometimes, the settlement of trades. RCHs are supervised by the BoE rather than the FCA.

At the time of writing, there are five RCHs in the UK:

1. **CME Clearing Europe Ltd** – this is a London-based clearing facility for OTC derivatives and an independent subsidiary of the CME Group.
2. **LCH.Clearnet Ltd** – this acts as central counterparty for trades executed on Euronext.liffe and for certain trades executed on the LSE. The LSE now owns 60% of LCH.Clearnet.
3. **Euroclear UK & Ireland Ltd (formerly CRESTCo)** – this firm is owned and operated by Euroclear and offers the facility – via the CREST system – to settle trades in dematerialised form. It is mainly known for UK and Irish equity clearing, and also provides clearing and settlement for a variety of other equities, bonds and funds.
4. **LME Clear Ltd** – a wholly-owned subsidiary of LME, clearing trades made on that exchange.
5. **ICE Clear Europe Ltd** – a subsidiary of ICE. It acts as a clearing house and central counterparty specifically for contracts executed on, or through, ICE Futures Europe.

CME Clearing Europe, LCH Clearnet and LME Clear are also recognised central counterparties, and must comply with the requirements laid down in EU Regulation 648/2012 (European Market Infrastructure Regulation (EMIR)), directly applicable regulations made under EMIR, and the recognition requirements set out in Part 5 and 6 of the Schedules to FSMA (Recognition Requirements for Investment Exchanges and Clearing Houses) Regulations 2001.

Recognised clearing houses which are not recognised central counterparties must comply with the recognition requirements in Parts 3 and 4 of the Schedule to the Financial Services and Markets Act 2000 (Recognition Requirements for Investment Exchanges and Clearing Houses) Regulations 2001.

As with recognition as an RIE, recognition as an RCH means that the clearing house does not need to become an authorised person in order to conduct financial services business in the UK. At the time of writing, there are also three recognised overseas clearing houses (ROCHs).

Requirements for Investment Exchanges and Clearing Houses Regulations 2001

In summary, the Regulations introduce:

- a reporting obligation for OTC derivatives
- a clearing obligation for eligible OTC derivatives
- measures to reduce counterparty credit risk and operational risk for bilaterally cleared OTC derivatives
- common rules for central counterparties (CCPs) and for trade repositories, and
- rules on the establishment of interoperability between CCPs.

1.2.9   Designated Professional Bodies (DPBs)

As stated previously, it is a criminal offence for a firm to engage in certain types of financial services activity without being authorised by the FCA.

Certain types of firm, such as accountants or solicitors, may well offer some financial services as an adjunct to their normal business. For example, a firm of accountants legitimately advising its client on how to optimise his tax affairs, might advise the sale of certain investments on which he has accumulated a certain level of gains. While the advice might be given with the aim of minimising the client's tax bill, the ancillary effect is to advise him on his investments, which is a regulated activity requiring authorisation.

Practicing accountants must be authorised by their professional body (such as the Institute of Chartered Accountants of England and Wales (ICAEW)). Given the standards required, and levels of supervision exercised by bodies such as the ICAEW, a further layer of authorisation from the FCA is seen as unnecessary; instead, the ICAEW has been granted designated professional body (DPB) status. This allows it to supervise its member firms in the code of conduct of some, limited, financial services business in addition to their normal accounting business. Firms which are subject to the requirements of a DPB are able to offer their clients these limited financial services without additional authorisation from the FCA.

Under Part XX (20) of the FSMA, firms are permitted to carry on regulated business under the supervision of a DPB and are known as exempt professional firms (EPFs).

The DPB status exists for ten bodies covering the following five professions:

- accountants
- solicitors
- actuaries
- chartered surveyors, and
- licensed conveyancers.

The Law Societies of England, Wales and Northern Ireland (for solicitors), the Royal Institution of Chartered Surveyors (RICS), the Council for Licensed Conveyancers and the Institute of Actuaries are all DPBs. The accountancy profession has a number of professional bodies that are granted designated status, including the ICAEW and the Association of Chartered Certified Accountants (ACCA).

1.2.10 Multilateral Trading Facilities (MTFs)

Later in this chapter, we will look in more depth at the impact of the Markets in Financial Instruments Directive (MiFID) – a European Directive which necessitated significant changes to the law and to the FCA Handbook and which came into force on 1 November 2007.

One major change was that a new activity became regulated under MiFID – that of operating a MTF.

An MTF is described by the FCA as being any system that *'brings together multiple parties (eg, retail investors or other investment firms) that are interested in buying and selling financial instruments and enables them to do so. These systems can be operated by an investment firm or a market operator. Instruments may include shares, bonds and derivatives. This is done within the MTF operators' system'*. Examples include firms such as Chi-X (the largest by volume) and LMAX Exchange. An MTF has also been described as an **exchange – lite**, but they do not have a listing process and do not have the ability to change the regulatory status of a security.

Prior to November 2007, firms which operated what were then known as Alternative Trading Systems (ATSs) in the UK, required specific authorisation to carry out the regulated activity of **arranging deals in investments**, which includes operating an organised marketplace/trading facility in financial instruments, other than by way of the formalised investment exchanges we have already considered.

In November 2007, the FCA (then the FSA) granted automatic permission for any authorised firm operating an ATS permission to operate an MTF under the new rules.

1.3 The General Prohibition

Learning Objective

1.1.3   understand the implications of the general prohibition (FSMA 2000 C.8, Part 2, S.19): the general prohibition offences; enforceability of agreements entered into with an unauthorised person

As we have seen, the FCA regulates investment exchanges and MTFs. In addition, it regulates firms which operate in financial markets.

FSMA 2000 C.8, Part 2, S.19 of the FSMA provides the **general prohibition** whereby carrying on regulated activities, or purporting to do so, without first being authorised by the FCA, or being subject to one of the exemptions available, is prohibited and is a criminal offence. (Regulated activities are described in Section 1.4.) The offence is punishable by a maximum penalty of two years in prison, and/ or an unlimited fine, on conviction in the Crown Court. It may be a defence for a firm to show that it has taken all reasonable precautions and exercised all due diligence to avoid committing the offence.

Any agreements made by a person in contravention of the general prohibition are unenforceable by that person against the other party to the agreement. This is also the case for agreements made as a result of the activities of someone who was contravening the general prohibition, even if that person was not a party to the agreement. The other party is entitled to recover any money or property transferred under the agreement and to compensation for any loss suffered.

Example

Mrs X buys shares in ABC PLC. The purchase is made following the recommendation of a firm of brokers, UNA Ltd. Mrs X subsequently discovers that UNA was not authorised under the FSMA.

Mrs X now has two choices:

- she could simply keep her shares in ABC and take no action against UNA, or
- she could sue UNA for the recovery of her money and damages (handing back her shares in ABC) because UNA has breached the general prohibition.

The relevant staff of UNA have also committed a criminal act, and on conviction are liable to imprisonment for up to two years, plus an unlimited fine. In practice, this operates as a particularly effective deterrent.

1.3.1 Regulated Activities

To understand whether a person is in breach of the FSMA general prohibition it is, of course, necessary to understand what the regulated activities themselves are. The FSMA provides that regulated activities involve two elements:

1. specified activities (such as dealing, arranging or advising)
2. specified types of investment (such as shares, bonds, deposits, contracts of insurance).

Thus, a regulated activity involves performing one or more specified activity in relation to one or more of the specified investments.

A firm which wishes to carry out a regulated activity must be either authorised or exempt (see above for examples of exempt persons). A firm which seeks authorisation must apply to the FCA, which will grant it a specific **permission** under Part 4A of the FSMA in relation to each regulated activity it is authorised to conduct. The FCA's register, shown on its website, shows all authorised firms together with their specific Part 4A Permissions.

1.4 The Regulated Activities

Learning Objective

1.1.4 Know what regulated activities (FSMA 2000 Part II, Regulated Activities Order (RAO) 2001) constitute designated investment business in the UK

Part II of the FSMA, Regulated and Prohibited Activities, includes the general prohibition, which simply states that no person can carry on a regulated activity in the UK, or purport to do so, unless he is either authorised or exempt. The specified investments and activities themselves are detailed in secondary legislation issued under the FSMA – principally the Regulated Activities Order (RAO) 2001, as amended most recently in 2010. This clarifies precisely what these regulated activities are.

You should note that the term **person** means natural persons (ie, humans) and all other types of legal person such as incorporated bodies, partnerships, trusts and other types of unincorporated associations.

As we have already noted, the RAO defines regulated activities by reference:

- first, to the activities a firm might carry on in relation to those investments
- and then, to the range of specified investments.

This means that when an activity listed below is not carried on in relation to one of the specified investments, it is not a regulated activity. However, not all of the activities can be related to all the investments – some are specific to just one type; eg, effecting a contract of insurance (activity) relates only to contracts of insurance (investment).

The specified activities are as follows:

1. **Accepting deposits** – mainly the preserve of banks and building societies, but other firms may find themselves caught under this activity.
2. **Issuing e-money** – ie, acting as the issuer of e-money, as it is described below in Section 1.5.
3. **Effecting or carrying out contracts of insurance as principal** – this essentially applies to insurers.
4. **Dealing in investments as principal or agent** – this applies only to certain of the specified investments. Dealing is buying, selling, subscribing for or underwriting the investments concerned. If the firm deals as principal (ie, on its own account), it applies only to those investments that are:
   - **securities** – shares, debentures and warrants; or
   - **contractually-based investments** such as options, futures, contracts for difference and life policies.

   If the firm deals as agent (ie, on behalf of someone else), it applies to **securities** or **relevant investments**. Relevant investments include contractually based investments (as for dealing as principal) and additionally rights under pure protection and general insurance contracts.
5. **Arranging deals in investments** – this covers:
   - bringing about deals in investments – that is, the involvement of the person is essential to bringing about/concluding the contract, and also
   - **making arrangements with a view to transacting in investments** (which may be quite widely interpreted as any arrangement pursuant to transactions in investments, such as making introductions).

   The arranging activities relate only to specified investments which are:
   - securities, eg, shares, debentures or warrants
   - relevant investments, eg, options, futures, contracts for difference (CFDs) and rights under insurance contracts
   - underwriting capacity of a Lloyd's syndicate or membership of a Lloyd's syndicate, and
   - rights to or interests in any of the above.

   A typical example might be a broker, making arrangements for its client to enter into a specific insurance contract.
6. **Arranging home finance transactions** – the arranging and making of arrangements in relation to mortgages, home reversion or home purchase plans, and regulated sale and rent-back agreements are captured in the same way as arranging deals in investments.
7. **Operating a multilateral trading facility (MTF)** – by an investment firm or a market operator, which brings together multiple third-party buying and selling interests in financial instruments – in the system and in accordance with non-discretionary rules. MTFs can be assimilated to alternative trading exchanges providing additional pools of liquidity to their members (usually banks, major mutual funds and large insurance companies).

8. **Managing investments** – this applies in respect of investments belonging to someone other than the manager and where the manager exercises discretion over the management of the portfolio. The portfolio must include, or be able to include, securities or contractually based investments. A typical example is a portfolio manager. Non-discretionary management (if the firm does not make the final decision) is not covered under this heading: it is captured under the separately defined regulated activities of dealing in investments and advising on investments.

9. **Assisting in the administration and performance of a contract of insurance** – this is activity carried on by an intermediary after conclusion of a contract of insurance, eg, loss assessors.

10. **Safeguarding and administering investments** – again, this applies in the context of securities (eg, shares, debentures) and contractually based investments (eg, options, futures, CFDs, qualifying insurance contracts). The firm must be holding the assets for someone else and it must be both safeguarding and administering the assets to be caught under this heading. A typical example is a custodian bank, which might hold title documents to investments, hold dematerialised investments in its name and administer the collection of interest/dividends or the application of corporate actions.

11. **Sending dematerialised instructions** – this covers firms which operate systems that allow for the electronic transfer of title in certain investments (again, securities and contractually based investments) and those which cause instructions to be sent on those systems. An example of such a system is CREST.

12. **Establishing, operating and winding up a CIS** – this activity captures persons who set up, operate/administer and wind up any type of CIS, whether an authorised scheme or an unregulated scheme. Acting as a trustee of an authorised unit trust (AUT), or as the depository or sole director of an open-ended investment company (OEIC), are also separate regulated activities.

13. **Establishing, operating and winding up a pension scheme** – this activity captures those who set up, operate/administer and wind up stakeholder pension schemes and personal pension schemes. These activities may be carried out by the scheme trustees and/or the scheme administrators.

14. **Providing basic advice on stakeholder products** – this is a special regulated activity, for those who advise only on stakeholder products. Stakeholder products conform to certain criteria for cost and accessibility.

15. **Advising on investments** – this covers giving advice on securities and relevant investments. It does not extend to giving advice about deposits, nor to occupational pensions schemes, nor to generic advice (eg, *'invest in the US, not in Europe'*). Neither does it extend to giving information – facts, which are not tailored to constitute a recommendation – instead of advice.

16. **Advising on home finance transactions** – advising on the merits of entering into, or varying the terms of, a regulated mortgage, a home reversion plan, a home purchase plan or a regulated sale and rent-back agreement is a regulated activity.

17. **Lloyd's market activities** – in addition to those mentioned above under arranging investments, there are three further Lloyd's-related regulated activities:
    - advising on syndicate participation
    - managing underwriting capacity as a managing agent
    - arranging deals in contracts of insurance at Lloyd's.

18. **Entering into a funeral plan contract** – a firm that enters into funeral plan contracts as provider (ie, being the person to whom the pre-payments are made) is conducting a regulated activity.

19. **Entering into and administering home finance transactions** – this captures the activity of regulated mortgage lenders, home reversion providers, home purchase providers and regulated sale and rent-back agreement providers.

20. **Dormant account funds** – the activities of meeting repayment claims and managing dormant account funds, carried on by dormant account fund operators, are regulated activities.

21. **Agreeing to carry on a specified activity** – is itself a regulated activity (and so a firm should not agree to carry on a regulated activity until it is properly authorised, notwithstanding that it may not intend to actually carry out that activity until it has its authorisation).

22. **Certain activities relating to entering forms of consumer credit as lender** – rights under any contract under which one person provides another with credit and contracts for hire of goods – rights under a contract for the bailment or hiring of goods to a person other than a body corporate.

23. **Providing credit reference services** – furnishing persons with information that is relevant to the financial standing of persons other than bodies corporate and is provided to that person for that purpose.

24. **Providing credit information services** – taking steps on behalf of a person other than a body corporate in connection with information relevant to that person's financial standing that is or may be held by a regulated person.

25. **Certain other activities relating to consumer credit** are regulated including credit broking, debt adjusting, debt counselling, debt collecting and debt administration.

26. **The setting of benchmarks** – providing information, administration and the determining or publishing a benchmark or publishing connected information.

Activities 4, 5, 7, 8, 11, 12, 13 and 14 are classified as **designated investment business**. Activities 9, 10, 15 and 21 are designated investment business only when they relate to designated investments. Broadly, designated investment business is a sub-set of regulated activities, which excludes commercial banking and insurance activities.

You will see later that certain rules (such as the Conduct of Business Sourcebook (COBS)) apply only to firms carrying out designated investment business, while others (such as the general prohibition) apply to all regulated activities.

1.5   The Specified Investments

Learning Objective

1.1.5   Know which designated investments are covered by the Regulated Activities Order (RAO) 2001 (as amended)

The following are defined as specified investments within the RAO:

1. **Deposits** – that is, money paid by one person to another, with or without interest being earned on it, and on the basis that it will be repaid when a specified event occurs (eg, when a demand is made). The obvious example is deposits held with banks and building societies. For clarity, the RAO sets out certain exclusions – for example, electronic money (covered separately below in point 2), money paid in advance for the provision of goods or services and money paid as a security deposit.

2. **Electronic money** – that is, monetary value (as represented by a claim on the e-money issuer) which is stored on an electronic device, issued on receipt of funds and accepted as a means of payment by third parties. In effect, it is an electronic substitute for notes and coins.

3. **Rights under contracts of insurance** – includes both long-term insurance contracts (eg, life assurance, endowment policies) and general insurance (eg, motor, building insurance). The FCA gives guidance on identifying a contract of insurance (since this is not always as simple as you might think) in the Perimeter Guidance (PERG) Sourcebook. (*Life insurance policies are designated investments.)

4. ***Shares** – defined widely as shares or stock in any company (wherever or however incorporated) or in any unincorporated body formed outside the UK. The RAO definition excludes shares in OEICs, since an OEIC is a CIS and is captured under a separate definition. It also excludes some building society and credit union shares, since these can behave like – and are, therefore, captured under – the definition of deposits.

5. ***Instruments creating or acknowledging indebtedness** – this includes debentures, debenture stock and loan stock and, as a **mopping-up** clause, specifies also *'any other instrument creating or acknowledging debt'*. Again the definition is wide, so the RAO provides for some exclusions – eg, trade bills, cheques and other bills of exchange, and (because they are separately captured) contracts of insurance and government and public securities.

6. ***Alternative finance investment bonds/alternative debentures** – a form of Sharia-compliant bond or **sukuk**.

7. ***Government and public securities** – eg, gilts and US Treasuries, local authority loan stocks. Again, certain instruments are excluded, such as trade bills issued by government bodies and National Savings & Investments (NS&I) deposits and products.

8. ***Instruments giving entitlements to investments** – essentially, warrants and similar instruments entitling the holder to subscribe for shares, debentures, government and public securities at a set price and on or between set date(s) in the future.

9. ***Certificates representing certain securities** – this item covers certificates and the like which confer rights in (but are not themselves) other instruments such as shares, debentures, gilts and warrants. It includes, eg, American depositary receipts (ADRs), which typically give holders rights over a certain number of a non-US company's shares. These ADRs are designed to offer the – typically, US-based – investor a more convenient way to invest in non-US company shares, because they are dealt in, and pay dividends in, US dollars. Also covered here are other depositary receipts, such as global depositary receipts (GDRs).

10. ***Units in a collective investment scheme** – this covers holdings in any CIS, whether it is an authorised scheme or an unregulated scheme. For example, it covers units in an AUT or shares in an OEIC – which you may also see described as an investment company with variable capital (ICVC). This is why OEICs are specifically excluded from the heading of **shares** above. Unregulated schemes can also take other legal forms, such as limited partnerships, and so limited partnership interests are included under this heading.

11. ***Rights under a stakeholder pension scheme** – stakeholder pensions are pension schemes set up under the Welfare Reform and Pensions Act 1999 which have to meet certain criteria and be run in a particular way.

12. ***Rights under a personal pension scheme** – these are pensions designed for individuals who do not belong to a company scheme and/or who wish to take control of their own investment decisions for their pension provisions (eg, self-invested personal pensions (SIPPs)). A wide range of investments may be held within a personal pension scheme.

13. ***Options** – options (the right, but not the obligation, to buy or sell a fixed quantity of an underlying asset for a fixed price on or between fixed dates) are covered only if they relate to:
    - securities or contractually based investments (eg, stocks, shares, bonds, or futures on similar instruments);
    - currencies;
    - certain precious metals, including gold and silver;
    - options on futures contracts and other CFDs (see in point 15 below).

14. ***Futures** – that is, contracts for the sale/purchase of an asset when delivery and settlement will be made at a future date, at a price agreed when the contract is made. The RAO excludes futures agreed for commercial purposes as opposed to those made for investment/speculative purposes; so

a contract to buy cocoa at an agreed price at some future date is not caught if it is carried out by a chocolate-maker to help him secure a certain price for the raw materials needed.

15. ***Contracts for difference** – eg, spread bets, interest rate swaps. These are contracts in which the investor's aim is to secure a profit (or avoid a loss) by making money by reference to fluctuations in the value of an index, or to the price of some other underlying property. The RAO excludes futures and options since these are separately caught.

16. **Lloyd's syndicate capacity and syndicate membership** – this relates in the main to the activities of Lloyd's member's agents and managing agents.

17. **Rights under a funeral plan contract** – ie, certain plans under which the customer pays for benefits which will pay for his (or someone else's) funeral.

18. **Rights under a regulated mortgage contract** – ie, mortgage loans secured by first legal mortgages on property, at least 40% of which is to be used for the borrower's, or some related party's, dwelling. This specified investment also includes **lifetime mortgages**, a type of equity release transaction.

19. **Rights under a home purchase plan** – home purchase plans are alternatives to mortgages, which allow people to buy their homes while complying with Islamic principles (financing via an interest-bearing mortgage is not permitted under a strict interpretation of these principles).

20. **Rights under a regulated sale and rent-back agreement** – whereby a person sells all or part of qualifying interest in land/property but remains in occupation of at least 40% of the land/property.

21. **Rights under a regulated home reversion plan** – in which the customer sells part or all of his home to the plan provider in return for a lump sum or series of payments; he retains the right to stay in his home until he dies or moves into residential care.

22. **Rights to or interests in anything that is a specified investment** listed, excluding rights under regulated mortgage contracts.

Among these specified investments, those marked with an asterisk (*) are classified as designated investments. In the final item, designated investments excludes rights under a long-term care insurance contract which is a pure protection contract.

1.6 Excluded Activities

Learning Objective

1.1.6 Know what are excluded activities in relation to designated investment business in the UK (PERG 2.8)

The FCA provides a number of exclusions from the requirement for authorisation within the Perimeter Guidance Sourcebook (PERG) (part of the FCA Handbook). Those who meet the terms of the exclusions do not need to obtain authorisation for carrying on the regulated activities in question. Some key examples of exclusions in relation to designated investment business in the UK are listed below.

1.6.1 Exclusions when Dealing as Principal

Absence of Holding Out

Dealing in investments as principal is a regulated activity, so that persons dealing on their own account in order to make profits are normally required to be authorised or exempt. However, this regulated activity is restricted to those persons who are holding themselves out to be, and acting as, **market makers** and who regularly solicit the public with the purpose of inducing them to deal. A person buying shares solely on his own account does not need to be authorised or exempt, unless he is **holding himself out** to be a dealer in the investments.

This means that:

- firms which are professional dealers, such as market makers, and which hold themselves out as such, are carrying on a regulated activity and require authorisation, but
- individuals or companies which are not in the business of dealing in investments, and which only invest for themselves in the hope of making profit, are exempt from requiring authorisation.

This exclusion relates to dealings in securities (shares and bonds) and contractually based investments (futures, options and CFDs) as long as they are entered into by an unauthorised person.

Other Exclusions

There are other exclusions where dealing as principal is not classified as a regulated activity:

1. A bank providing finance to another person and accepting an instrument acknowledging the debt.
2. A company or other organisation issuing its own shares, warrants or debentures or purchasing its own shares in accordance with certain provisions of the Companies Act 1985 (Treasury shares).
3. Using options, futures and CFDs for corporate risk management purposes, as long as the company's business is mainly unregulated activities and the sole or main purpose of the deals is to limit identifiable risks.
4. Entering into transactions as principal for, or in connection with:
   - the sale of a body corporate
   - transactions between members of a group or joint enterprise
   - the sale of goods or supply of services
   - while acting as bare trustee (nominee, in Scotland)
   - in connection with an employee share scheme
   - an overseas person
   - an incoming e-commerce provider.

1.6.2 Exclusions when Providing Advice in Newspapers

There is a particular exclusion from the regulated activities of advising on investments that is available to newspapers and other media. There is a particular exclusion from the regulated activities of advising on investments that is available to newspapers and other media such as *Investment Week* and *Citywire*. If a newspaper includes investment advice and that advice is not the principal purpose of the newspaper, it is excluded from the regulated activity of advising on investments. The existence of money and city pages or subsections within a newspaper does not make the principal purpose of the paper anything other than the provision of news, so there is no need for authorisation.

If the principal purpose of a publication is the provision of investment advice, with a view to encouraging investors or prospective investors to undertake investment activity, then authorisation is required. This is the case for periodicals that tip certain investments and are often sold on a subscription basis. They are often referred to as tipsheets and include publications like *Warrants Alert* (highlighting warrants that offer good value to the investor).

The FCA recognised the impact of social media in its guidance consultation GC14/6 noting that digital and, in particular, social media are now becoming the media of choice in many cases for customer communications and specifically for financial promotions, noting the positive benefit from using social media but highlighting that this has to be based on compliance.

The guidance consultation intended to:

- clarify and confirm the approach to the supervision of financial promotions (as defined in the legislation) in social media
- help firms understand how they can use these media and comply with the rules
- remind firms that the rules are intended to be media-neutral to ensure that consumers are presented with certain minimum information, in a fair and balanced way, at the outset of firms' interaction with them
- set out specific areas that firms need to consider, and provide some solutions and illustrative examples.

1.6.3 Trustees, Nominees and Personal Representatives

There is an exclusion from the need for authorisation if the person carrying on a regulated activity is:

- acting as representative of another party
- not generally holding himself out as carrying on regulated activities, and
- not receiving additional remuneration for providing these investment services.

This exclusion can apply to the following types of designated investment business:

- dealing in investments as principal
- arranging deals in investments and making arrangements with a view to transactions in investments
- managing investments
- safeguarding and administering investments
- sending dematerialised instructions
- advising on investments
- assisting in the administration and performance of a contract of insurance which is a life policy.

It is important to note that this exclusion is not available where the person is carrying on, dealing, arranging or advising activity in connection with a contract of insurance.

1.6.4 Employee Share Schemes

Companies may wish to set up schemes enabling their employees to hold shares in the company they work for. There is an exclusion available from the requirement to be authorised to operate such schemes that is available to the company, any company in the same group or any trustee who holds certain types of securities or debentures under the scheme. However, the exclusion isn't available to third parties who may be involved in operating the scheme, such as third-party administrators. The exclusions cover four types of activity:

- dealing in investments as principal

- dealing in investments as agent
- arranging deals in investments and making arrangements with a view to transactions in investments
- safeguarding and administering investments.

1.6.5 Overseas Persons

There are a number of exclusions for overseas persons carrying on regulated activities, providing that they do not do so from a permanent place of business in the UK. These exclusions apply only if the business is carried on through an authorised, or exempt, UK person, or if they are the result of a legitimate approach, such as where a UK client makes an unsolicited approach to an overseas person. The exclusions cover mainly the following types of designated investment business:

- dealing in investments as principal
- dealing in investments as agent
- arranging deals in investments
- advising on investments
- agreeing to carry on the regulated activities of managing investments, arranging deals in investments, safeguarding and administering investments or sending dematerialised instructions
- operating a multilateral trading facility.

1.7 Exempt Persons

Learning Objective

1.1.7　Know who constitute exempt persons in relation to designated investment business in the UK (PERG 2.10)

In certain circumstances, specific types of persons carrying on regulated activities may be exempt from the requirement for authorisation. The relevant provisions are found in the FSMA and in the statutory instrument FSMA Exemption Order 2001. This order provides exemption for the BoE and other central banks.

These exemptions generally relate to specific regulated activities and may be restricted to certain circumstances or subject to certain conditions.

An example of an exemption being restricted to certain circumstances might be if some other authorised person has accepted responsibility for the regulated activities (such as appointed representatives).

An example of an exemption being subject to certain conditions might be a requirement that the regulated activity is not carried on to make a profit.

Exempt persons can be split into two groups:

- those specifically described as exempt persons under the FSMA (such as RCHs and RIEs), and
- those that are not described as exempt persons under the FSMA, but who may nonetheless be exempt from the requirement to apply to the FCA for authorisation – such as a member of a DPB, carrying on the regulated activities in particular circumstances (see Section 1.2.9 on DPBs).

This distinction is significant; certain legal provisions apply only to transactions involving exempt persons, and not to non-exempt persons who are only free from the need to apply for authorisation because of the specific circumstances of their activity.

The classes of exempt persons set out in PERG 2.10 are discussed further below.

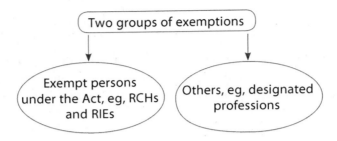

1.7.1 Appointed Representatives

An appointed representative is a representative of an authorised firm who is not an employee of that firm nor under a contract for services for the firm (self-employed). It can be any type of person (ie, as an individual or a business entity). It must be a party to a contract with an authorised person that allows it to carry on certain regulated activities and the authorised person must have accepted responsibility in writing for the conduct of these regulated activities.

The FCA rules do not apply directly to appointed representatives because they are not authorised persons in their own rights. Instead, any business conducted by the appointed representative for whom the authorised person has accepted responsibility will be treated as having been conducted by the authorised person. The authorised person:

- must itself have permission (authorisation) to perform the regulated activities undertaken by its authorised representatives, and
- is potentially liable for the actions of its representatives, and subject to FCA discipline. Note that, although appointed representatives do not themselves need to be authorised, the individuals involved may require approval from the FCA if they are fulfilling controlled functions at an appointed representative firm. These are persons performing governing functions (directors, partners) and individuals who will be dealing directly with clients.

The FCA expects authorised firms to conduct thorough reviews of the suitability and conduct of their appointed representatives. The exemption from authorisation that appointed representatives enjoy (S.39 of the FSMA and the FSMA (Appointed Representatives) Regulations 2001) comes at the price of imposing on the appointing firm the responsibility for vetting and monitoring, which the FCA would normally conduct itself.

The provisions that govern the appointment and monitoring of appointed representatives are in the FCA's Supervision Manual (Chapter 12). The principal provision is as SUP 12.3.2G, which states that: *'the firm is responsible, to the same extent as if it had expressly permitted it, for anything that the appointed representative does or omits to do, in carrying on the business for which the firm has accepted responsibility'.*

Appointed representatives are exempt persons in relation to the following types of designated investment business, defined under Part III of the RAO, under the Appointed Representatives Regulation 2001:

- arranging deals in investments and making arrangements with a view to transactions in investments;
- advising on investments
- giving basic advice on stakeholder products
- safeguarding and administering assets
- assisting in the administration and performance of a contract of insurance that is a life policy
- arranging the safeguarding and administration of assets
- agreeing to carry on a regulated activity.

In particular, appointed representatives are not permitted to deal in investments either as agent or principal, or to manage investments.

1.7.2 Recognised Investment Exchanges (RIEs) and Recognised Clearing Houses (RCHs)

The FSMA gives the FCA the responsibility of recognising, regulating and supervising investment exchanges, while the BoE has a similar role with regards to clearing houses.

To be recognised by the FCA/BoE, these exchanges and clearing houses need to demonstrate that they are **fit and proper** for their purpose. Once recognised, the exchanges are referred to as RIEs and the clearing houses are referred to as RCHs. RIEs and RCHs are exempt persons in that they do not need to seek authorisation from the FCA to do regulated activities – they are, instead, recognised. This was discussed earlier in Section 1.2.6.

1.7.3 Miscellaneous Exempt Persons

The Treasury has established certain exemptions from the need to be authorised for particular persons. Some of these exemptions are restricted in that they only apply in certain circumstances.

For example:

- supranational bodies of which the UK or another European Economic Area (EEA) member state is a member, and
- central banks of the UK or another EEA member state.

These are exempted from the need to be authorised to carry on any regulated activity, apart from effecting or carrying out contracts of insurance. Prime examples are the BoE, the European Investment Bank (EIB) and the International Monetary Fund (IMF).

In contrast, certain bodies are exempted from the need to be authorised for the sole regulated activity of accepting deposits; these include municipal banks, local authorities and charities.

1.7.4 Members of Lloyd's and the Professions

Members of the Lloyd's insurance market and firms regulated by the DPBs (see Section 1.2.9) are allowed to perform limited regulated activities without being authorised. They are not exempt persons but the general prohibition of the FSMA does not apply to them. These provisions are discussed in more detail in the following paragraphs.

Members of Lloyd's

Several activities carried on in connection with business at Lloyd's are regulated activities.

These include:

- advising on syndicate participation
- acting as a managing agent for one or more syndicates, and
- arranging deals in insurance contracts.

However, the FSMA disapplies the general prohibition for members of Lloyd's in relation to contracts of insurance written at Lloyd's. This is further extended to those members that ceased to be underwriting members at any time on or after 24 December 1996; these former members can carry out insurance contracts underwritten at Lloyd's without the need for authorisation.

The reason for this exemption is that the FCA expects the activities at Lloyd's to be suitably supervised and executed by the Society of Lloyd's, and so additional FCA authorisation of members is deemed to be unnecessary. The FCA does, however, have certain powers to impose rules on the members (or former members) of Lloyd's if it is felt necessary.

Members of the Professions

As we saw in Section 1.2.9, there are five professions (accountants, solicitors, actuaries, chartered surveyors and licensed conveyancers) where individual firms are permitted to carry on particular regulated activities without the need for authorisation. Firms are required to apply to their relevant designated professional body (such as the ICAEW, the Law Society and the RICS) for permission to conduct these activities.

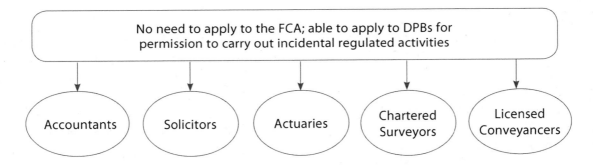

The DPB must operate a set of rules with which its members must comply, and the regulated activity must be only incidental to the provision of professional services. For example, a firm of accountants providing tax advice might give a client advice as to which investments might best be sold to avoid the accrual of a tax liability.

There are other restrictions to the activities carried out by member firms of DPBs. For example, such firms are allowed to receive pecuniary reward only from their client (ie, they should not receive commissions from the providers of products held or bought by the client). Moreover, certain types of designated investment business may not be carried out by the members, namely:

- dealing in investments as principal, ie, acting as market maker
- establishing, operating or winding-up CISs or stakeholder pension schemes acting as a stakeholder pension scheme manager.

With regard to managing investments, the firm may exercise discretion to sell investments but may only purchase investments if the decision is taken, or advice is given, by an authorised person.

Advising on investments can only be done in specified circumstances in order for it to be exempt.

1.7.5 Exempt Persons

Exempt persons who are appointed representatives or miscellaneous persons cannot be both exempt in relation to some regulated activities and authorised in relation to others. That is, if a firm is already authorised and wishes to perform additional regulated activities that might otherwise fall under the appointed representatives/miscellaneous persons exemptions, it cannot claim those exemptions. It must extend its authorisation to include all the regulated activities it carries on.

2. The Role of the Financial Conduct Authority (FCA) and the Prudential Regulation Authority (PRA)

Learning Objective

1.2.1 Know the FCA's general duties (Financial Services Act 2012 c. 21, Part 2, Section 6, 1B) and the PRA's general objective (Financial Services Act 2012 c. 21, Part 2, S.6, 2B)

1.2.2 Know the eight regulatory principles to be applied by both the FCA and PRA (Financial Services Act 2012 c. 21, Part 2, S.6, 3B)

1.2.3 Know the powers of the FCA and PRA with regard to rule making in respect of their powers regarding: authorisation; supervision; enforcement; sanctions; disciplinary action

2.1 The Strategic, Operational and Statutory Objectives

2.1.1 The FCA's General Duties

The FCA has a single strategic objective and three operational objectives within the Financial Services Act of 2012. These are:

- **Strategic objective** – ensuring that financial markets work well.

- **Operational objectives**:
  - ○ **The consumer protection objective** – securing an appropriate degree of protection for consumers. This does not necessarily mean preventing all risk of loss to consumers. In considering what is the appropriate degree of protection, the FCA should have regard to the different degrees of risk involved in different kinds of investment, the differing levels of experience and expertise of consumers, the needs of the consumers for advice and accurate information and the general principle that consumers should take responsibility for their decisions.
  - ○ **The integrity objective** – protecting and enhancing the integrity of the UK financial system. The integrity of the financial system includes the following:
    - – soundness, stability and resilience
    - – not being used for a purpose connected with financial crime
    - – not being affected by behaviour that amounts to market abuse
    - – the orderly operation of the financial markets
    - – the reliability and transparency of the price formation process in those markets; and
    - – the suitability of the listing rules.
- **The competition objective** – promoting effective competition in the interests of consumers in the markets for regulated financial services or services provided by an RIE in carrying on regulated activities in respect of which it is exempt from the general prohibition. The FCA may have regard to matters including:
  - ○ the needs of different consumers who use or may use those services, including their need for information that enables them to make informed choices
  - ○ the ease with which consumers who obtain those services can change the person from whom they obtain them
  - ○ the ease with which new entrants can enter the market
  - ○ how far competition is encouraging innovation.

Part 9A of FSMA empowers the FCA to make rules that are legally binding on authorised firms concerning regulated and unregulated activities. Such rules must appear to the FCA to be necessary or expedient for the purpose of advancing one or more of its operational objectives.

Other Powers and Accountability

The PRA has similar rule-making powers; however the powers only extend to PRA-authorised persons. In addition to rule-making powers, FSMA empowers either regulator to:

- grant authorisation to persons applying for Part 4A permission, vary a firm's permission and cancel authorisation
- supervise authorised persons on an ongoing basis to ensure that they continue to meet the regulators' authorisation requirements and that they comply with the Handbook rules and other regulatory obligations
- employ a range of disciplinary measures and sanctions to punish or limit the activities of firms that fail to comply
- enforce the regulatory framework – the general approach is one of credible deterrence, using enforcement strategy as a tool to change behaviour in the industry.

The FCA's objectives also provide for a degree of accountability:

- **Annual report** – the FCA's annual report to the Treasury contains an assessment of how well or otherwise the FCA has met its statutory objectives. The report is scrutinised by various Parliamentary committees.
- **Rules** – the FCA has to show how the rules it makes relate to the statutory objectives.

- **Judicial review** – if the FCA fails to consider the objectives, or incorrectly interprets the objectives, it can be challenged in the courts.
- **Regulatory failure** – the FCA and PRA will be held accountable if breaches of the objectives occurred or were made worse because of a serious failure on the part of the regulator.

Under FSMA, the relevant regulator (the FCA and/or the PRA) is required to maintain arrangements to supervise compliance with the requirements imposed on authorised persons. The supervisory approach has to work to ensure the statutory objectives are met.

The FCA's supervision efforts focus on the conduct of both FCA-authorised and PRA-authorised firms, plus prudential regulation for those authorised firms that are not authorised by the PRA. The PRA supervises the prudential aspects of those firms that it authorises. A structured approach to supervision is adopted which is outlined in more detail in Chapter 2, Section 4.

2.1.2   The PRA's Obligations

The PRA's general objective is to be advanced primarily by:

- seeking to ensure that the business of PRA-authorised persons is carried on in a way which avoids any adverse effect on the stability of the UK financial system, and
- seeking to minimise the adverse effect that the failure of a PRA-authorised person could be expected to have on the stability of the UK financial system.

The objective is contributing to the securing of an appropriate degree of protection for those who are or may become policyholders. For example, on November 13 2014, the Prudential Regulation Authority (PRA) sent a Dear CEO letter to general insurance firms, reminding them of their obligations to set adequate technical provisions noting that some firms had chosen to lower premium rates, extend their terms and scope of cover offered or have weakened their underwriting criteria in order to remain competitive in the current market conditions.

The PRA has also been given an insurance objective that only relates to the effecting or carrying out of contracts of insurance as principal to the extent it is a PRA-regulated activity. The objective is contributing to the securing of an appropriate degree of protection for those who are or may become policyholders.

The PRA states that it advances its objectives using both regulation and supervision using three characteristics:

- A **judgement-based approach** – using judgement in determining whether financial firms are safe and sound, whether insurers provide appropriate protection for policyholders and whether firms continue to meet the threshold conditions.
- A **forward-looking approach** – assessing not just against current risks, but also against those that could plausibly arise in the future. When the PRA judges it necessary to intervene, it will generally aim to do so at an early stage.
- A **focused approach** – focusing on those issues and those firms that pose the greatest risk to the stability of the UK financial system and policyholders.

This involves firms having resilience against failure and, in the event they do fail in the course of business, avoiding harm resulting from disruption to the continuity of provision of financial services.

The Financial Services Banking Reform Act introduced some reform to Section 2B of FSMA 2000 (the PRA's general objective) making a new continuity objective part of that general objective, when the PRA is dealing with ring-fencing matters, noting that the PRA must ensure that ring-fenced bodies do not do things that put the continuity of core services in the UK at risk and are also insulated from external risks. Such risks include, for example, the fall in value of trading assets, or foreign assets.

2.1.3 The Principles of Good Regulation

The strategic and operational objectives are supported by a set of Principles of Good Regulation which the FCA (and in certain cases also the PRA) must have regard to when pursuing their functions under the FSMA. The FSMA, as amended by the Financial Services Act 2012, requires the regulators to follow eight principles when carrying out their work. The principles are:

1. **Efficiency and economy** – they need to use their resources in the most efficient and economical way. As part of this the Treasury can commission value-for-money reviews of their operations.
2. **Proportionality** – they must ensure that any burden or restriction imposed on a person or activity is proportionate to the benefits they expect as a result. To judge this, they take into account the costs to firms and consumers. One of the main techniques used is to carry out a cost-benefit analysis of their proposed regulatory requirements.
3. **Sustainable growth** – they must ensure there is a desire for sustainable growth in the economy of the UK in the medium- or long-term.
4. **Consumer responsibility** – consumers should take responsibility for their decisions.
5. **Senior management responsibility** – a firm's senior management is responsible for the firm's activities and for ensuring that its business complies with regulatory requirements. This secures an adequate but proportionate level of regulatory intervention by holding senior management responsible for the risk management and controls within firms. Firms must make it clear who has what responsibility and ensure that their business can be adequately monitored and controlled.
6. **Recognising the differences in the businesses carried on by different regulated persons** – where appropriate, they exercise their functions in a way that recognises differences in the nature of, and objectives of, businesses carried on by different persons subject to requirements imposed by, or under, the FSMA.
7. **Openness and disclosure** – they should publish relevant market information about regulated persons or require them to publish it (with appropriate safeguards). This reinforces market discipline and improves consumers' knowledge about their financial matters.
8. **Transparency** – they should exercise their functions as transparently as possible. It is important that they provide appropriate information on their regulatory decisions, and that they are open and accessible to the regulated community and the general public.

2.2 Principles for Businesses

Learning Objective

1.2.4 Understand the importance of the Principles for Businesses (PRIN 1.1.2, 1.1.7, 2.1.1)

The FCA's detailed rules are published in the FCA Handbook. This contains a number of sourcebooks or manuals, grouped in handbook blocks. The high level standards block of the handbook contains the sourcebook Principles for Businesses (PRIN), which sets out 11 principles that authorised firms must observe in carrying out their business. Some of the principles apply to all authorised firms, no matter what sort of regulated business they do; some apply only to firms carrying on specified types of business.

If a firm breaches any of the principles that apply to it, it will be liable to disciplinary sanctions. However, the onus will be on the FCA to show that the firm has been at fault.

The 11 Principles for Businesses are:

1. **Integrity** – a firm must conduct its business with integrity.
2. **Skill, care and diligence** – a firm must conduct its business with due skill, care and diligence.
3. **Management and control** – a firm must take reasonable care to organise and control its affairs responsibly and effectively, with adequate risk management systems.
4. **Financial prudence** – a firm must maintain adequate financial resources.
5. **Market conduct** – a firm must observe proper standards of market conduct.
6. **Customers' interests** – a firm must pay due regard to the interests of its customers and treat them fairly. (Note that the FCA defines the term customers differently to clients. The term client covers a variety of parties doing business with the firm, including professional counterparties. The term customer applies, very broadly, to those clients who are not professionals and who may, therefore, need protection.)
7. **Communications with clients** – a firm must pay due regard to the information needs of its clients and communicate information to them in a way which is clear, fair and not misleading.
8. **Conflicts of interest** – a firm must manage conflicts of interest fairly, both between itself and its customers, and between customers and other clients.
9. **Customers: relationships of trust** – a firm must take reasonable care to ensure the suitability of its advice and discretionary decisions for any customer who is entitled to rely upon its judgment.
10. **Clients' assets** – a firm must arrange adequate protection for clients' assets when it is responsible for them.
11. **Relations with regulators** – a firm must deal with its regulators in an open and co-operative way and must disclose to the FCA appropriately anything relating to the firm of which the FCA would reasonably expect notice.

2.2.1 Treating Customers Fairly (TCF)

It should be apparent from a reading of the above that a general overriding theme of **fair play** runs through the principles. This is coupled with a recognition that there is often an information imbalance between the firm and its customers (since the firm is usually more expert in its products and services than its customers).

This theme is reinforced through the FCA's treating customers fairly (TCF) initiative. This was launched in response to a study undertaken in 2000–01, to consider what a fair deal for customers should actually mean. At the time, this was considered mainly in the context of post-sales relationships and the FCA's responsibilities under the Unfair Terms in Contracts Regulations 1999, although it was subsequently widened to embrace all parts of the customer relationship.

While the initiative placed new emphasis on the fair treatment of customers, and in particular a focus on getting the right outcomes for them, the FCA is at pains to remind firms that fair treatment has always been one of its Principles for Businesses – it is embedded in Principle 6 above – and that the TCF agenda is really no more than a clearer way of focusing firms' attention on what really matters.

The FCA has defined six consumer outcomes to explain to firms what it believes TCF should do for its consumers. These are that:

1. consumers can be confident that they are dealing with firms where the fair treatment of customers is central to the corporate culture
2. products and services marketed and sold in the retail market are designed to meet the needs of identified consumer groups and are targeted accordingly
3. consumers are provided with clear information and are kept appropriately informed before, during and after the point of sale
4. if consumers receive advice, the advice is suitable and takes account of their circumstances
5. consumers are provided with products that perform as firms have led them to expect, and the associated service is both of an acceptable standard and as they have been led to expect
6. consumers do not face unreasonable post-sale barriers imposed by firms to change product, switch provider, submit a claim or make a complaint.

To help firms, the FCA has published on its website illustrative examples for each of the outcomes.

The FCA has carried out reviews on all firms to assess how well they are meeting the above outcomes, and also to ensure that firms have appropriate management information in place to monitor their own performance for the fair treatment of clients. This has been largely been taken forward by the principles of conduct risk. For example through its firm systematic framework supervisory tool, the FCA aims to be able to assess a firm's culture throughout the advice process, from the initial client contact to the ongoing service.

In changing the former Advanced, Risk-Responsive Operating FrameWork (ARROW) approach, the FCA has changed its model of supervision. The main steps in the FCA's risk assessment process are as follows:

- **Firm systematic framework (FSF)** – preventative work through structured conduct assessment of firms (considered here and later in this workbook).
- **Event-driven work** – dealing faster and more decisively with problems that are emerging or have happened and securing customer redress or other remedial work where necessary. This covers issues that occur outside the firm assessment cycle, and uses better data monitoring and intelligence.
- **Issues and products** – fast, intensive campaigns on sectors of the market or products within a sector that are putting or may put consumers at risk. This approach is driven by sector risk assessment, which looks at what is currently and prospectively causing poor outcomes for consumers and market participants. It uses data analysis, market intelligence and input from the firm assessment process.

In April 2015, the FCA released a practical structural change to its authorisations and supervision departments. The split into 'retail and authorisations' and 'investment, wholesale and specialists' supervision divisions attempted to address the *increasingly diverse sectors, where risks may be very different across sectors but common across firms within a sector'*. This provided a greater emphasis on sector and market-wide analysis.

Following this, in September 2015, the FCA announced changes to its supervisory model, including how it classified firms to support this sector-based approach.

The FCA stated that it would continue to look at the way individual firms and people behave, but will also increasingly look at how markets work as a whole, with greater emphasis on sector and market-wide analysis.

Part of the change to its model was a move away from the C1–C4 conduct categories that were previously used. Firms are now categorised as either:

- **Fixed portfolio** firms will continue to be subject to a programme of firm or group-specific supervision (Pillar I).
- **Flexible portfolio** firms will be subject to event-driven reactive supervision (Pillar II) and thematic issue or product supervision (Pillar III) only.

The FCA states that flexible portfolio firms will be proactively supervised through a combination of market-based thematic work, as well as communication, engagement and education activity aligned to the key risks the FCA identifies for the sector. The firms moving into the flexible portfolio will no longer have a named supervisor, and their first point of contact will be the customer contact centre. The move from designated supervisory contact to primary contact centre coverage was first introduced in 2003, with the contact centre's expansion from D categorised firms to also cover A–C. This gradual progression away from designated supervisor best reflects the FCA's vastly increased remit over the last decade.

For fixed portfolio impacted firms, Pillar 1 proactive supervision ordinarily comprises a 12- to 36-month cycle covering firm meetings, reviews of management information, an annual strategy meeting and other proactive firm work. Deep dive assessments will look at how a firm's business operates in practice and can be scheduled as part of the supervision strategy. In relation to business model and strategy analysis (BMSAs), the FCA will focus attention on where it sees common indicators of heightened risks.

The Firm Systematic Framework (FSF) is designed to assess a firm's conduct risk, and aims to answer the question: are the interests of customers and market integrity at the heart of how the firm is run? It does this by using a common framework across all sectors, which is targeted to the type of firm.

The common features involve:

- **Business model and strategy analysis (BMSA)** – to give a view on how sustainable the business is in respect of conduct and of where future risks may lie.
- Assessment of how the firm embeds fair treatment of customers and ensures market integrity in the way it conducts its business.

The assessment has four modules:

- **governance and culture** – to assess how effectively a firm identifies, manages and reduces conduct risks
- **product design** – to determine whether a firm's products or services meet customer needs and are targeted accordingly
- **sales or transaction processes** – to assess firms' systems and controls, and
- **post-sales/services and transaction handling** – to assess how effectively a firm ensures its customers are treated fairly after the point-of-sale, service or transaction, including complaints handling.

2.3 Statements of Principle and Code of Practice for Approved Persons

Learning Objective

1.2.7 Know the Statements of Principle and Code of Practice for Approved Persons (APER 1.1A.1 1.2.3, 1.2.3A 2.1A,2 2.1B.2 3.1.1A, 3.1.1B-3.1.7A, 3.1.7B, 4.1-4.7)

We have seen above that the FCA authorises firms to carry out regulated activities. However, a firm is a collection of individuals, and some of these individuals are considered to occupy roles which are critical to the effective control and operation of the firm and to its capacity to meet the requirements of authorisation. These individuals must be approved by the FCA to fulfil their role, and so they are known as **approved persons**.

These important roles are known as the **controlled functions**, and they break down into two types:

1. **Significant influence functions (SIFs)** – functions that are governing or managerial. These include the directors of the firm and other key personnel.
2. **Customer functions** – functions involving interaction with the customers of the firm, such as an investment adviser or investment manager.

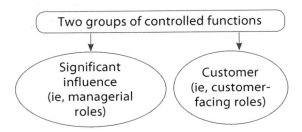

A more detailed breakdown of these controlled functions is provided in Section 2.6.1. In an authorised firm, only persons approved by the FCA may fill these roles.

In a similar manner to the principles for businesses, the high level standards block of the handbook contains a sourcebook, statements of principle and code of practice for approved persons (APER), which sets out the fundamental obligations of approved persons. These show the seven statements of principle as well as a code of practice for approved persons. This code of practice describes conduct which, in the opinion of the FCA, does not comply with the statements of principle and also outlines factors that should be taken into account in determining whether or not an approved person's conduct complies with a statement of principle.

2.3.1 Statements of Principle for Approved Persons

The statements of principle state that an approved person must:

(For All Functions)

1. Act with integrity in carrying out his controlled function.
2. Act with due skill, care and diligence in carrying out his controlled function.
3. Observe proper standards of market conduct in carrying out his controlled function.
4. Deal with the FCA and with other regulators in an open and co-operative way and disclose appropriately any information of which the FCA would reasonably expect notice.

The new Accountability Regime, discussed in Section 2.8, has brought in an enhanced level of responsibility for those captured that goes beyond the Approved Persons regime.

(Additional Principles for SIFs)

5. Take reasonable steps to ensure that the business of the firm for which he is responsible in his controlled function is organised so that it can be controlled effectively.
6. Exercise due skill, care and diligence in managing the business of the firm for which he is responsible in his controlled function.
7. Take reasonable steps to ensure that the business of the firm for which he is responsible in his controlled function complies with the relevant requirements and standards of the regulatory system.

The following sections (2.3.2 to 2.3.8) are taken directly from the code of practice and show how it expands on the (relatively broad) principles set out above.

2.3.2 Code of Practice for Statement of Principle 1

In the opinion of the FCA, any of the following is a failure to comply with the requirement for an approved person to act with integrity in carrying out their controlled function:

1. Deliberately misleading (or attempting to mislead) a client, the firm (including the firm's auditors or appointed actuary) or the FCA by either act or omission. This includes deliberately:
   - falsifying documents
   - misleading a client about the risks of an investment
   - misleading a client about the charges or surrender penalties of investment products
   - misleading a client about the likely performance of investment products by providing inappropriate projections of future investment returns
   - misleading a client by informing him that products only require a single payment when that is not the case
   - mismarking the value of investments or trading positions
   - procuring the unjustified alteration of prices on illiquid or off-exchange contracts
   - misleading others within the firm about the creditworthiness of a borrower
   - providing false or inaccurate documentation or information, including details of training, qualifications, past employment record or experience
   - providing false or inaccurate information to the firm (or to the firm's auditors or appointed actuary);
   - providing false or inaccurate information to the FCA
   - destroying, or causing the destruction of, documents (including false documentation) or tapes or their contents, relevant to misleading (or attempting to mislead) a client, the firm or the FCA;
   - failing to disclose dealings where disclosure is required by the firm's personal account-dealing rules, and
   - misleading others in the firm about the nature of risks being accepted.

2. Deliberately recommending an investment to a customer, or carrying out a discretionary transaction for a customer, if the approved person knows that he is unable to justify its suitability for that customer.

3. Deliberately failing to inform a customer, the firm (or its auditors or appointed actuary) or the FCA of the fact that their understanding of a material issue is incorrect. This includes deliberately failing to:
   - disclose the existence of falsified documents
   - rectify mismarked positions immediately.

4. Deliberately preparing inaccurate or inappropriate records or returns in connection with a controlled function, such as:
   - performance reports for transmission to customers which are inaccurate or inappropriate (eg, by relying on past performance without giving appropriate warnings)
   - inaccurate training records or details of qualifications, past employment record or experience
   - inaccurate trading confirmations, contract notes or other records of transactions or holdings of securities for a customer, whether or not the customer is aware of these inaccuracies or has requested such records.

5. Deliberately misusing the assets or confidential information of a client or the firm such as:
   - front running client orders (ie, handling the firm's own orders before those of its client, or before the firm's broker recommendations are released to clients, so as to benefit from price movements that may arise from client dealing activity)
   - carrying out unjustified trading on client accounts to generate a benefit to the approved person (sometimes known as **churning**)
   - misappropriating a client's assets, including wrongly transferring cash or securities belonging to clients to personal accounts
   - using a client's funds for purposes other than those for which they are provided;
   - retaining a client's funds wrongly, and
   - pledging the assets of a client as security or margin in circumstances where the firm is not permitted to do so.

6. Deliberately designing transactions so as to disguise breaches of requirements and standards of the regulatory system.

7. Deliberately failing to disclose the existence of a conflict of interest in connection with dealings with a client.

8. Deliberately not paying due regard to the interests of a customer.

9. Deliberate acts, omissions or business practices that could be reasonably expected to cause consumer detriment.

2.3.3 Code of Practice for Statement of Principle 2

In the opinion of the FCA, any of the following is a failure to comply with the requirement for an approved person to act with due skill, care and diligence in carrying out their controlled function.

1. Failing to inform a customer or the firm (or the firm's auditors or appointed actuary) of material information in circumstances where he was aware, or ought to have been aware, of such information and the fact that he should provide it. Examples include:
   - failing to explain the risks of an investment to a customer
   - failing to disclose details of the charges or surrender penalties of investment products
   - mismarking trading positions
   - providing inaccurate or inadequate information to the firm, its auditors or appointed actuary
   - failing to disclose dealings where disclosure is required by the firm's personal account dealing rules.

2. Recommending an investment to a customer, or carrying out a discretionary transaction for a customer, where he does not have reasonable grounds to believe that it is suitable for that customer.

3. Undertaking, recommending or providing advice on transactions without reasonable understanding of the risk exposure of the transaction to the customer. For example, recommending transactions in investments to a customer without a reasonable understanding of the liability of that transaction.
4. Undertaking transactions without a reasonable understanding of the risk exposure of the transaction to the firm. For example, trading on the firm's own account without a reasonable understanding of the liability of that transaction.
5. Failing without good reason to disclose the existence of a conflict of interest in connection with dealings with a client.
6. Failing to provide adequate control over a client's assets, such as failing to segregate a client's assets or failing to process a client's payments in a timely manner.
7. Continuing to perform a controlled function despite having failed to meet the standards of knowledge and skills as required by the FCA.
8. Failing to pay due regard to the interests of a customer, without good reason.

2.3.4   Code of Practice for Statement of Principle 3

Statement of Principle 3 requires an approved person to observe proper standards of market conduct in carrying out their controlled function. In terms of interpreting what might be regarded as **proper standards of market conduct**, the FCA states that compliance with its Code of Market Conduct will tend to show compliance with Statement of Principle 3.

2.3.5   Code of Practice for Statement of Principle 4

Statement of Principle 4 requires an approved person to deal with the FCA and other regulators in an open and co-operative way and to disclose appropriately any information of which the FCA would reasonably expect notice.

The FCA does not consider the following behaviours by an approved person to comply with Statement of Principle 4:

1. Failing to report promptly in accordance with his firm's internal procedures (or, if none exists, direct to the FCA) information which it would be reasonable to assume would be of material significance to the FCA, whether in response to questions or otherwise.
2. Failing without good reason to:
    a. inform a regulator of information of which the approved person was aware in response to questions from that regulator
    b. attend an interview or answer questions put by a regulator, despite a request or demand having been made
    c. supply a regulator with appropriate documents or information when requested or required to do so and within the time limits attaching to that request or requirement.

2.3.6   Code of Practice for Statement of Principle 5

Statement of Principle 5 requires an approved person performing a SIF to take reasonable steps to ensure that the business of the firm for which he is responsible in their controlled function is organised so that it can be controlled effectively.

The FCA expects this to include the following:

1. **Reporting lines** – the organisation of the business and the responsibilities of those within it should be clearly defined, with reporting lines clear to staff. If staff have dual reporting lines there is a greater need to ensure that the responsibility and accountability of each individual line manager is clearly set out and understood.
2. **Authorisation levels and job descriptions** – if members of staff have particular levels of authorisation, these should be clearly set out and communicated to staff. It may be appropriate for each member of staff to have a job description of which he is aware.
3. **Suitability of individuals** – if an individual's performance is unsatisfactory, the appropriate approved person performing a SIF should review carefully whether that individual should be allowed to continue in that position. The approved person performing the SIF should not let the financial performance of the individual (or group) prevent an appropriate investigation into the compliance with the requirements and standards of the regulatory system.

Failure to comply with Principle 5 may include weaknesses and failings in any of these areas, eg:

- failure to apportion responsibilities
- poor systems and controls
- failure to act upon relevant management information
- failure to review the competence of individuals.

2.3.7 Code of Practice for Statement of Principle 6

Statement of Principle 6 requires an approved person performing a SIF to exercise due skill, care and diligence in managing the business of the firm for which they are responsible in his controlled function.

In the opinion of the FCA, the following behaviour by an approved person does not comply with Statement of Principle 6:

1. Failing to take reasonable steps adequately to inform himself about the affairs of the business for which he is responsible, including:
   - permitting transactions without understanding the risks
   - permitting expansion of the business without assessing the risks
   - inadequate monitoring of highly profitable or unusual transactions or practices
   - not testing the veracity of explanations from subordinates; not obtaining independent, expert opinion where necessary.
2. Delegating the authority for dealing with an issue or a part of the business to an individual or individuals (whether in-house or outside contractors) without reasonable grounds for believing that the delegate had the necessary capacity, competence, knowledge, seniority or skill to deal with the issue or to take authority for dealing with that part of the business.
3. Failing to take reasonable steps to maintain an appropriate level of understanding about an issue or part of the business that he has delegated to an individual or individuals (whether in-house or outside contractors), including:
   - disregarding a delegated issue
   - not obtaining adequate reports
   - not testing the veracity of explanations from subordinates.
4. Failing to supervise and monitor adequately the individual or individuals (whether in-house or outside contractors) to whom responsibility for dealing with an issue or authority for dealing with a part of the business has been delegated, including:
   - failing to take action where progress is unreasonably slow or unsatisfactory explanations are given
   - failing to review the performance of an outside contractor.

2.3.8 Code of Practice for Statement of Principle 7

Statement of Principle 7 requires an approved person performing a SIF to take reasonable steps to ensure that the business of the firm for which they are responsible in his controlled function complies with the relevant requirements and standards of the regulatory system.

In the opinion of the FCA, the following behaviour by an approved person does not comply with the provisions of Principle 7:

- Failing to take reasonable steps to implement adequate and appropriate systems and controls in respect of the firm's regulated activities.
- Failing to take reasonable steps to monitor compliance with the relevant requirements and standards of the regulatory system.
- Failing to inform himself of the reason for any suspected or actual breaches of the relevant regulatory provisions.
- Failing to take reasonable steps to ensure that procedures and systems are reviewed and if necessary improved, following identification of a breach.
- For the Money Laundering Reporting Officer (MLRO), failure to perform his duties.

2.4 FCA Supervision

Learning Objective

1.2.5 Understand the approach of the FCA to supervision and the role of risk-based supervision (SUP 1A.3)

2.4.1 Tools of Supervision

The FCA has a range of supervisory tools available to it that it classifies under four headings:

- **Diagnostic tools** – designed to identify, assess and measure risk.
- **Monitoring tools** – to track the development of identified risk, wherever this arises.
- **Preventative tools** – to limit or reduce identified risks and so prevent them crystallising or increasing.
- **Remedial tools** – to respond to risks when they have crystallised.

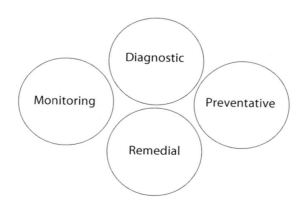

Some tools involve the FCA in a direct client relationship with firms, such as supervisory visits by FCA staff. Others do not involve the firms directly; for example, the FCA may make public statements to consumers about the riskiness of particular types of products, without singling out a specific provider.

2.4.2 Risk Diagnosis, Monitoring and Prevention

Under the FSMA, the FCA is required to maintain arrangements to supervise compliance with the requirements imposed on authorised persons. Specifically, the FSMA states that the FCA should: *'maintain arrangements designed to enable it to determine whether persons on whom requirements are imposed by or under this Act are complying with them'*.

The way in which it approaches this task is drawn from the FSMA and incorporates two fundamental principles. These are:

1. It is the responsibility of a firm's management to organise and control the firm effectively and maintain adequate risk management systems, with the ultimate aim of acting in compliance with its regulatory requirements.
2. The FCA will attempt to balance any burden or restriction placed on firms with the benefits that are likely to result (ie, it will take proportionate action, and not use a regulatory sledgehammer to crack a nut).

In accordance with the second principle, the FCA adopts a risk-based approach to supervision. This means that it focuses its resources on mitigating those risks which pose a threat to the achievement of its statutory objectives (with most resource being expended on the greatest risks) and that it has regard to the efficient and economic use of its resources.

The regulatory philosophy which originally guided the FCA's approach to policy formulation and supervision was principles-based regulation. The FCA characterises this approach as evidence-based and risk-based. In formulating policy and executing supervision, the FCA seeks to ensure that this is done in partnership with and with extensive input from consumers and the industry.

The FSA extensively reviewed its supervisory process following the collapse of Northern Rock in 2008, and concluded that, although the FSA's core supervisory principles were supported by the recent financial crisis, changes were nevertheless required, involving a move to outcomes-focused supervision and drawing upon the lessons from the global credit crisis.

The FCA implemented these changes through its supervisory enhancement programme and refers to the resulting enhanced process as **intensive supervision**.

The intended outcomes of the supervisory enhancement programme are for better, more effective and consistent supervisions as defined by:

- an integrated and consistent supervisory process across all relationship-managed firms
- a focus on big-picture risks: business models and strategy
- a balanced approach to prudential and conduct risks
- an increased focus on macro-prudential and cross-sector risks
- an effective relationship management capability
- a willingness to make judgments on the future risks and to require firms to mitigate them in advance of them crystallising.

Delivering Effective, On-the-Ground, Intensive Supervision and Credible Deterrence

The FCA has radically changed the way it operates, compared with the FSA. In particular it has revised both the regulatory philosophy and the operating model which enables its delivery. The underlying principle of the old-style FSA was that it would not intervene until something went wrong. This was well supported by society and the City at the time. The new model of supervision requires the FCA to intervene in a proactive way when it believes that the results of a firm's actions will pose a risk to the FCA's statutory objectives. This therefore requires the FCA to adopt a more intrusive, confrontational and direct regulatory style than before and to make judgments that are undoubtedly more difficult, and may be disputed by firms (and in some cases found to be wrong).

The outcomes-focused intensive supervision model has two key features.

Firstly, a significant enhanced analysis and risk identification capacity which focuses on business model risk and interacts with macro-prudential analysis. For this, the FCA requires more and better quality people and more sophisticated systems and analysis. Comprehensive conduct business model analysis is now being undertaken by FCA supervisors, supported by sector teams and conduct specialists, who also contribute wider market knowledge and horizon risk scanning. This is combined with mystery shopping and on-site visits, to increase the probability of identifying issues before they gain an industry-wide hold.

Secondly, there is a greater focus on outcome testing, rather than ensuring that firms have the appropriate systems and controls. This approach also requires earlier and more direct regulatory intervention.

Underpinning both of these is a greater scrutiny of senior management competence, where historically the FSA only judged probity. The FCA now seeks to assess both technical competence and the ability of individuals to contribute to effective governance. As with other aspects of the new approach, this requires the FCA to make judgements that at times will be at variance with those of the firms.

A final aspect of the new supervisory approach is the aim to deliver credible deterrence, including a consistent and more transparent framework for calculating financial penalties.

2.4.3 Risk-Based Approach

The risk-based approach discussed above means that the FCA assesses individual firms for the risk each one presents to the FCA's objectives. This helps the FCA determine what level of supervisory attention should be directed at each firm.

The FCA stated that following the financial crisis it has become clear that there are various issues with culture and business practices in many areas of the financial services industry and the FCA seeks to ensure that firms are considering consumers and market integrity throughout their operations and services.

The FCA seeks to ensure this by looking closely at the culture and practices of firms from a variety of aspects with a focus on market level understanding of conduct on a sector and subsector basis and to mitigate risks accordingly.

The FCA's work will be divided into three separate pillars:

1. Proactive firm supervision

An assessment of whether firms have the interests of their clients and the integrity of the market at the heart of their business (Pillar 1 supervision is only applicable to fixed portfolio firms).

Pillar 1 work will consist of four separate evaluation and supervision methods:

Business model and strategy analysis (BMSA); an analysis of business models and strategies in order to understand possible risks to consumers and market integrity. Factors which the FCA has stated will serve as indicators for heightened risk comprise:

- fast growth
- high levels of profitability
- cross-selling dependent strategies
- products with unclear features
- products being sold into undesignated markets for their purpose, and
- inherent conflicts of interest.

Proactive engagement; the FCA's regular engagement with firms in order to maintain an understanding of the key aspects of their operations to identify emerging risks and take preemptive measures in response. Proactive engagement consists of three main elements:

- meetings with key individuals
- regular reviews of management information, and
- annual strategy meetings.

Deep dive assessments; focussing on four risk groups:

- culture and governance
- product design
- sales and transaction processes, and
- post-sales/services and transaction handling.

Firm evaluation; a summary of the FCA's review based on previous evaluations. Taking all factors into account, the FCA judges and explains its view in regards to the risks posed by a firm and their causes. The FCA's strategy and work programme for the firm's next supervision cycle are aimed at addressing and mitigating those risks.

2. Reactive supervision

Upon becoming aware of a significant risk to consumers or markets (or upon damage being suffered), ensuring mitigation of such risk and, if necessary, using the FCA's formal powers to hold firms or individuals accountable to those who have been treated unfairly. Reactive, event driven supervision will apply to both fixed and flexible portfolio firms.

3. Issues and products supervision

Pillar 3 comprises sectoral analysis of events and potential drivers of poor outcomes for consumers and markets. This work ranges from large and detailed studies, such as thematic reviews, to smaller sample-based work. Given that Pillar 1 proactive supervision does not apply to flexible portfolio firms, Pillar 3 supervision is the FCA's prime form of proactively supervising flexible portfolio firms.

In conducting market supervision, the FCA also adheres to, and asks firms to adhere to, the following ten principles:

1. ensuring fair outcomes for consumers and markets
2. being forward-looking and pre-emptive
3. being focused on the big issues and causes of problems
4. taking a judgement-based approach
5. ensuring firms act in the right spirit
6. examining business models and culture
7. emphasising individual accountability
8. being robust when things go wrong
9. communicating openly
10. having a joined-up approach.

These ten principles are reflected throughout the regulator's three-pillar approach to supervising the markets and are applicable to all firms.

The FCA has also set a strategic objective of ensuring that the relevant markets function well and have embodied this through providing an appropriate degree of protection for consumers while protecting and enhancing market integrity and promoting effective competition.

Both fixed portfolio firms and flexible portfolio firms must evaluate the systems and controls they have in place in light of the above principles, with adherence to the FCA's strategic objectives.

2.4.4 Main Steps in Risk Assessment

In changing the former ARROW approach, the FCA has changed its model of supervision. The main steps in the FCA's risk assessment process are as follows:

- **Firm systematic framework (FSF)** – preventative work through structured conduct assessment of firms.
- **Event-driven work** – dealing more quickly and more decisively with problems that are emerging or have happened and securing customer redress or other remedial work where necessary. This covers issues that occur outside the firm assessment cycle and uses better data monitoring and intelligence.
- **Issues and products** – fast, intensive campaigns on sectors of the market or products within a sector that are putting or may put consumers at risk. This approach is driven by what we call sector risk assessment, which looks at what is currently and prospectively causing poor outcomes for consumers and market participants. It uses data analysis, market intelligence and input from the firm assessment process.

1. **The Firm Systematic Framework (FSF)**

This is designed to assess a firm's conduct risk, and aims to answer the question: are the interests of customers and market integrity at the heart of how the firm is run? It does this by using a common framework across all sectors, which is targeted to the type of firm.

The common features involve:

- Business model and strategy analysis (BMSA) – to give a view on how sustainable the business is in respect of conduct, and of where future risks may lie.
- Assessment of how the firm embeds fair treatment of customers and ensures market integrity in the way it conducts its business.
  The assessment has four modules:
  - governance and culture – to assess how effectively a firm identifies, manages and reduces conduct risks
  - product design – to determine whether a firm's products or services meet customer needs and are targeted accordingly
  - sales or transaction processes – to assess firms' systems and controls, and
  - post-sales/services and transaction handling – to assess how effectively a firm ensures its customers are treated fairly after the point of sale, service or transaction, including complaints handling.
- Deciding what actions are required by the firm to address issues identified.
- Communication to the firm, setting out the assessment and actions required.

2. Event-driven work
Having fewer supervisors allocated to specific firms means more flexibility to devote resources to situations in firms where there is heightened risk to consumers; or where consumers have experienced some loss and quick action is required to stop the situation from worsening.

3. Issues and products
Being more flexible in how the FCA deploys supervisors means it can react promptly to emerging issues, and carry out more reviews on products and issues across a sector or market. The FCA uses a sector risk assessment (SRA) to drive this issue and product work. This provides an assessment of the conduct risks across a sector (such as the investment intermediary sector, or the retail banking sector). This complements firm-specific work, so together they identify risks, whether they are cross-firm issues, firm-specific issues or product issues. The FCA also uses a range of data, information and intelligence from firms, consumers and trade bodies to identify the biggest risks and to prioritise its work.

The key questions the FCA uses the SRA to answer are:

- What are the cross-firm and product issues that are behind poor outcomes for consumers or endanger market integrity?
- What is the degree of potential harm?
- What is the discovery or mitigation work proposed?

Specialist sector teams work together to deliver these assessments, making appropriate use of external data and market intelligence.

2.5 Senior Management Arrangements, Systems and Controls (SYSC)

Learning Objective

1.2.5 Understand the approach of the FCA to supervision and the role of risk based supervision (SUP 1A.3)

1.2.6 Know the senior management responsibilities: purpose (SYSC 1.2.1, 1.2.1A); apportionment of responsibilities (SYSC 2.1.1); recording the apportionment (SYSC 2.2.1); systems and controls (SYSC 3.1.1); compliance (SYSC 6.1.1-5), internal audit (SYSC 6.2.1, 6.2.1A) and risk functions (SYSC 7.1.2/3/5)

The FCA imposes certain requirements on the directors and senior managers of authorised firms. These are set out in the high level standards block of the handbook in the sourcebook Senior Management Arrangements, Systems and Controls (SYSC).

The requirements, and their purpose, are as follows:

1. **Senior management responsibility** – to encourage firms' directors and senior managers to take responsibility for their firm's arrangements on matters likely to be of interest to the FCA (because they are relevant to the FCA's ability to discharge its regulatory obligations).
2. **Effective organisation and control** – to amplify Principle for Businesses 3 (discussed in Section 2.2), under which a firm must take reasonable care to organise and control its affairs responsibly and effectively, with adequate risk management systems.
3. **Apportionment of responsibility** – to encourage firms to vest responsibility for an effective and responsible organisation in specific directors and senior managers, so that everyone knows who is responsible for what activities, so that functions are not, therefore, in danger of falling between stools (each director/manager regarding another as being accountable for a given activity or function, for example, so that no one person assumes responsibility for its oversight).
4. **Common standards** – to create a common platform of organisational systems and controls for all firms. Originally the standards only applied to firms subject to the Capital Requirements Directive (CRD) and MiFID.

After public consultation in 2008, the FCA (the FSA at that time) extended these requirements to firms that are not subject to the CRD or MiFID. These firms are called **non-scope** or **non-common-platform** firms and the requirements are in the form of guidance rather than rules. This means that, in most cases, non-common-platform firms should read the rules and requirements outlined below, replacing the word **must** with **should**.

2.5.1 Apportionment of Responsibilities

As part of the above requirements set out in SYSC, the FCA requires all firms to take reasonable care to maintain a clear and appropriate apportionment of significant responsibilities among their directors and senior managers in such a way that:

* it is clear who has those responsibilities, and
* the business and affairs of the firm can be adequately monitored and controlled by the directors, relevant senior managers and governing body of the firm.

2.5.2 Recording the Apportionment

Firms must make a record of the arrangements they have made to satisfy the FCA's requirement to apportion responsibilities among directors and senior managers. They must also take reasonable care to keep this record up to date and retain the record for six years from the date on which it was superseded by a more up-to-date record.

2.5.3 Systems and Controls

The FCA requires all firms to take reasonable care to establish and maintain such systems and controls as are appropriate to their business. Clearly, the nature and extent of these appropriate systems and controls will depend on a variety of factors, such as the nature, scale and complexity of the business, geographical diversity, the volume and size of the transactions undertaken and the degree of risk associated with each area of business operations.

2.5.4 Compliance

The systems and controls mentioned above include taking reasonable care to establish and maintain effective systems and controls for compliance with applicable requirements and standards under the regulatory system, and for countering the risk that the firm might be used to further financial crime (including, but not limited to, money laundering).

A common-platform firm must maintain a permanent and effective compliance function which operates independently. The compliance function is responsible for monitoring and assessing the adequacy and effectiveness of the measures and procedures put in place by the firm in order to comply with regulatory standards.

The compliance function should advise and assist the persons responsible for carrying out the firm's regulated activities to comply with the firm's regulatory obligations and should have the necessary authority, resources, expertise and access to all information that is relevant for the performance of its role. A firm must appoint a compliance officer, who is responsible for its compliance function.

2.5.5 Governance Arrangements

Firms must have robust governance arrangements, which include a clear organisational structure with well defined, transparent and consistent lines of responsibility, effective processes to identify, manage, monitor and report the risks it is, or might be, exposed to, and internal control mechanisms, including sound administrative and accounting procedures for effective control. These arrangements, processes and mechanisms must be comprehensive and proportionate to the nature, scale and complexity of a firm's activities.

Firms must also establish, implement and maintain systems and procedures that are adequate to safeguard the security, integrity and confidentiality of information, taking into account the nature of the information in question.

Firms must also monitor and evaluate on a regular basis the adequacy and effectiveness of their systems, internal control mechanisms and arrangements established and take appropriate measures to address any deficiencies.

2.5.6 Responsibility of Senior Personnel

Senior personnel, including the supervisory function, within a firm are responsible for ensuring that the firm complies with its obligations under the regulatory system. In particular, senior personnel must assess and periodically review the effectiveness of the policies, arrangements and procedures put in place to comply with the firm's obligations under the regulatory system and take appropriate measures to address any deficiencies.

2.5.7 Other Personnel

Firms must employ staff with the skills, knowledge and expertise necessary for them to carry out their roles and to discharge the responsibilities allocated to them.

2.5.8 Internal Audit

Firms must, if appropriate and proportionate in view of the nature, scale and complexity of their business and the nature and range of investment services and activities undertaken, establish and maintain an internal audit function which is separate and independent from the other functions and activities of the firm.

2.5.9 Financial Crime and Anti-Money Laundering

Firms must ensure that they have adequate and appropriate policies and procedures to enable them to identify, assess, monitor and manage money laundering risks and must ensure that these are comprehensive and proportionate to the nature, scale and complexity of their activities.

Firms must appoint an individual as the MLRO, with responsibility for oversight of their compliance with the FCA's rules on systems and controls against money laundering. The MLRO should have an appropriate level of authority and independence within the firm and have access to resources and information sufficient to enable him to carry out that responsibility.

2.5.10 Risk Control/Function

Firms must establish, implement and maintain adequate risk management policies and procedures, including effective procedures for risk assessment, which identify the risks relating to the firm's activities, processes and systems and if appropriate set the level of risk tolerated by the firm.

Firms must also monitor the adequacy and effectiveness of their risk management policies and procedures, the level of compliance by the firms and their relevant persons with the arrangements, processes and mechanisms adopted and the adequacy and effectiveness of measures taken to address any deficiencies on those policies, procedures, arrangements, processes and mechanisms.

2.5.11 Record-Keeping

Firms must arrange for orderly records to be kept of their business and internal organisations, including all services and transactions undertaken by them, which must be sufficient to enable the FCA or any other relevant competent authority to monitor firms' compliance with the requirements. These records must be kept for a period of at least five years if they relate to MiFID business; for non-MiFID business the retention period is at least three years.

Records must be maintained by firms in a medium that allows the storage of information in a way that is accessible for future reference by the FCA or any other competent authorities.

2.6   The Controlled Functions

Learning Objective

1.2.8   Understand the FCA's controlled functions (SUP10A.4): the five functional areas and the main roles within each; the four areas of significant influence functions (SUP 10A.5.1, 10A.6.1, 10A.7.1, 10A.8.1, 10A.9.1/2, 10A.10.1/3); the requirement for FCA approval prior to appointment; the on-going requirement to be fit and proper; the consequences of a qualified versus clean withdrawal on termination of employment (SUP 10A.12)

1.2.9   Understand the obligations to notify the FCA (SUP 15.3)

As discussed briefly earlier, the FCA calls certain functions within authorised firms **controlled functions**. The FCA lists five types of controlled functions in the FCA Handbook; these are outlined below, along with the description of the 16 individual roles.

2.6.1   Controlled Functions

Following the introduction of the Accountability Regime (refer to Section 2.8) the FCA will be running a two-tier system until such time as the Accountability Regime is rolled out to all regulated firms (around 2018). The Accountability Regime applies to UK banks, building societies and credit unions, foreign banks and insurance companies. All other regulated firms will be covered by the existing Approved Persons Regime. The five types of controlled function are:

1. **Governing functions** – these are the persons responsible for directing the affairs of the business. If the business is a company, they will be the directors of that company. If the business is a partnership, they will be the partners. It is important to remember, however, that the deciding factor is not just whether the person has the title of director – someone who acts as a director, even if he is not formally registered as such (a shadow director) will also require FCA approval because of the influence he exerts over the firm.
2. **Required functions** – these are specific individual functions which the FCA considers to be fundamental to effective control within an authorised firm, as appropriate to the nature of their business. For example, every firm should have appointed someone to fulfil the compliance oversight function and the money laundering reporting functions.
3. **Systems and control functions** – these are the functions which provide the governing body with the information it needs to meet the requirements of Principle 3 of the Principles for Businesses.

4. **Significant management function** – this function occurs only in larger firms where there is a layer of management below the governing body which has responsibility for a significant business unit, eg, the Head of Equities, the Head of Fixed Income and the Head of Settlements.

All of the above groups are described by the FCA as **significant influence functions (SIFs)** because the persons fulfilling these roles exercise a significant influence over the conduct of a firm's affairs.

5. **Customer function** – this function involves giving advice on dealing, arranging deals and managing investments. The individuals have contact with customers in fulfilling their role. Examples of customer functions are an investment adviser or investment manager. Customer functions are not SIFs.

The chart below sets out the specific role descriptions within the controlled functions. When studying this table bear in mind that the exam syllabus requires you to understand only the main roles given in the right-hand column of the table.

You may remember from previously in this chapter (Section 2.2) that Principle 3 of the Principles for Businesses (Management and Control) requires that firms take reasonable care to organise and control their affairs responsibly and effectively. It is this principle that underpins the approved persons regime for individuals performing controlled functions.

Firms' senior management should ensure that the individuals they have occupying relevant roles are **fit and proper** for those roles (see Section 2.7). Indeed, any assessment of the ongoing fitness and propriety of the firm itself will incorporate the extent to which it fulfils this obligation and will include assessing the competence of the staff to ensure they are suitable for their roles. The FCA now interviews applicants for approval for SIFs, to ensure that they are aware of, and able to discharge, their regulatory responsibilities.

The apportionment and oversight function is the function of acting in the capacity of a director or senior manager responsible for either or both of the apportionment function and the oversight function set out in SYSC 2.1.3 and SYSC 4.4.5 R. However, in requiring someone to apportion responsibility, a common-platform firm should not apply for that person or persons to be approved to perform the apportionment and oversight function.

The table below sets out Part 1 of the FCA-controlled functions (FCA-authorised persons and appointed representatives).
The table below sets out Part 1 of the FCA-controlled functions (FCA-authorised persons and appointed representatives).

Type	CF	Description of controlled function
FCA-governing functions*	1	Director function
	2	Non-executive director function
	3	Chief executive function
	4	Partner function
	5	Director of unincorporated association function
	6	Small friendly society function
FCA-required functions*	8	Apportionment and oversight function
	10	Compliance oversight function
	10A	CASS operational oversight function
	11	Money laundering reporting function
	40	Benchmark submission function
	50	Benchmark administration function
Systems and control function*	28	Systems and controls function
Significant management function*	29	Significant management function
Customer-dealing function	30	Customer function
	31	Mortgage customer function
*FCA-significant influence functions		

The table below sets out Part 2 of the FCA-controlled functions (PRA-authorised persons).

Type	CF	Description of FCA controlled function
FCA-required functions*	8	Apportionment and oversight function
	10	Compliance oversight function
	10A	CASS operational oversight function
	11	Money laundering reporting function
	40	Benchmark submission function
	50	Benchmark administration function
Significant management function*	29	Significant management function
Customer-dealing function	30	Customer function
*FCA-significant influence functions		

The table below sets out the PRA-controlled functions for a PRA-authorised firm.

Type	CF	Description of PRA controlled function
PRA-governing functions*	1	Director
	2	Non-executive director function
	3	Chief executive function
	4	Partner
	5	Director of an unincorporated association
	6	Small friendly society
PRA-required functions*	12	Actuarial function
	12A	With-profits actuary function
	12B	Lloyd's actuary function
Significant management function*	28	Systems and controls function
PRA-significant influence functions		

When a person submits their PRA SIF application, they will be required to declare if they also need approval for one of the FCA functions (see table above). This information is required so that the PRA can assess the person's suitability to perform both roles. As FCA consent is required before the PRA can approve an application, the FCA will also be involved in the assessment process. On approval by the PRA the individual's PRA-controlled function will include the FCA role. Only the PRA-controlled function will be shown on the public register.

Both the PRA and the FCA can refuse the application.

To give an example, if someone is appointed to be both a chief executive and a (board level) executive director, they will only need to apply to the PRA for the chief executive function (CF3). They do not also need separate approval for CF1, as they would have done under the FSA. However, the PRA's chief executive function will also cover the individual's actions as an executive director.

2.6.2 Clean and Qualified Withdrawal

Firms are required to submit a form to the FCA no later than seven business days after an approved person ceases to perform a controlled function. In most cases, this is a clean withdrawal.

However, firms must notify the FCA as soon as they become aware, or have information which reasonably suggests, that they will submit a qualified form in respect of an approved person.

A form is **qualified** if the information contained relates to the fact that the firm has dismissed or suspended the approved person from its employment, it relates to the resignation by the approved person while under investigation by the FCA or otherwise reasonably suggests that it may affect the FCA's assessment of the approved person's fitness and propriety.

The notification must be made in writing by either fax or email and should be made where possible within one business day of the firm's becoming aware of the information.

2.6.4　Notification Requirements

A regulated firm must notify the appropriate regulator (either the FCA or the PRA depending on the regulated firm) immediately it becomes aware, or has information which reasonably suggests, that any of the following has occurred, may have occurred or may occur in the foreseeable future:

1. the firm failing to satisfy one or more of the threshold conditions (as set out in FSMA), or
2. any matter which could have a significant adverse impact on the firm's reputation, or
3. any matter which could affect the firm's ability to continue to provide adequate services to its customers and which could result in serious detriment to a customer of the firm, or
4. any matter in respect of the firm which could result in serious financial consequences to the UK financial system or to other firms.

The circumstances which may give rise to any of these events are wide-ranging and the probability of any matter resulting in such an outcome, and the severity of the outcome, may be difficult to determine. However, the FCA and the PRA expect firms to consider properly all potential consequences of events. The FCA's Principle 11 covers everything that the regulator might reasonably need to know in the proper discharge of its duties, which effectively places the onus on the regulated community to disclose anything of relevance.

Over and above the standard applications to perform controlled functions and applications to vary a firm's permission, for example, which are standalone processes, and the GABRIEL reporting system, transaction reporting, and other required disclosures, the regulator needs to know anything that may impact achieving their objectives.

This would include whether there is any variance from the information supplied to it earlier, either through the original application for authorisation and the business plan provided, or subsequent information given, or anything else of relevance.

In practice, firms provide (or should provide) information of relevance, in a timely manner. If, at a subsequent monitoring visit the FCA discovers matters pertaining to the above that it would or should have had prior sight, this raises more questions about being open and co-operative or, if ignorance is cited, a wider question of competence.

It's much more straightforward and compliant to apprise the FCA on an ongoing basis of anything relevant.

2.7 The Fit and Proper Test

Learning Objective

1.2.10 Understand the criteria applied to ensure approved persons are fit and proper to conduct investment business with retail and professional clients (FIT 1.3, 2.1, 2.2 & 2.3)

As discussed above, persons performing controlled functions need to be first approved by the FCA, which will assess whether they are considered to be fit and proper to perform that function.

In assessing fitness and propriety within the approved persons' regime, the FCA will consider a number of factors, of which the most important will be the person's:

- honesty, integrity and reputation
- competence and capability, and
- financial soundness.

During the application process, the FCA may discuss the candidate's fitness and propriety with the firm and may retain notes of such discussions. In making its assessment the FCA will consider the controlled function to be fulfilled, the activities of the firm and the permission which has been granted to the firm. If any information comes to light that suggests that the individual might not be fit and proper, the FCA will take into account how relevant and important it is.

The following criteria are among those which will be considered when assessing an individual's fitness and propriety; they do not, however, constitute a definitive list of the matters which may be relevant.

2.7.1 Honesty, Integrity and Reputation

The FCA will have regard to whether a person has been:

- convicted of a criminal offence; particular consideration will be given to offences of fraud, dishonesty and financial crime
- the subject of an adverse finding or settlement in a civil case, again with particular consideration given to cases involving financial businesses and fraud
- the subject of previous investigation or disciplinary proceedings by the FCA or another regulatory authority;
- the subject of a justified complaint in relation to regulated activities
- refused a licence to trade, or had a licence or registration revoked
- involved in an insolvent business
- disqualified as a director, or dismissed from a position of trust.

The person must be able to demonstrate a readiness and willingness to comply with the requirements and standards of the regulatory system.

The FCA will treat each application on its merits, considering the seriousness and circumstances of any matters arising, as well as (in some cases) the length of time which has elapsed since the matter arose.

The FCA will consider previous convictions or dismissals/suspensions from employment for drugs, alcohol abuse or other abusive acts only if they relate to the continuing ability of the person to perform the controlled function for which they are employed.

2.7.2 Competence and Capability

In assessing an applicant's competence and capability, the FCA will have particular regard to whether the person:

- satisfies the relevant requirements laid down in the FCA's Training and Competence Sourcebook;
- has demonstrated the experience and training needed for them to fulfil the controlled function applied for, and
- has sufficient time to perform the controlled function and meet its responsibilities.

2.7.3 Financial Soundness

When assessing an applicant's financial soundness, the FCA will have particular regard to whether the person has:

- been subject to any judgment to repay a debt or pay another award that remains outstanding, or was not satisfied within a reasonable period
- filed for bankruptcy, been adjudged bankrupt, had their assets sequestrated or made arrangements with their creditors.

The FCA will not normally require a statement of a person's assets and liabilities – the fact that a person may be of limited financial means will not of itself impact their suitability to perform a controlled function.

2.8 Accountability Regime

Learning Objective

1.2.11 Understand the new Accountability Regime (Senior Managers Regime) regime for banks – Senior Managers, Certificate Regime and Conduct Rules

1.2.12 Know how the Senior Managers Regime applies to individuals, including approval by the PRA/ FCA, fit and proper certificates and the notification of breaches of the Conduct Rules

Both the FCA and PRA (the regulators) believe that holding individuals to account is a key component of effective regulation. In June 2012 Parliament established the Parliamentary Commission on Banking Standards (PCBS) to consider and report on:

- professional standards and the culture of the UK banking sector, taking account of regulatory and competition investigations into the LIBOR rate-setting process, and
- lessons to be learned about corporate governance, transparency and conflicts of interest and their implications for regulation and for government policy.

The recommendations of the PCBS implemented changes required by amendments which the Financial Services (Banking Reform) Act 2013 (the Act) made to the FSMA.

The PCBS concluded that public trust in banking was at an all-time low and recommended a series of measures to restore trust and improve culture. These recommendations proposed a new framework for approving and holding individuals to account which would include:

- a Licensing Regime (which subsequently became the Certification Regime under the Banking Reform Act) operating alongside the Senior Persons Regime and applying to other bank staff whose actions or behaviour could significantly harm the bank, its reputation or its customers, and
- replacing the existing Statements of Principle and Code of Conduct for Approved Persons with a set of enforceable Conduct Rules which would apply to a wider range of employees than those subject to regulatory approval.

These changes are significant and include:

- A new **Senior Managers Regime** (SMR) for individuals who are subject to regulatory approval, which will require firms to allocate a range of responsibilities to these individuals and to regularly vet their fitness and propriety. This will focus accountability on a narrower number of senior individuals in a firm than under the current Approved Persons Regime (APR).
- A **Certification Regime** which will require relevant firms to assess the fitness and propriety of certain employees who could pose a risk of significant harm to the firm or any of its customers.
- A new set of **Conduct Rules**, which will apply to persons in the combined scope of the SMR and the Certification Regime.

The new Conduct Rules will apply to persons in the combined scope of the SMR and the Certification Regime.

The FCA will also apply them to most employees of relevant firms (other Conduct Rules staff) based in the UK or who deal with customers in the UK. This means that the Conduct Rules will cover all employees who are able to affect the FCA's objectives. It will also prevent gaming of the Certification Regime and raise overall conduct standards in the industry.

The scope of this new regime applies to credit institutions and dual-regulated firms. Here are the rules in summary:

Senior Managers Regime

Chairmen and non-executive directors will now be included as **senior management functions** and will be explicitly held to account for boardroom decisions and deemed potentially culpable for poor decisions as executive directors.

The Senior Management Functions, therefore, need to show and demonstrate an increased understanding of the key business and strategic activities of the entities for which they are responsible, and their associated risks.

A number of differing classifications have been introduced:

- **Prescribed Responsibilities** will be allocated to the most senior of those performing **Senior Management Functions**. Captured individual will be recorded as part of the individual statements of responsibility describing the most senior executives' roles, and demonstrated through day-to-day management, adding to the scope and accountability of current roles and control and information arrangements.

- A **Management Responsibilities Map** will introduce the concept of documenting a firm's management and governance arrangements, including how the statements of responsibility have been allocated. This will provide enhanced transparency of individual accountability and increase the reporting lines and quality and specificity of management information requirements of those affected.
- A **Presumption of Responsibility** (originally a measure, but subsequently replaced with a **duty of responsibility** would have reversed the burden of proof, and demanded improved evidence of oversight to show that **reasonable steps** have been taken to prevent, stop or remedy breaches).
- **Parallel regimes** will operate for organisations with both banking and non-banking activities. Whilst the new regimes will apply to banking, there will be expectations of consistency in the way governance operates as a whole.

Conduct Rules and Certification Regime

A new framework of behavioural standards will be introduced against which individual conduct will be judged through Conduct Rules applicable to all individuals (but not ancillary staff), with a requirement to notify the regulator of breaches and any formal disciplinary action taken. This is a much wider burden than required by current regulation.

A new **Certification Regime** will be created to cover material risk-takers, those performing significant harm functions and anyone supervising a certified person. This captures a larger number of individuals than the current approved persons regime and requires firms to certify these employees as fit and proper on an ongoing basis. Material risk takers are regularly referred to regulatory initiatives and seek to capture individuals not captured by other prescriptive means.

Senior managers must provide annual attestation that the firm has complied with the regime, and that those covered by the Certification Regime remain **fit and proper** through arrangements designed and managed by the firm. This will introduce an administrative and evidential burden on firms rather than the regulators, consistent with the evidential burden being introduced by the SMR.

Subsequent Developments

In a subsequent development in October 2015, the government announced important changes to this regime. The regime scope was extended to the whole of the financial services industry in the UK, and the most aggressive part of the regime was scaled back. The **presumption of responsibility** will be replaced with a **duty of responsibility**.

Senior managers will continue to have an obligation to prevent regulatory breaches, but the senior manager will be guilty of misconduct only if the FCA demonstrates (ie, proves and it is accepted) that the senior manager failed to do this. Senior managers will still need to take steps to prevent regulatory breaches, and to show that they have done so.

This announcement follows the Fair and Effective Markets Review in June 2015, which recommended that the regime should be extended to cover firms active in fixed income, commodity and currency markets. As of October 2015, this will now therefore be applied consistency across the industry (ie, across all sectors of the financial services industry, including insurers, investment firms, asset managers, insurance and mortgage brokers and consumer credit firms), with many more regulatory consultations due as this develops. The government has suggested that regulators should ensure that the regime will appropriately reflect firms' diverse business models and be proportionate to the size and complexity of firms.

For banks, building societies, credit unions and PRA-regulated investment firms the regime will come into force on 7 March 2016. For other firms, the intention is that it will come into operation during 2018. More developments are expected.

2.9 Information and Investigatory Powers

Learning Objective

1.2.13 Know the FCA's powers to require information (FSMA 2000 C.8, Part 11, S.165) and its investigatory powers (Enforcement Guide (EG) 3)

S.165 of the FSMA 2000 provides the FCA with statutory powers to require firms to provide it with specific information or documents, to support its supervisory and enforcement functions. The request may be made by the FCA or one of its employees or agents. The firm must comply with the FCA's request within such reasonable timescale as the FCA shall prescribe and in any format that the FCA may reasonably require. It may also require the production of a report by a skilled person.

The Enforcement Guide (EG) (within the FCA Handbook) provides greater clarification of the way that these powers may be used in practice and the considerations that the FCA will take into account when deciding which of its investigatory powers to use. In particular, it clarifies the circumstances when it might consider appointing investigators to conduct an investigation into the affairs of a firm, exchange or CIS.

S.166–8 of the FSMA gives the FCA further information-gathering powers, as follows:

- **Section 166** – the FCA has power to require a firm and certain other persons to provide a report by a skilled person. This may be used to support either its supervision or enforcement functions.
- **Section 167** – if the FCA has general concerns about the conduct or state of affairs of a firm or appointed representative, it may appoint investigators.
- **Section 168** – if the FCA has concerns about any person, such that it considers that specific regulatory breaches have occurred, it may appoint investigators. This includes where:
  - a person may be guilty of an offence under Ss.177/191 (failing to co-operate with the FCA) or 398(1) (misleading the FCA)
  - an offence may have been committed under S 24(1) (false claim to be authorised or exempt); or S.297 (misleading statement and practices)
  - there may have been a breach of the general prohibition of regulated activities or a contravention of S.21 or S.238 of the FSMA (restrictions on financial promotions).

In addition, the FCA may undertake the appointment of a person to carry out investigations in particular cases where it appears to them that a person may:

- be carrying out authorised activities when they are not authorised to do so (S.20 of the FSMA)
- be guilty of an offence under prescribed regulations relating to money laundering
- have contravened a rule made by the FCA

- not be a fit and proper person to perform functions in relation to a regulated activity carried on by an authorised or exempt person
- have performed or agreed to perform a function in breach of a prohibition order

or if:

- an authorised or exempt person may have failed to comply with a prohibition order (S.56(6))
- a person for whom the FCA has given approval under S.59 (approval for particular arrangements) may not be a fit and proper person to perform the function to which that approval relates or a person may be guilty of misconduct for the purposes of S.66 (disciplinary powers).

2.10 FCA Enforcement Regime

Learning Objective

1.2.14 Know the role, scope and consequences of the Regulatory Decisions Committee's (RDC) responsibility for decision making and its interaction with the FCA's Enforcement Division and Financial Crime Division (DEPP 1.2, 3.1–3.4, 4.1)

1.2.15 Know the FCA's disciplinary powers with respect to DEPP 2.2, 2.3, DEPP 2 Annex 1G, 2G, DEPP 5.1, EG 7.1–7.5, EG 7.10–7.19, EG 8, EG 9.3–9.18, EG 9.25–9.28, EG11: authorised firms; approved persons/individuals subject to the new Accountability Regime for Banks (Senior Managers Regime, Certificate Regime and Conduct Rules); other persons directly or indirectly involved

2.10.1 FCA Statutory Notices

The FSMA gives the FCA the power to issue a range of notices to authorised firms and/or approved persons, collectively referred to as **statutory notices**. These are as follows:

- **Warning notices** give details about any action the FCA proposes to take and why it proposes to do so. They also give the recipient the right to make representations as to why the FCA should not take this action.
- **Decision notices** give details of the action that the FCA has decided to take, leaving room for appeal by the recipient.
- **Further decision notices** may follow the issue of a decision notice if the FCA has agreed with the recipient to take a different action to that proposed in the original decision notice. The FCA may issue a further decision notice only with the consent of the recipient.

In addition, the FCA can issue the following notices, but they are not referred to as **statutory notices**. These are:

- **Notices of discontinuance** confirm that where the FCA has previously sent a warning notice and/or a decision notice, it has decided not to proceed with the relevant action.
- **Final notices** set out the terms of the final action which the FCA has decided to take and the date that it is effective from. They are also – unlike warning and decision notices – published by the FCA on its website.
- **Supervisory notices** give details of the supervisory action that the FCA has taken, or proposes to take. These notices need to be preceded by the issue of a warning notice or decision notice,

and they are also published by the FCA. A typical supervisory notice might limit a firm's Part IV permission (authorisation) with immediate effect. Hence it would seem reasonable for the FCA to alert the public to the fact that the firm is no longer permitted to carry on certain activities.

2.10.2 The Regulatory Decisions Committee (RDC)

In the interests of fairness, the FSMA requires that when the FCA takes regulatory decisions and issues statutory notices, it follows procedures that are: *'designed to secure, among other things, that the decision which gives rise to the obligation to give any such notice is taken by a person not directly involved in establishing the evidence on which that decision is based'.*

Regulatory decisions are, therefore, made by a relatively independent committee, the Regulatory Decisions Committee (RDC), rather than by the FCA enforcement division that has initiated and carried out the original investigation.

The RDC is a committee of the FCA's board, is part of the FCA and is accountable to the FCA board; however, it is independent to the extent that it is separate from the FCA's executive management structure. Only the chairman is an FCA employee; the rest of the members are outside the FCA and are either current or retired practitioners with financial services knowledge and experience, or non-practitioners appointed to the RDC for a fixed period.

The RDC meets in private, either in its entirety, or more commonly as a panel, depending on the issue under review. In either case, the chairman or deputy must be present, together with at least two other RDC members. The RDC also has its own legal advisers and support function, so it is not advised on cases by the FCA's enforcement team's legal advisers.

The RDC has responsibility for statutory decisions, such as to:

- specify a narrower description of a regulated activity than that applied for in a Part 4A permission (authorisation), or limit a Part 4A permission in a way which would make a fundamental change
- refuse an application for a Part 4A permission, or to cancel an existing Part 4A permission
- refuse an application for approved person status, or withdraw an existing approval
- make a **prohibition order** in relation to a person, which prohibits them from employment in financial services; or else refuse to vary such an order
- exercise the FCA's powers to impose a financial penalty, make a public statement on the misconduct of an approved person, issue a public censure against an authorised person, or make a restitution order against a person.

If a statutory notice decision is not made by the RDC it will be made under the executive procedures of the FCA. These executive procedures enable the FCA to use statutory powers if individual guidance or voluntary agreement is felt to be inappropriate. A typical example of when these executive procedures may be used is if the FCA has particular concerns and therefore requires a firm to submit reports, such as those on trading results, customer complaints, or reports detailing the firm's management accounts.

2.10.3 Disciplinary Processes and Measures

The FCA may address instances of non-compliance with their requirements using three forms of formal disciplinary sanction:

1. public statements of misconduct (relating to approved persons, ie, individuals)
2. public censures (relating to authorised persons, ie, firms)
3. financial penalties (fines).

The imposition of regulatory enforcement measures (such as fines and public statements/censures) assists the FCA in meeting its statutory objectives.

In addition to these formal measures, the FCA can take a lower-key approach if it feels this is more appropriate. It could, for example:

* issue a private warning, or
* take supervisory action, such as:
    ○ varying or cancelling a firm's Part 4A permissions, or removing its authorisation entirely
    ○ withdrawing an individual's approved person status
    ○ prohibiting an individual from performing a particular role in relation to a regulated activity.

These may be used if the FCA considers it necessary to take protective or remedial action (rather than disciplinary action), or if a firm's ability to continue to meet its threshold conditions, or an individual approved person's fitness and propriety, are called into question.

When the FCA is considering formal discipline against an authorised firm and/or an approved person, it is required by the FSMA to issue one or more notices (these are the statutory notices we looked at earlier). As we saw, these notices fall into two categories: warnings and decisions.

Warning notices are not in themselves disciplinary events, since for an action to be regarded as disciplinary action a decision must have been made – and a warning is just that, no more and no less. Indeed, the decision notices themselves may not be absolutely final. They may be:

* discontinued by the issue of a notice of discontinuance
* varied with agreement in a further decision notice, or
* simply confirmed in a final decision notice.

2.10.4 Criteria for Disciplinary Action

In determining whether to take regulatory enforcement measures, the FCA will consider the full circumstances which may be relevant to the case. This will include, but not be limited to, the following:

* The nature and seriousness of the suspected breach:
    ○ Was it deliberate or reckless?
    ○ Does it reveal serious or systemic weakness of the management systems or internal controls of the firm?
    ○ How much loss, or risk of loss, was there to consumers and other market users?
* The conduct of the firm after the breach:
    ○ How quickly, effectively and completely was the breach brought to the attention of the FCA?

- Has the firm taken remedial steps since the breach was identified? For example, by identifying and compensating consumers who suffered loss, taking disciplinary action against the staff involved, addressing systemic failures and taking action to avoid recurrence of the breach in the future.
- The previous regulatory record of the firm or approved person.
  - Has the FCA (or a previous regulator) taken any previous disciplinary action?

2.10.5 The Measures

1. Private Warnings

These are issued by the FCA when it has concerns regarding the behaviour of the firm or approved person, but decides it is not appropriate to bring formal disciplinary action. It may include cases of potential (but unproven) market abuse, or if the FCA considers making a prohibition order but decides not to do so.

In such circumstances, the FCA believes it is helpful to let the recipient know that they came close to disciplinary action and the private warning serves this purpose. The circumstances giving rise to a private warning may include a minor matter (in nature or degree), or if the firm or approved person has taken full and immediate remedial action. The benefit of a private warning is that it avoids the reputational damage that follows more public sanctions, such as a fine or public censure.

The private warning will state that the FCA has had cause for concern but, at present, does not intend to take formal disciplinary action. It will also state that the private warning will form part of the FCA's compliance history. It will require the recipient to acknowledge receipt and invite a response.

2. Variation of Permission

The Part 4A permission granted to the firm by the FCA can be varied on the FCA's own initiative. Three circumstances are envisaged by the regulator:

1. If it appears to the FCA that the firm is failing (or is likely to fail) to meet the threshold conditions in relation to one or more of the regulated activities which the firm has permission to undertake. For example, a firm has an inadequate level of financial resources.
2. If it appears to the FCA that the firm has failed to carry on one or more of the regulated activities that they have permission to undertake for a period of at least 12 months.
3. If the FCA deems it desirable to vary or cancel the person's Part 4A permission in order to protect the interests of consumers and potential consumers.

The FCA's powers to vary and cancel a person's Part 4A permissions are exercisable in the same circumstances. However, the statutory procedure for the exercise of each power is different and this may determine how the FCA acts in a given case.

When it considers how it should deal with a concern about a firm, the FCA has regard to its regulatory objectives and the range of regulatory tools that are available to it. It also has regard to:

1. the responsibilities of a firm's management to deal with concerns about the firm or about the way its business is being or has been run, and
2. the principle that a restriction imposed on a firm should be proportionate to the objectives the FCA is seeking to achieve.

Examples of circumstances in which the FCA will consider varying a firm's Part 4A permission because it has serious concerns about a firm, or about the way its business is being or has been conducted, include when:

1. in relation to the grounds for exercising the power under S.45(1)(a) of the Act, the firm appears to be failing, or appears likely to fail, to satisfy the threshold conditions relating to one or more, or all, of its regulated activities, because for instance:
   - the firm's material and financial resources appear inadequate for the scale or type of regulated activity it is carrying on – for example, if it has failed to maintain professional indemnity insurance or if it is unable to meet its liabilities as they have fallen due, or
   - the firm appears not to be a fit and proper person to carry on a regulated activity because:
     - it has not conducted its business in compliance with high standards which may include putting itself at risk of being used for the purposes of financial crime or being otherwise involved in such crime
     - it has not been managed competently and prudently and has not exercised due skill, care and diligence in carrying on one or more, or all, of its regulated activities, or
     - it has breached requirements imposed on it by or under the Act (including the Principles and the rules), for example, in respect of its disclosure or notification requirements, and the breaches are material in number or in individual seriousness
2. in relation to the grounds for exercising the power under S.45(1)(c), it appears that the interests of consumers are at risk because the firm appears to have breached any of Principles 6 to 10 of the FCA's Principles (see PRIN 2.1.1R) to such an extent that it is desirable that limitations, restrictions, or prohibitions are placed on the firm's regulated activity.

3. Withdrawal of a Firm's Authorisation

The FCA will consider cancelling a firm's Part 4A permission in two particular circumstances:

1. if the FCA has very serious concerns about a firm, or the way its business is conducted, or
2. if a firm's regulated activities have come to an end, but it has not applied for cancellation of its Part 4A permission.

The grounds on which the FCA may exercise its power to cancel an authorised person's permission under S.45 of the Act are the same as the grounds for variation. They are set out in S.45(1) and described in EG 8.1. Examples of the circumstances in which the FCA may cancel a firm's Part 4A permission include:

1. non-compliance with a Financial Ombudsman Service (FOS) award against the firm
2. material non-disclosure in an application for authorisation or approval or material non-notification after authorisation or approval has been granted. The information which is the subject of the non-disclosure or non-notification may also be grounds for cancellation
3. failure to have or maintain adequate financial resources, or failure to comply with regulatory capital requirements
4. non-submission of, or provision of false information in, regulatory returns, or repeated failure to submit such returns in a timely fashion
5. non-payment of FCA fees or repeated failure to pay FCA fees except under threat of enforcement action;
6. failure to provide the FCA with valid contact details or to maintain the details provided, so that the FCA is unable to communicate with the firm
7. repeated failures to comply with rules or requirements
8. failure to co-operate with the FCA in a way that is of sufficient seriousness that the FCA ceases to be satisfied that the firm is fit and proper, for example, failing without reasonable excuse to:

a. comply with the material terms of a formal agreement made with the FCA to conclude or avoid disciplinary or other enforcement action, or

b. provide material information or take remedial action reasonably required by the FCA.

S.45(2A) of the Act sets out further grounds on which the FCA may cancel the permission of authorised persons which are investment firms.

Depending on the circumstances, the FCA may need to consider whether it should first use its own-initiative powers to vary a firm's Part 4A permission before going on to cancel it. Among other circumstances, the FCA may use this power if it considers it needs to take immediate action against a firm because of the urgency and seriousness of the situation.

4. Withdrawal of Approval

As well as having the power to withdraw authorisation from the firm, the FCA has the power to withdraw the approval of particular individuals who fulfil controlled functions. The FCA is required to first issue a warning notice to the approved person and the firm, followed by a decision notice. The FCA's decision can be referred to the Upper Tribunal (see Section 2.10).

The FCA recognises that withdrawing approval will often have a substantial impact on those concerned. When considering withdrawing approval it will take into account the cumulative effect of all relevant matters, including the following:

- the competence and capability of the individual (embracing qualifications and training) – does he have the necessary skills to carry out the controlled function he is performing?
- the honesty, integrity and reputation of the individual. Is he open and honest in dealings with consumers, market participants and regulators? Is he complying with his legal and professional obligations?
- the financial soundness of the individual. Has he been subject to judgment debts or awards which have not been satisfied within a reasonable period?
- whether he failed to comply with the statements of principle, or was knowingly involved in a contravention of the requirements placed on the firm
- the relevance, materiality and length of time since the occurrence of any matters indicating the approved person is not fit and proper
- the degree of risk the approved person poses to consumers and the confidence consumers have in the financial system
- the previous disciplinary record and compliance history of the approved person
- the particular controlled function and nature of the activities undertaken by the approved person.

The FCA will publicise the final decision notice in relation to the withdrawal of approval, unless this would prejudice the interests of consumers.

5. Prohibition of Individuals

Under Section 56 of the FSMA, the FCA has the right to make a **prohibition order** against an individual. This order can prohibit the individual from carrying out particular functions, or from being employed by any authorised firm, if the FCA considers it necessary for the achievement of its four statutory objectives. The prohibition order may relate just to a single specified regulated activity or to all regulated activities. It may also relate to the individual's ability to work for a particular class of firms or to all firms.

Prohibition orders are generally used by the FCA in cases which they see as more serious than those that would merit mere withdrawal of approval, ie, there may be a greater lack of fitness and propriety. The FCA will consider all the factors listed above which could otherwise have resulted in a withdrawal of approval. It will also consider factors such as whether the individual has been convicted of, or dismissed or suspended from employment for, the abuse of drugs or other substances or has convictions for serious assault. The FCA might feel it appropriate to issue a prohibition order against someone who continues to fulfil a controlled function after approval has been withdrawn.

As with withdrawal of approval, the FCA is required first to issue a warning notice to the approved person and the firm, followed by a decision notice. The FCA decision can be referred to the Upper Tribunal (see Section 2.10). Generally, it will publish the final decision notice in relation to the prohibition of an individual.

6. Public Censure and Statement of Misconduct

The FCA is empowered under the FSMA to issue a **public censure** to firms it considers have contravened a requirement imposed on by, or under, the Act. For approved persons, the FSMA may issue a public statement of misconduct if a person has failed to comply with the Statements of Principle, or has been knowingly involved in a firm's contravention of a requirement imposed on it by, or under, the Act.

As with other disciplinary actions, the steps required of the FCA are to:

- issue a warning notice (including the terms of the statement or censure the FCA is proposing to issue)
- follow this by a decision notice
- subsequently provide the right to go to tribunal (see Section 2.10).

7. Financial Penalties

As an alternative to public censures/statements of misconduct, the regulator is able to impose financial penalties on firms contravening requirements imposed on them by, or under, the FSMA, and on approved persons failing to comply with the Statements of Principle, or having been knowingly involved in a firm's contravention of requirements.

The regulator provides guidance as to the criteria used to determine whether to issue public censures/ statements (and no fine), rather than impose a financial penalty. It includes the following factors:

- If the firm or person avoided a loss or made a profit from their breach, a financial penalty is more appropriate to prevent the guilty party from benefiting from its/their actions.
- If the breach or misconduct is more serious in nature or degree, a financial penalty is likely to be imposed.
- Admission of guilt, full and immediate co-operation and taking steps to ensure that consumers are fully compensated may lessen the likelihood of financial penalty.
- A poor disciplinary record or compliance history may increase the likelihood of a financial penalty, as a deterrent for the future.
- Whether the firm has followed the regulator's guidance.

As is usual for disciplinary matters, there will be a warning notice, decision notice and final decision notice and ordinarily the final decision will be made public by the regulator issuing a press release. However, in circumstances where it would be unfair on the person, or prejudicial to the interests of consumers, the regulator may choose not to issue a press release.

When the regulator publishes a notice of financial penalty on its website it will also publish the rationale for the decision and the specific rules that were breached. SIF holders should regularly review the notices to keep themselves informed of the regulator's approach and to help them mitigate against similar failings in their own firm.

2.10.6 Redress

In order to meet its statutory objectives, the FCA may seek redress for consumers from any person, whether authorised or not, who has breached a relevant requirement of the Act. In deciding whether to do so, the FCA will consider the other ways that those consumers might obtain redress and whether the alternatives might be more efficient or cost-effective.

Redress for consumers is achieved by gaining restitution, meaning the repayment of the profits made by the person, or the losses suffered by the consumers. Decisions whether to apply to the civil courts for restitution orders under the Act will be made by the RDC chairman or, in an urgent case when the chairman is not available, by an RDC deputy chairman. In an exceptionally urgent case the matter will be decided by the director of enforcement at the FCA, or in their absence, another member of the FCA's executive of at least director-of-division level. The FCA has to apply to the court for redress; the court will quantify and direct to whom restitution should be paid.

The FCA's general approach is to judge the need for restitution on the facts of each case. If a firm has offered redress to the consumers already, or if the FCA considers it more efficient or cost-effective for consumers to pursue other means of redress, it may not use its powers of restitution. For example, if the consumers were themselves financial institutions, they would probably pursue legal action themselves rather than expect the FCA to seek redress through a restitution order.

The FCA's powers to gain redress for customers are granted to it under the FSMA.

The following sections of the FSMA relate to the FCA's powers in this regard, and indeed to the ability of clients to sue for damages in their own right where a firm is in breach.

- **Section 56** FSMA gives the FCA the power to issue a prohibition order.
- **Section 71** FSMA gives a private individual the power to sue, if he suffers loss as a result of a breach of any of section 56(6), 59(1) or 59(2).
- **Section 56(6)** involves a firm allowing an individual to act in contravention of a prohibition order.
- **Section 59(1)** involves a firm allowing an individual to carry on a controlled function as part of that firm's regulated activities, without the appropriate approved person status.
- **Section 59(2)** involves a firm allowing an individual to carry on a controlled function under an arrangement with a contractor, without the appropriate approved person status.
- **Section 150** FSMA gives a private individual the right to sue a firm if he suffers loss as a result of that firm having contravened an FCA rule.

2.11 The Upper Tribunal

As has been noted previously, any person who receives a decision notice (including a supervisory notice) has the right to refer the FCA's decision to review by a Tribunal. The individual or firm has 28 days from the receipt of the notice in which to do so, and during this period the FCA cannot take the action it has proposed; it must allow the individual or firm the full 28 days to decide whether to refer the decision to the Tribunal.

The original tribunal was the Financial Services and Markets Tribunal, established in 2001. As of April 2010, this has been subsumed into the Upper Tribunal, Tax and Chancery Chamber. The Tribunal is a superior court of record and is administered by the Ministry of Justice. It is independent of the FCA.

The Tribunal will carry out a full rehearing of the case, in public if appropriate, and will determine on the basis of all available evidence whether the FCA's decision (including the amount of any financial penalty) was appropriate. The rehearing may include evidence that was not available to the FCA at the time. The Tribunal's decision is binding on the FCA. While the Tribunal has to date generally not overturned many of the FCA's decisions, it has been known to do so – an important factor in demonstrating that it is independent in its decision-making and prepared to challenge the FCA if it sees fit.

It is possible for a firm or individual to appeal a decision of the Tribunal itself (but only on a point of law; and with the permission of either the Tribunal itself or the Court of Appeal).

3. Company Law

3.1 Schemes of Arrangement and Reconstruction

A scheme of arrangement is a statutory procedure allowed for under Part 26 of the Companies Act 2006, whereby a company makes a compromise arrangement with its shareholders and/or creditors, allowing it to restructure itself. The company (through its directors) proposes a new corporate structure for itself; shareholders and/or creditors approve the structure; the courts then approve the structure; and the new structure is immediately in effect.

A scheme of arrangement can be used for the following purposes:

- acquiring a company or business
- merging two or more companies or businesses
- acquiring shares owned by minority investors
- restructuring a business (such as creating a new holding company)
- a management buy-out/-in of a company
- demerging/splitting a company into separate entities
- reconstructing a group into two or more separate companies
- effecting a moratorium amongst a company's creditors (eg, an agreement to postpone payments to them).

Under a reconstruction, a business is preserved and is carried on by substantially the same people, subsequent to the reorganisation. Typically, such a procedure may be used to rescue a company that is in financial difficulties, to give the company a fresh start.

An amalgamation is a situation where two companies combine, either by forming a new company encompassing both the original businesses or by one company acquiring the shares of the other (known as a merger by absorption). The majority of public company takeovers are now effected through these types of scheme of arrangement.

3.1.1 Procedures for Schemes of Arrangement

There are three main stages:

1. **Explanatory statement** – this is dispatched to shareholders and creditors at the same time as a notice convening members' and creditors' meetings. It explains the effect of the scheme, including all information reasonably necessary to enable the shareholder or creditor to decide how to vote. The statement normally takes the form of detailed document, including a letter from the company's chairman or financial advisers. This includes details of the transaction, its purpose, its expected outcome and of any impact on the personal interests of the directors of the company.
2. **Members' and creditors' meetings** – the company, a creditor, the liquidator or a shareholder must apply to the court for permission for a meeting to be held for each of the classes of the interested parties concerned (ie, creditors, shareholders). The scheme must be approved by a majority in number, and 75% in value, of the creditors or class of creditors or shareholders present and voting either in person or by proxy at each meeting.
3. **Court approval** – after the proposal has been approved by shareholders and creditors, an application is made to the court to sanction the scheme. The court will ensure that the arrangement is such that a member of the class concerned and acting in respect of his interest might reasonably approve the arrangement.

Once the scheme is sanctioned by the court, a copy of the court order must be filed within seven days with the Registrar of Companies. At this stage the scheme becomes effective, binding on all creditors and shareholders of the class that voted in favour of the scheme, whether or not that individual creditor or shareholder voted in favour. The Articles of Association of the merged or reconstructed company must be updated.

The following table shows the advantages and disadvantages of a scheme of arrangement over an alternative method of reconstruction:

Advantage	Disadvantage
Once approved, the scheme is binding on all shareholders	Timing – obtaining court approval can be a lengthy procedure
Stamp duty may be saved (in the case of a capital reduction scheme)	Cost – legal counsel is required; documentation is more extensive
A scheme effects an immediate transfer of shares	Schemes can be complex to prepare and difficult for shareholders and creditors to understand
A takeover effected by a scheme is not bound by the normal Takeover Code timetable, but by the more flexible timetable for schemes of arrangement in Appendix 7 of the Code: see Chapter 4	For a takeover, a scheme can only be used for a recommended bid and not for a hostile bid. The target company and directors control the timing and implementation of the scheme; the bidding company is therefore taking a risk that the scheme is withdrawn – eg, if a higher offer is received or anticipated
If used in a takeover, a 75% shareholder vote is required to give certainty of 100% of the shares in favour	Only 75% of those voting (in person or by proxy) are required to approve the scheme for it to proceed – may be disadvantageous to small minorities

3.2 Provisions Relating to Squeeze Out and Sell Out

Learning Objectives

1.3.2 Know the provisions contained in the Companies Act 2006 relating to squeeze out and sell out (S.974–985)

1.3.4 Know the provisions contained in the Companies Act 2006 relating to pre-emption rights (CA85 S.89 and CA06 S.561, 565–566, 568)

3.2.1 Squeeze-Outs and Sell-Outs

Sections 974–985 of the Companies Act 2006 make provisions for the problem of residual minority shareholders after a takeover bid.

Section 979 of the Act provides the **squeeze-out** provisions which apply to all companies. They provide that where a bidder has offered to acquire all of the shares in a company not currently held by him, and has acquired or agreed to acquire both 90% of the shares to which his offer related and 90% of the voting rights attached to the shares, he may oblige the holders of the remaining shares to sell their shares to him, at the price offered in the original takeover offer. The bidder must give shareholders notice of his intention to exercise the squeeze-out rights within three months of the last date on which the offer can be accepted, or within six months of the date of the offer if earlier.

Section 983 of the Act provides the **sell-out** rights, which allow that where the bidder has acquired or contracted to acquire at least 90% in value of all of the shares in the target company, those shareholders who did not accept the offer have the right to oblige the bidder to acquire their shares. Sell-out rights must be exercised within three months from either (a) the end of the period within which the offer can be accepted or (b) the date of the notice to shareholders informing them of their right to exercise their sell-out rights; whichever is the later.

Note that both the timescale and the threshold for sell-out rights are different from those for squeeze-out rights.

3.2.2 Pre-emption Rights

Pre-emption rights are a fundamental principle of UK company law, and are set out in Section 561 of the Act. These provide that whenever a company issues new equity shares wholly in exchange for cash, it must offer these shares in the first instance to their existing shareholders, pro-rata to their existing shareholdings in that company. The basic principle is that a shareholder should be able to protect his proportion of the total equity of a company by having the opportunity to subscribe for any new issue of equity securities.

It should be noted that pre-emption rights apply only to issues of new shares in exchange for cash; if shares are issued in exchange for other shares or assets (such as in a share-for-share acquisition or vendor placing) pre-emption rights do not apply. Note also that private companies may exclude pre-emption rights from their Articles of Association, but that listed companies may not.

Rights issues and open offers are examples of pre-emptive issues, as shares are offered to all shareholders in proportion to their existing holdings. A secondary placing is a non-pre-emptive issue, as shares are offered to new, incoming shareholders.

Pre-emptive issues are subject to the following provisions:

- Under Section 562, any pre-emptive offer must be communicated to shareholders, and allow no less than 14 days to accept the offer of new shares. Companies may elect to offer a longer notice period.
- In a rights issue, shareholders may elect to accept all or part of their entitlement (and make the required payment); they may sell their entitlement to a third party; or they may ignore the offer. In an open offer, shareholders may not sell their entitlement to a third party.
- Any shares which are not taken up by shareholders in a rights issue may be sold by the company in the market, and any surplus over the rights issue price paid to those non-participating shareholders. In an open offer, any surplus received is not paid to non-participating shareholders.

3.2.3 Disapplication of Pre-emption Rights by Listed Companies

If a company wishes to issue new shares on a non-pre-emptive basis (ie, to new shareholders) it must obtain shareholder approval for the disapplication of pre-emption rights. This must be granted by way of a special resolution, passed either at the company's annual general meeting (AGM) to provide a general disapplication for issues over the course of the year, or at a separate general meeting, for the purpose of a specific new share issue. In the latter case, 14 days' notice is generally required. Sections 569–573 provide the requirements for this process.

Under the Companies Act, shareholders in listed companies may pass a special resolution disapplying pre-emption rights for a maximum period of five years. This maximum period is also confirmed in the Listing Rules.

However, listed companies are normally restricted by the guidance of the investor protection committees, which allows them to seek a general approval to disapply pre-emption rights only for the issue of new shares amounting to a maximum of 5% of the issued share capital in any one year, or 7½% on a rolling three-year basis. Any disapplication of pre-emption rights which exceeds these levels will require specific shareholder approval at a general meeting.

The Listing Rules do not normally permit non-pre-emptive issues to be made at a price which represents a discount of more than 10% to the middle market price of the shares. Any discount greater than 10% requires shareholder approval at a general meeting.

3.3   Provisions Relating to the Reduction of Share Capital

Learning Objective

1.3.3   Know the provisions contained in the Companies Act 2006 relating to the reduction of share capital (S.641)

It is a central principle of company law that a company's share capital (ie, the money subscribed for shares) belongs to the company, and not to its shareholders, and cannot therefore be used to make distributions to shareholders. This principle of capital maintenance exists primarily as a protection for the company's creditors. Any company seeking to reduce its capital must comply with the requirements of the Act.

The Act specifically mentions three circumstances where a company might seek to reduce its share capital. This might be done in order to:

- extinguish or reduce the liability of shareholders on shares which are not fully paid up
- cancel share capital which is not represented by assets
- return capital to shareholders which is in excess of the company's requirements.

Chapter 10 of the Act sets out the provisions for the reduction of share capital.

A private company may reduce its share capital, providing that the Articles of Association do not prohibit this, and providing that shareholders approve a special resolution in favour of the reduction. This special resolution must be supported by a directors' statement of solvency. The company must have at least one shareholder remaining after the reduction of capital.

A public limited company (PLC) is also required to pass a special resolution to reduce its capital, but in this case the special resolution must be confirmed by the court. The resolution may not provide for a reduction to take place at a date which is later than the date of the resolution.

3.4 Investigations by Inspectors

Learning Objective

1.3.5 Know the provisions contained in the Companies Act 2006 relating to investigations by inspectors (S.1035–1039)

The Companies Act 2006 (Sections 1035–1039) gives members the right to apply to the Department for Business, Innovation and Skills (BIS) for an inspector to investigate the company's affairs.

3.4.1 Criteria

An inspector may be appointed by the Secretary of State for Business, Innovation and Skills on his own initiative or on the application of:

- at least 200 members or the holders of at least 10% of issued shares, or
- the company itself, if it has passed an ordinary resolution approving such an action.

Any applicant must provide £5,000 security for costs and must furnish the BIS with evidence to support their claim.

The Companies Act also gives the BIS the power to exercise its investigative powers at its own discretion in any of the following four circumstances:

- the company may have been conducting its affairs with intent to defraud creditors or in a manner prejudicial to members, or for unlawful or fraudulent purposes
- promoters or managers may be guilty of fraud or any other act of misconduct
- the company has failed to provide proper information to the members
- the company was formed for any fraudulent or unlawful purpose or engaged in prejudicial acts.

The BIS has no obligation to warn the company or reveal the circumstances which led to the investigation.

3.4.2 The Inspector's Powers

The inspectors have very wide powers to obtain and require disclosure of information. They may also question any person on oath, obtain a warrant to search premises, and finally inform the Secretary of State for Business, Innovation and Skills of any matters coming to their attention during the investigation.

3.4.3 The Secretary of State's Powers

The Secretary of State for Business, Innovation and Skills has the power to:

- give directions to an inspector as to the subject matter to be investigated (eg, area of operation, specific transactions or a period of time)
- terminate an investigation when criminal offence matters have been passed to a prosecuting authority
- set requirements for the contents and time limit of the inspector's report.

3.5 Financial Assistance

Learning Objective

1.3.6 Know the provisions contained in the Companies Act 2006 relating to financial assistance for the acquisition of a public company's own shares (S.678–680)

Sections 678–680 of the Act prohibit a public company, or its subsidiary, from directly or indirectly giving financial assistance to a third party for the purchase of its own shares, or to reduce or discharge a liability incurred by a purchaser or a third party for the purpose of acquisition. The provision of financial assistance is a criminal offence.

Financial assistance includes:

* a gift
* provision of a guarantee, security, indemnity, release or waiver
* any other form of assistance, whereby the company's net assets are reduced to a material extent.

A wide number of transactions fall within the definition of financial assistance; a common example is where a target company allows its assets to be pledged as security for the bidder's acquisition finance.

Any financial assistance in contradiction of these rules is void, and therefore, all contracts in connection with it have no legal effect. The company and its officers may be liable to a fine and/or two years' imprisonment on conviction in the Crown Court. Directors who initiate financial assistance agreements are in breach of their duties and are liable to the company for any losses.

3.5.1 Exceptions

There are certain exceptions when transactions that would satisfy the definition of financial assistance are permitted. These are when:

* the principal purpose of the transaction is not the provision of financial assistance
* the financial assistance is an incidental part of a larger purpose
* the assistance is lending in the ordinary course of the company's business
* a loan is made to employees as part of an employee share scheme.

In addition, it should be noted that the provisions relate only to public companies and not to private companies, and that they relate to assistance for the acquisition of shares and not to acquisitions of business assets.

3.6   Shareholder Rights

Learning Objectives

1.3.7   Know the main statutory rights of shareholders in the Companies Act 2006 (S.303–306, 314–315, 338–340, 994–998)

1.3.8   Know the provisions contained in the Companies Act 2006 relating to company meetings (S.284, 303–305, 307–310, 318–319)

While directors are responsible for making decisions regarding the day-to-day running of the business, decisions that affect the structure of a company or the rights of members are decided upon in a meeting of the shareholders.

The Companies Act contains general provisions concerning the conduct and structure of company meetings which apply in the absence of any provisions to the contrary in the company's Memorandum and Articles. The two types of meeting are AGMs and general meetings (GMs). The latter were, until 2009, referred to as extraordinary general meetings (EGMs).

3.6.1   Notice Period for Meetings

Public companies must hold an AGM within six months of the financial year end. The Companies Act provides shareholders with the right to attend, speak and vote at the AGM and to appoint a proxy to vote (but not speak) on their behalf at the meeting.

Private companies do not have to hold an AGM unless provided for in their articles.

Notice for an Annual General Meeting (AGM)

For all public companies, shareholders must be given at least 21 calendar days' notice of an AGM, with a 14-day notice period required for the AGM of a private company.

Notice for a General Meeting (GM)

All members of the company and each director is entitled to receive notice of a company meeting (Section 310). Under Sections 308–9, notice of a GM must be given in hard copy form, electronic form or by means of a website, or by a combination of these means. However, if notice is given by means of a website, members must be advised of the existence of the notification on the website, and the notification must remain on the website until the end of the meeting.

Under the Companies Act 2006 Section 307 the minimum notice period for GMs for listed companies (those listed on an EEA state regulated market, such as the LSE main market, but excluding AIM and ISDX Growth Market-traded companies) was extended to 21 clear calendar days. However, a listed company may reduce the required notice period for a meeting which is not an AGM to 14 days if shareholders pass a resolution at their AGM each year, allowing the shortening of the general notice period, and providing that the company allows shareholders to vote at such meetings via electronic means. Most traded companies have adopted this approach.

For all other companies, the notice period for any general meeting which is not an AGM is generally 14 calendar days.

General meetings of public companies may be held at short notice, providing that shareholders representing at least 95% of voting rights agree to the notice period. For private companies the threshold is 90% of shareholders. However, short notice for an AGM of a public company must be agreed unanimously by all shareholders.

3.6.2 Shareholders or Court Calling a Meeting

Under S.303, shareholders representing 5% or more of the voting shares may require the directors to convene a GM. This applies to both public or private companies. This limit was introduced following the introduction of the Shareholder Rights Directive in 2009.

The request to call a GM must state the general nature of the business to be dealt with, and may include the text of a resolution to be moved at the meeting. It may be made in hard copy form or in electronic form, and must be authenticated by the person or persons making it. If directors receive a S.303 request to call a meeting, they must call the meeting within 21 days from the date of receipt of the notice, and it must be held no more than 28 days from the notice convening the meeting.

Under S.305 of the Act, if directors do not call a meeting when required to do so, the shareholders who requested the meeting (or any of them representing more than 50% of the total rights of those shareholders) may call the meeting, and are entitled to be reimbursed their reasonable expenses in relation to this.

Under S.306, the court has the power to call a GM if it is impractical to call one in the normal manner or to conduct it in the proper manner. It may make such orders as it considers fit for the conduct of the meeting, including setting a quorum of one.

3.6.3 Resolutions

Decisions proposed and voted on at general meetings are known as **resolutions**.

- **Ordinary resolutions** require only a simple majority (greater than 50%) of votes cast at the meeting in order to be carried. Examples where an ordinary resolution is required include approval of the annual financial statements, appointment and removal of auditors, appointment and removal of directors and approval of a dividend.
- A **special resolution** requires a 75% majority of votes cast to be passed. Examples include resolutions for changing the company's name, waiving pre-emption rights, de-listing a public company, share buy-backs, changes to the Articles of Association and voluntary winding up (liquidation) of the company.

Unless specified to the contrary in the company's articles, each shareholder is entitled to one vote in respect of each share held.

Resolutions are generally proposed by the company's directors and are set out in the notice of the general meeting. However, they may be proposed by the members; the company has a duty to circulate and propose shareholders' resolutions, providing that the request is made by either:

- shareholders representing at least 5% of voting rights, or
- at least 100 shareholders holding at least £100 paid-up shares each.

The costs of circulating the notice of this resolution must be paid by the requesting members unless notice is given before the end of the previous financial year.

In addition, shareholders may require the company to circulate to all shareholders a statement of not more than 1,000 words, regarding a matter to be dealt with at a meeting, or a matter referred to in a proposed resolution to be dealt with at that meeting. This right may be exercised by shareholders representing at least 5% of the total voting rights, or at least 100 shareholders who hold shares with an average paid up sum of at least £100 per shareholder.

3.6.4 Meetings

A meeting can only validly pass resolutions if it is quorate (ie, has the requisite number of attendees). A quorum is two members unless otherwise stated in the company's Articles. Any member so elected may act as chairman at any meeting.

Any shareholder entitled to attend and vote at a company's meeting is entitled to appoint another person (who need not be a shareholder) as his proxy to attend and vote in his place. In a public company, a proxy may attend and vote, but may not exercise the shareholder's right to speak.

3.6.5 Unfair Prejudice

Under Sections 994-8 a shareholder may petition the court, if he considers that the company's affairs are being conducted in a way that is unfairly prejudicial to the interest of some or all the shareholders, or that it is proposing some prejudicial act or omission. If the court is satisfied that the petition is well-founded, it may take steps to regulate the company's affairs in the future, or require the company to take steps to remedy the matter or matters complained of. This could include the alteration of the company's articles, in which case the amended articles must be delivered to the Registrar of Companies within 14 days of the court order.

3.7 Interests in Shares

Learning Objective

1.3.9 Know the provisions contained in the Companies Act 2006 relating to notices by a company requiring information about interests in its shares (S.793–795)

S.793 of the Act provides a public company (listed or unlisted) with the power to issue a notice to a person who it knows, or has reasonable cause to believe, has an interest in its shares or has had an interest in the previous three years.

The notice requires the shareholder to disclose, confirm or deny his interest, and, if he confirms it, to disclose information about his interest, including information about any other person who has an interest in those shares.

If a shareholder has sold his shares in the last three years, he must identify the person they were sold to, the date of the transaction and the broker used (if applicable).

In the absence of a response within a reasonable time, companies may disenfranchise (ie, remove the voting/dividend rights of) defaulting shareholders. If a shareholder provides false information, he is liable to a maximum penalty of two years in jail on conviction, and/or an unlimited fine.

This process may be used by companies if there are suspicions of undisclosed substantial shareholdings, or as a routine **shareholder management** process. Only the company secretary may send out the enquiry notices (rather than shareholders or third parties).

3.8   Requirements to be a Public Limited Company (PLC)

Learning Objective

1.3.10   Know the provisions contained in the Companies Act 2006 relating to requirements to be a public company (S.90, 92, 94)

1.3.11   Know the provisions contained in the Companies Act 2006 relating to restrictions on public offers by a private company (S.755, 760)

The Companies Act specifies two types of limited company:

- public limited companies, and
- private companies.

Under Part 7 of the Companies Act 2006, a PLC must:

- have a minimum of two shareholders
- have a minimum issued share capital of £50,000 on which all the share premium and at least 25% of the nominal value have been paid up
- have a memorandum of association which states that it is a public company
- be correctly registered as public.

Such companies must have either PLC or Public Limited Company at the end of their names.

Public companies are allowed to sell their shares to the public, and may apply for FCA listing or admission to another market such as AIM. However, a public company does not have to be listed, and a great many are not.

All other companies are private companies and must have either Ltd or Limited at the end of their names. Private companies may place restrictions on who may be a shareholder, reducing the opportunity of any shareholder to sell his shares. They require a minimum of only one member/shareholder.

3.8.1 Company Constitution

Since a company as an entity has a relationship with its directors, its shareholders, its potential investors and the outside world, it needs a constitution which publicly sets out the terms on which it interacts with other parties. This is provided by two documents – the memorandum of association and the articles of association.

The Memorandum of Association

The memorandum of association is the external rulebook of the company governing its relationship with the outside world. It should state:

- the company's name
- the location of the company's registered office
- that the company's liability is limited
- if the company is to become a PLC, then the memorandum must state this
- the objectives of the company – trading objectives and permitted activities of the company.

However, following the implementation of the relevant sections of the Companies Act 2006 in October 2009, the memorandum has been reduced in significance, with greater importance being given to the articles. In particular, there is now a general assumption that the company has unlimited capacity to transact business, unless there are specific limits imposed in the articles.

The Articles of Association

This is the internal rulebook of the company governing the relationship between the company and its members (shareholders). There are standard terms for articles contained within Table A of the Companies Act, but each company can create its own rules.

Once established, the provisions are binding on the shareholders in their relationship with the company and with each other. They may only be altered on the passing of a special resolution in a general meeting.

The articles typically include:

- the company's name, registered office and form
- details of each class of shares, including voting, redemption and distribution rights
- provisions for general meetings, including resolutions, notice, short notice, quorum and chair
- directors' requirements, including meetings and maintenance of registers
- actions which are permitted or prohibited for the company and its directors, such as pre-emption rights, transfer restrictions, borrowings, trading activities.

3.8.2 Restrictions on Public Offers by a Private Company

Under S.755 of the Companies Act 2006 it is an offence for a private company to offer securities to the public. If shares are, however, sold to the public the allotment is valid, but the company and its officers are liable to fines for a breach of this section. Thus private companies can only issue their shares to people known to them, such as employees, private investors and family members.

An exception to this rule is if the private company commits to re-register as a public company within six months of the date the shares are issued.

Under S.90, a private company may be re-registered as a public company providing that a special resolution to re-register it is passed, and that it meets the following conditions:

- it meets the requirements to be a public company set out at the beginning of S.3.8, in relation to its share capital
- it has not previously been re-registered as unlimited
- it makes the necessary changes to its name and articles to comply with the provisions for public companies
- it obtains a balance sheet, dated no earlier than seven months before the application to re-register as a public company, including both an unqualified audit report and a written statement from the company's auditor that the amount of the company's net assets at the balance sheet date was not less than the aggregate of its called-up share capital and undistributable reserves
- that there was no change in the financial position of the company between the balance sheet date and the date of application for re-registration which changes this position.

An application for re-registration as a public company must be made to the Registrar of Companies, and be accompanied by copies of the special resolution, amended articles, balance sheet and statements referred to above; together with a statement that the requirements for re-registration as a public company have been complied with.

3.9   Directors' Duties

Learning Objective

1.3.12   Know the duties of directors, in particular in relation to conflicts of interest (S.170–175)

3.9.1   Duties of Directors

The Companies Act specifies the duties of directors at Ss.170–175. These duties are extended to shadow directors: that is, persons who are not officially directors, but in accordance with whose wishes a company is accustomed to act. The main duties of directors are as follows:

- A director of a company must act in accordance with the company's constitution and only exercise powers for the purpose for which they are conferred.
- Directors must act in the way they consider, in good faith, is most likely to promote the success of the company for the benefit of its shareholders as a whole, having regard for:
  - the long-term consequences of their actions; the interests of the company's employees
  - the need to foster the company's business relationships with suppliers, customers and others
  - the impact of the company's operations on the community and environment
  - the company's reputation for high standards of business conduct; and the need to act fairly.
- Directors should exercise independent judgement.

- Directors should exercise such care, skill and diligence as might reasonably be expected from a person with the general knowledge, skill and experience that might reasonably be expected from a person carrying out those functions, and the general knowledge, skill and experience that the director actually has.
- Directors have a duty to avoid conflicts of interest. This subject is covered in more detail in Section 3.9.2.

3.9.2 Conflicts of Interest

Directors of companies have a duty under Section 175 of the Companies Act to avoid situations in which they have, or could have, a direct or indirect interest that conflicts, or may possibly conflict, with the interests of the company.

This covers a very broad range of situations where:

- the director's interest may be actual or potential, and direct or indirect, and
- the conflict with the company's interests may be actual or potential.

An example of this occurring is if one of the board members (ie, a director, chairman or chief executive) has outside interests in their own name, or if they are a NED of another company. The director should avoid having an interest in, or directorship of, another firm that is either in direct competition or undertaking the same business.

However, if such a conflict of interest is anticipated, it can be authorised in advance either by a vote of a majority of directors (where the interested director does not vote), or by the passing of an ordinary resolution by shareholders in general meeting. Directors can only authorise a conflict if their articles permit this.

If a conflict has already arisen, it can be ratified by a vote of shareholders as above, but not by a vote of the directors, for example where a conflict arose from unforeseen events.

3.10 Overseas Companies

Learning Objective

1.3.13 Understand the relevance of local law when dealing with companies established outside the UK

European directives provide pan-European requirements for all companies operating within the EU. Each EU member state incorporates these requirements in its own domestic law. Companies which operate within the EU must comply with the specific law of the countries within which they operate. In addition, however, they must comply with the domestic law of their country of incorporation.

Take the example of a UK company authorised in the UK, and operating an investment business in both the UK and France. The UK is referred to as its **home state** and France is its **host state**. The company must comply with host state regulations in France so far as its French operations are concerned, comply with home state regulations with regard its authorisation and activities in the UK, but also observe the provisions of the UK's Companies Act in so far as its relations with its shareholders and directors are concerned.

4. Money Laundering, Counter-Terrorism and Bribery

4.1 Money Laundering

Learning Objective

1.4.1 Know that the UK legislation on money laundering and counter terrorism funding can be found in the Proceeds of Crime Act (POCA) 2002, the Money Laundering Regulations 2007, the Terrorism Act 2000, the Counter Terrorism Act 2008 (S.7) and that the guidance to these provisions can be found in the Joint Money Laundering Steering Group (JMLSG) Guidance Notes

1.4.2 Understand the terms money laundering, criminal conduct and criminal property and the application of money laundering to all crimes (POCA 2002 s.340)

Money laundering is the process of turning **dirty** money (money derived from criminal activities) into money which appears to be from legitimate origins. Dirty money is difficult to invest or spend, and carries the risk of being used as evidence of the initial crime. Laundered money can more easily be invested and spent without risk of incrimination.

There are three stages to a successful money laundering operation:

1. **Placement** – introduction of the money into the financial system; typically, this involves placing the criminally derived cash into a bank or building society account, a bureau de change or any other type of enterprise which can accept cash, such as a casino.
2. **Layering** – involves moving the money around in order to make it difficult for the authorities to link the placed funds with the ultimate beneficiary of the money. This may involve buying and selling foreign currencies, shares or bonds in rapid succession, investing in CISs, or insurance-based investment products, or moving the money from one country to another.
3. **Integration** – at this final stage, the layering has been successful and the ultimate beneficiary appears to be holding legitimate funds (clean money rather than dirty money). The money is regarded as integrated into the legitimate financial system.

Broadly, the anti-money laundering provisions apply to all crimes. They are aimed at identifying customers and reporting suspicions at the placement and layering stages, and keeping adequate records which should prevent the integration stage being reached.

4.1.1 Anti-Money Laundering Provisions

Increasingly, anti-money laundering provisions are being seen as the front line against drug dealing, organised crime and the financing of terrorism. Much police activity is directed towards making the disposal of criminal assets more difficult and monitoring the movement of money.

The UK rules and regulations in relation to money laundering come from a variety of sources.

The **primary legislation** is provided in:

- the Proceeds of Crime Act (POCA) 2002
- the Serious Organised Crime and Police Act (SOCPA) 2005
- the Counter-Terrorism Act (CTA) 2008 (Schedule 7), and
- the Terrorism Act (TA) 2000.

Secondary legislation is provided in the Money Laundering Regulations 2007, which give effect to the Third Money Laundering Directive.

Specific rules for financial services firms are provided in the FCA Handbook, in the SYSC Sourcebook.

Finally, the Joint Money Laundering Steering Group (JMLSG) Guidance provides guidance on how to implement the requirements of the money laundering regulations.

The Proceeds of Crime Act (POCA) 2002

POCA 2002 is widely drafted. It specifies that money laundering relates to criminal property – that is, any benefit (money or otherwise) that has arisen from criminal conduct. Property is criminal property only if the alleged offender knows or suspects it is criminal property. The broad requirement is for firms to report suspicions of money laundering to the authorities. POCA is described in more detail in Section 4.2.

The Serious Organised Crime and Police Act (SOCPA) 2005

This act amended certain sections of POCA. In particular, one feature of POCA was that **criminal conduct** was deemed to include anything which would have been an offence had it been done in the UK, regardless of where it had actually happened. This resulted in the often-cited **Spanish bullfighter** problem – bullfighting is illegal in the UK, but not in Spain, meaning that, arguably, a financial institution should regard deposits made by a Spanish bullfighter as the proceeds of crime, even if they represent his legitimate earnings in Spain.

SOCPA addresses this difficulty – in part at least – in that there is a defence for alleged offenders if they can show that they know, or believe on reasonable grounds, that the conduct was not criminal in the country where it happened. However, the Secretary of State has reserved the right to prescribe certain offences as **relevant criminal conduct** which may be legal where they occurred, but are illegal in the UK and still need to be reported. For example, the government may specify serious tax evasion or drug cultivation as types of criminal conduct which do need to be reported, despite occurring overseas.

The Terrorism Act 2000 (TA) 2000

This act contains the law relating to financing terrorism. It provides the criminal offences of raising, receiving, owning or using finance or property for terrorist activity, entering into an arrangement as a result of which finance is made available for terrorist activity, or facilitating the concealment or movement of such finance or property.

The maximum penalty on conviction in the Crown Court is 14 years' imprisonment, an unlimited fine or both. The court may also order the forfeiture of the property or finance concerned. There is, however, a defence if a person can show that they reported their suspicions, intended to report suspicions but had a good reason not to do so, or acted with the express permission of the police.

There is also a statutory obligation to report any suspicious transaction in relation to terrorist financing, and in particular suspicions that a person may be providing funds for terrorism, using and possessing funds or property for the purposes of terrorism, or laundering money which is terrorist property. These obligations should be interpreted with the help of the JMLSG Guidance. A failure to report is an offence punishable by up to five years' imprisonment, an unlimited fine, or both.

The scope of the Act is not limited to terrorist acts in the UK, or acts against the government. It is discussed in more detail below in Section 4.5.

The Counter-Terrorism Act (CTA) 2008

The CTA came into force in November 2008, and includes provisions relating to terrorist financing and money laundering, including giving HMT new powers to direct firms in the financial sector to take certain actions in respect of business with parties in a non-EEA jurisdiction, where they have concerns that money laundering, proliferation of nuclear/biological weapons or terrorist financing is being carried on. Non-compliance with the provisions of a Treasury direction include civil penalties or criminal prosecution, with a maximum penalty of two years' imprisonment or an unlimited fine or both. It is discussed in more detail below in Section 4.5.

The Money Laundering Regulations 2007

These are relatively detailed regulations, which implement the provisions of the Third Money Laundering Directive. They deal predominantly with the processes which firms must adopt in order to combat money laundering. For example, they deal with firms' requirements for systems and training to prevent money laundering and their obligations to check the identity of new customers. They are discussed in more detail below.

The FCA Senior Management Arrangements, Systems and Controls (SYSC) Sourcebook

This provides high level standards of governance for FCA authorised firms on the obligations of senior management in implementing the anti-money laundering provisions in the UK financial services industry.

The Joint Money Laundering Steering Group (JMLSG) Guidance Notes

The Joint Money Laundering Steering Group is made up of 17 leading UK trade associations in the financial services industry, including the British Bankers' Association (BBA), the Council of Mortgage Lenders (CML) and the Association of British Insurers (ABI). Its aim is to promulgate good practice in countering money laundering and to give practical assistance in interpreting the money laundering regulations. This is primarily achieved by the publication of industry guidance on implementing risk management, anti-terrorist financing and anti-money laundering provisions. The guidance notes are not mandatory but do highlight industry best practice. They are also approved by the Treasury, which means that if a firm can show that it adhered to them, the courts will take this into account as evidence of compliance with the legislation.

Additionally, the FCA has confirmed that it will take into account whether a firm has followed the relevant provisions of the guidance when considering whether to take action against it, and when considering whether to prosecute a breach of the money laundering regulations.

The most recent Guidance Notes (2009) reflected the changes introduced since the Money Laundering Regulations 2007. In overview, the JMLSG Guidance Notes:

- require that firms take a risk-based and proportionate approach to the prevention of money laundering
- simplify the identity verification requirements for many customer types
- allow for greater reliance on identification verification carried out by other firms.

The JMLSG's 2009 guidance is divided into three parts.

- **Part I** sets out advice on the identification requirement for all types of customer.
- **Part II** gives sector-specific guidance for various types of firm.
- **Part III** (published in October 2010) provides specialist advice for financial firms including guidance on how to meet certain general regulatory obligations, or determining the equivalence of particular overseas jurisdictions or markets.

The preface of the JMLSG Guidance states that: *'The FCA Handbook confirms that the FCA will have regard to whether a firm has followed relevant provisions of this guidance when considering whether to take action against a regulated firm (SYSC 3.2, SYSC 5.3, and DEPP 6.2.3); and when considering whether to prosecute a breach of the money laundering regulations (see EG 12.1–2). The guidance therefore provides a sound basis for firms to meet their legislative and regulatory obligations when tailored by firms to their particular business risk profile. Departures from this guidance, and the rationale for so doing, should be documented, and firms will have to stand prepared to justify departures, for example to the FCA.'* http://www.jmlsg.org.uk/industry-guidance/article/jmlsg-guidance-current.

The following sections discuss certain aspects of these regulations in more detail.

The FCA launched Part 1: A firm's guide to preventing financial crime in April 2015.

In late 2015, the European Banking Authority (EBA) launched a public consultation on two guidelines, seeking to promote a common understanding of the risk-based approach to anti-money laundering and countering the financing of terrorism.

Issued in conjunction with the European Securities and Markets Authorities (ESMA) and the European Insurance and Occupational Pensions Authority (EIOPA) – known as the Joint Supervisory Committee – the consultation is addressed to competent authorities responsible for supervising credit and financial institutions' compliance with anti-money laundering and counter terrorist financing obligations.

4.2   Money Laundering Offences and Penalties

Learning Objectives

1.4.4   Understand the main offences set out in POCA 2002, Part 7 S.327, 328, 329, 330, 333 (assistance, ie, concealing, arrangements, acquisition, use and possession; failure to report; tipping off)

1.4.5   understand the implications of Part 7 regarding the objective test in relation to reporting suspicious transactions

1.4.6   understand that appropriate disclosure (internal for staff and to the National Crime Agency (NCA) for the firm) is a defence

1.4.7   Know the maximum penalties for committing the offences set out in POCA 2002

POCA 2002 establishes five offences:

1. **Concealing** – it is an offence for a person to conceal or disguise criminal property.
2. **Arrangements** – that is, being concerned in an arrangement which the person knows, or suspects, facilitates the acquisition, retention, use or control of criminal property for another person. Being concerned in an arrangement may be widely interpreted – it could include a person advising on a transaction, for example.
3. **Acquisition, use and possession** – acquiring, using or having possession of criminal property, if the person knows or suspects that the property arose out of criminal conduct.
4. **Failure to disclose** – there is a duty on employees in the regulated sector to make reports where they know or suspect that another person is engaged in money laundering or terrorist financing activity. It is an offence for employees to fail to disclose such information. Three conditions need to be satisfied for this to be an offence:
    a.   the person knows or suspects (or has reasonable grounds to know or suspect) that another person is committing an offence
    b.   the information giving rise to the knowledge or suspicion came to him during the course of business in a regulated sector (described below)
    c.   the person does not make the required disclosure to a nominated officer such as the firm's MLRO as soon as is practicable.
5. **Tipping-off** – this is a particular offence applying only to persons in working in the regulated sector, and it involves disclosing a suspicious activity report or investigation. It is committed where a person knows or suspects that by disclosing the information this is likely to prejudice the investigation, and the information came to them in the course of business in the regulated sector. It is possible to commit this offence even if you do not know that a report has actually been made.

4.2.1   Application of the Offences

The first three offences (concealing, arrangements, and acquisition, use and possession) apply to all persons and businesses (not just financial services firms). A person found guilty of any of these offences will on conviction in a Crown Court be sentenced to imprisonment for up to 14 years or an unlimited fine or both.

Offences 4 and 5 (failure to disclose and tipping-off) apply only to persons in the regulated sector. The regulated sector in this context is wider than the financial services community, as it includes a wide range of organisations involved in handling substantial amounts of cash. It includes authorised firms, estate agents, bureaux de change, consumer credit institutions, law firms, casino operators, accountants, high-end auctioneers and insolvency practitioners. A person in the regulated sector who is found guilty of failure to disclose or tipping off will, on conviction in a Crown Court, be sentenced to imprisonment for up to five years or an unlimited fine or both.

A person may commit the offence of failure to disclose suspicions of money laundering, even if they did not in fact suspect money laundering; they may commit this offence if they did not suspect money laundering, but there were reasonable grounds to know or suspect it. The test as to whether there are reasonable grounds is called the objective test and considers whether a reasonable person would have known or been suspicious, even though the offender protests their innocence.

4.2.2 Defences

As further detailed below, a person has a defence against the first three offences (concealing, arrangements, and acquisition, use and possession) if he makes the required disclosure to the MLRO or, if the person was the MLRO, to the National Crime Agency (NCA). The MLRO is discussed in more detail in Section 4.4 below.

Part 7 of POCA concerns investigations, and S.342 describes the offence of prejudicing investigations, which applies generally, that is, not only to those working in the regulated sector. A person commits this offence if they:

- make a disclosure that is likely to prejudice an investigation, or
- falsify, conceal, destroy or otherwise dispose of documents relevant to an investigation, or permit such falsification.

The offence is not committed if:

- the person did not know or suspect that the disclosure would prejudice an investigation
- the disclosure was made in the performance of a duty under POCA or other similar enactment
- the person is a legal adviser acting in his professional capacity in advising his client or in contemplation of legal proceedings (apart from where the disclosure is made with the purpose of furthering a criminal purpose)
- the person did not know or suspect that documents were relevant to the investigation
- the person did not intend to conceal from an investigator any facts disclosed by the documents.

These offences are punishable by a fine and a jail term of up to five years.

4.3 Senior Management Obligations

1.4.3 Know the obligations placed on senior management in relation to anti-money laundering regulation, including the obligation to arrange regular money laundering training for individuals

1.4.8 Understand: the necessity to obtain documentation proving identity and to record the Know Your Customer (KYC) process; the necessity to verify identity and the existence and nature of the entity; the types of documents that would be appropriate and the consequences of failure to obtain such KYC documentation

1.4.9 Understand the requirement to identify both source of funds and source of wealth

The Money Laundering Regulations 2007 apply to a wide range of organisations, as well as the financial services community, including authorised firms, estate agents, bureaux de change, consumer credit institutions, law firms, casino operators, accountants, high-end auctioneers and insolvency practitioners. As mentioned previously, this is referred to as the regulated sector. The supervision of the regulated sector is split between the FCA (for most financial services firms) and HMRC.

The regulations contain specific requirements intended to prevent money laundering by firms. These are in three main areas:

1. **Due diligence** – including identifying customers.
2. **Internal policies and procedures** – including record keeping, training of staff and reporting of suspicions of money laundering.
3. **Supervision and registration** – this provides the powers of the supervisors (FCA and HMRC).

It is an offence, punishable on conviction in the Crown Court by a jail term of up to two years and/or a fine, for firms or their officers to fail to comply with the money laundering regulations. In deciding whether an offence has been committed the court must consider whether the firm followed the relevant guidance of the JMLSG at the time.

The specific requirements outlined above are reflected in the FCA's rules for authorised firms, which provide more detail on the requirements.

4.3.1 The FCA's Requirements

The FCA's SYSC Sourcebook contains high-level requirements for firms to maintain adequate systems and controls to prevent them being used for purposes connected with financial crime. In particular, SYSC 3.2.6R requires them to take reasonable care to establish and maintain effective systems and controls for compliance with applicable regulatory requirements (including the money laundering regulations, POCA and TA 2000) and for countering the risk that the firm might be used to further financial crime.

4.3.2 Systems and Controls

Authorised firms are required to ensure that they establish and maintain effective systems and controls to enable them to identify, assess, monitor and manage money laundering risk. They must carry out regular assessments of the adequacy of these systems and controls. This includes being able to identify the source of both wealth and funds, which firms should be able to verify and confirm as part of their client take-on process and procedures, ie, **know your client (KYC)** documentation.

Money laundering risk is the risk that a firm may be used to launder the proceeds of crime. In identifying its money laundering risk, and in establishing its systems and controls, a firm should consider a range of factors, including:

- its customer, product and activity profiles
- its distribution channels
- the complexity and volume of its transactions
- its processes and systems, and
- its operating environment.

A firm should ensure that the systems and controls include appropriate:

- training for its employees in relation to money laundering prevention
- provision of information to its governing body and senior management, including a report at least annually by the firm's MLRO on the operation and effectiveness of those systems and controls
- documentation of its risk management policies and risk profile in relation to money laundering
- measures to ensure that money laundering risk is taken into account in its day-to-day operation and also with the development of new products, the taking-on of new customers, and changes in its business profile, and
- measures to ensure that new client identification procedures do not unreasonably deny access for persons who may not be able to produce detailed evidence of identity.

Each authorised firm must give a director or senior manager (who may also be the MLRO) overall responsibility for the establishment and maintenance of effective anti-money laundering systems and controls.

A firm must also appoint an MLRO, who is responsible for receiving and assessing internal suspicion reports, and for determining – after a proper investigation – whether to report them to NCA. The MLRO is a controlled function and therefore subject to the approved persons' regime.

The firm must ensure that its MLRO has an appropriate level of authority and independence within the firm and has access to resources and information sufficient to enable them to carry out their responsibilities. The MLRO acts as a central point for all activity within the firm relating to anti-money laundering and should be based in the UK.

Depending on the nature, scale and complexity of its business, it may be appropriate for a firm to have a separate compliance function (which may be heavily involved in monitoring the firm's compliance with its anti-money laundering procedures). The organisation and responsibilities of a compliance function should be documented. A compliance function should be staffed by an appropriate number of competent staff who are sufficiently independent to perform their duties. It should be adequately resourced and should have unrestricted access to the firm's relevant records.

As mentioned earlier, when considering whether a breach of its rules on systems and controls against money laundering has occurred, the FCA will look to see if the firm has followed relevant provisions in the guidance for the UK financial sector, provided by the JMLSG. It has stated that: *'The guidance ... provides a sound basis for firms to meet their legislative and regulatory obligations when tailored by firms to their particular business risk profile. Departures from this guidance, and the rationale for so doing, should be documented, and firms will have to stand prepared to justify departures, for example to the FCA'.*

Relevant aspects of the guidance are summarised below.

4.3.3   The Joint Money Laundering Steering Group (JMLSG) Requirements – Systems and Controls

Senior management of firms must appoint an appropriately qualified senior member of staff who will have overall responsibility for the maintenance of the firm's anti-money laundering systems and controls.

In order to determine the arrangements and controls needed by a firm for these purposes, its senior management must perform a risk assessment. This should consider such factors as:

- the nature of the firm's products and services
- the nature of its client base, and
- the ways in which these may leave the firm open to abuse by criminals.

Firms must also have an anti-money laundering policy statement in place; this provides a framework to the firm and its staff and must identify named individuals and functions responsible for implementing particular aspects of the policy. The policy must also set out how senior management undertakes its assessment of the money laundering and terrorist financing risks the firm faces and how these risks are to be managed.

The anti-money laundering policy statement might include such matters as:

Guiding Principles

1. Customers' identities need to be satisfactorily verified before the firm accepts them.
2. A commitment to the firm knowing its customers appropriately – both at acceptance and throughout the business relationship – through taking appropriate steps to verify a customer's identity and business.
3. Staff will need adequate training and need to be made aware of the law and their obligations.
4. There should be recognition of the importance of staff reporting promptly their suspicions internally.

Risk Mitigation Approach

1. A summary of the firm's approach to assessing and managing its money laundering and terrorist financing risk.
2. Allocation of responsibilities to specific persons and functions.
3. A summary of the firm's procedures for carrying out appropriate identification and monitoring checks on the basis of their risk-based approach.

4. A summary of the appropriate monitoring arrangements in place to ensure that the firm's policies and procedures are being carried out.

4.3.4   The Joint Money Laundering Steering Group (JMLSG) Guidance – Know Your Customer

Chapter 5 of the JMLSG Guidance is a practical guide to the due diligence required for different types of customer, to establish their identity before commencing business with them.

Customer identities should be verified in advance whenever the firm is entering into a business relationship with a party, or undertaking a transaction of €15,000 or more outside of a business relationship. Additional due diligence should be carried out whenever the firm suspects money laundering or terrorist financing, even in relation to existing customers.

In general, firms should vary their customer due diligence according to the level of risk of money laundering or terrorist financing they are exposed to. Fewer checks need be carried out for low-risk customers, such as EEA-regulated firms or governments, or for the sale of low-risk products (referred to as simplified due diligence); more checks are required for customers posing a higher risk of money laundering; for example, if the customer applies for a service online, or is in a position which exposes them to corruption (enhanced due diligence).

The stages of customer due diligence are:

1. obtaining evidence of identity of the customer and any beneficial owner
2. verifying evidence of identity to ensure that the evidence is valid
3. obtaining information to enable the firm to understand the nature and purpose of the relationship intended; monitoring the relationship; and identifying suspicious transactions.

For personal customers, the standard identification requirement is to ascertain the customer's name, residential address and date of birth. This may be satisfied by the production of a valid passport or photo-card driving licence and utility bill or bank statement. Firms should maintain records of the evidence and verification. In addition, firms should ascertain the source of the customer's wealth and/or funds.

In ascertaining the source of funds, the firm should establish whether the funds are to be paid from (for example) a bank account, credit or debit card or solicitors' account and ensure that this is an expected source. A firm may also enquire as to the source of the customer's wealth, to ensure they understand how the customer obtained the funds in question; for example, from earnings, inheritance, savings, company sale or another source. In both cases, the firm should take a risk-based approach, carrying out more detailed verification in high-risk transactions.

For a corporate customer, firms should obtain evidence of its full name, registered number, registered office and business address, in the form of, eg, a certificate of incorporation, articles of association or bank details. If should also verify the identity of any beneficial owner of the company.

If an exemption to the KYC requirements does not apply, then satisfactory identification evidence should be obtained, and verified, as soon after first contact between the firm and the customer as is reasonably practicable. If there is a delay between the forming of the business relationship and the verification of the customer's identity (for example, in the case of non-face-to-face business), firms' risk management procedures should limit the extent of the relationship. They could do this, eg, by placing restrictions on the transactions the customer can enter into, or on the transfer of funds, until verification is complete.

Additionally, firms should monitor their business relationships on an ongoing basis, to build up a clear understanding of the customer's circumstances and investment patterns.

If a firm cannot satisfactorily verify a customer's identity, it should not proceed with the business relationship, and should consider whether this should cause it to make a report to NCA. If it is simply the case that the customer cannot produce the correct documents or information, the firm may consider whether there is any other way it can satisfy itself as to their identity.

4.4   The Money Laundering Reporting Officer (MLRO) and Reporting Suspicions

Learning Objective

1.4.10   Understand the importance of being able to recognise a suspicious transaction and the requirement for staff to report to the Money Laundering Reporting Officer (MLRO) and for the firm to report to e National Crime Agency (NCA)

Under POCA 2002, it is an offence to fail to disclose a suspicion of money laundering. Obviously this requires the staff at financial services firms to be aware of what constitutes a suspicion. There is therefore a requirement under the money laundering regulations that all relevant employees must be trained to recognise and deal with what may be a money laundering transaction. This training should cover the law relating to money laundering and terrorist financing; how to recognise money laundering and terrorist financing (including the main risk areas for their own firm); and what procedures they must follow if they become aware of any suspicious activity. The training should be tailored to the firm's own business and structure, but should form part of a programme of regular, ongoing training, whose effectiveness is monitored.

Firms are also required to ensure that business relationships are understood, and monitored, sufficiently well that their staff will recognise patterns of activity which are not in keeping with the customer's anticipated profile.

The disclosure of suspicions is made, ultimately, to the NCA; however, disclosure goes through two stages. Firstly, any employee with a suspicion should disclose that suspicion to his firm's MLRO, who reviews matters, and decides whether the suspicion should be passed on to NCA.

It is important to appreciate that, by reporting to the MLRO, the employee with the suspicion has fulfilled his responsibilities under the law – he has disclosed his suspicions. Similarly, by reporting to NCA, the MLRO has fulfilled his responsibilities under the law.

The MLRO's responsibilities are set out in the SYSC Sourcebook of the FCA Handbook. As an approved person, the MLRO is subject to the approved persons regime. The MLRO is primarily responsible for ensuring a firm adequately trains staff in knowing and understanding the regulatory requirements and how to recognise and deal with suspicious transactions.

4.4.1 MLRO or Nominated Officer (NO)?

Under the FCA rules, all firms (except for sole traders, general insurance firms and mortgage intermediaries) must appoint an MLRO with responsibility for oversight of its compliance with the FCA's rules on systems and controls against money laundering.

The money laundering regulations require all affected firms (which includes some non-FCA firms) to appoint a **nominated officer (NO)** to be responsible for receiving internal money laundering disclosures from staff members, and to make external reports to the NCA if necessary. The nominated officer is also responsible for receiving internal disclosures under POCA and the Terrorism Act 2000.

Although the obligations of the MLRO under the FCA requirements are different from those of the nominated officer under POCA, the Terrorism Act or the Money Laundering Regulations 2007, in practice the same person tends to carry on both roles – and is usually known as the MLRO.

The new NCA is responsible for the financial crime activities of the Serious Fraud Office (SFO), but not those of the FCA.

4.5 Terrorism and Money Laundering

Learning Objective

1.4.11 Understand the difference between laundering the proceeds of crime and the financing of terrorist acts

1.4.12 Understand the purpose of Her Majesty's Treasury's (HMT) sanctions list

4.5.1 The Terrorism Act 2000

In light of the war against terrorism, legislation in the form of the Terrorism Act 2000 was introduced. This defines terrorism as *'the use or threat of action, designed to influence the government or to intimidate the public, which is made for the purpose of advancing a political, religious or ideological cause, and which:*

- *involves serious violence against a person or serious damage to property*
- *endangers a person's life or creates a serious risk to the health or safety of the public, or*
- *is designed seriously to interfere with, or seriously to disrupt, an electronic system.'*

Note that if the threat or action involves firearms or explosives, it is classed as terrorism, regardless of whether it was designed to influence the government or intimidate the public (or a section of the public).

Many of the requirements introduced by the Terrorism Act are similar to the anti-money laundering provisions encountered earlier. A person commits an offence if he enters into, or becomes concerned with, an arrangement that facilitates the retention or control of terrorist property by concealment, removal from the jurisdiction, transfer to nominees or in any other way.

The person may have a defence if he can prove that he did not know, and had no reasonable cause to suspect, that the arrangement related to terrorist property. There is a duty to report suspicions and it is an offence to fail to report if there are reasonable grounds to have a suspicion. The Terrorism Act 2000 and Anti-Terrorism Crime Security Act 2001 specify that a failure to report is liable to a term of up to five years in jail, plus a fine.

4.5.2 The Counter-Terrorism Act (CTA) 2008

The CTA became law on 26 November 2008, adding further to the government's armoury of legislation to tackle terrorism. Of particular interest is Schedule 7, which gives new powers to the Treasury to issue directions to firms in the financial sector.

In summary, directions can be given to individual firms; to firms that fit a particular description; or to the sector as a whole, concerning individuals or institutions who are doing business or are resident in a particular non-EEA country or regarding the government in that country. Directions can relate to customer due diligence and ongoing monitoring, systematic reporting on transactions and business relationships, and limiting or ceasing business:

- **Customer due diligence and monitoring** – the provisions are broadly similar to the requirements already imposed under the money laundering regulations. However, the Treasury is now able, for example, to direct that customer due diligence be undertaken again or completed before entering into a business relationship (where it might otherwise be conducted in parallel); or to direct that enhanced measures be carried out. It may also direct that specific activity monitoring be carried out.
- **Systematic reporting** – until now, reporting orders have only been available to law enforcement and must be obtained through the courts. Under the CTA, the Treasury itself can now require information to be provided concerning business relationships and transactions involving the specified person(s), on a one-off or periodic basis.
- **Limiting or ceasing business** – the Treasury's powers under the money laundering regulations (Regulation 18) are limited to where the Financial Action Task Force (FATF) has applied countermeasures. The CTA powers are more flexible and allow directions to be imposed in a wider range of situations (see below).

Under the CTA, the Treasury may issue directions when one or more of the following are met:

- The FATF has advised that countermeasures should be applied to a country (as per the money laundering regulations).
- The Treasury reasonably believes that money laundering/terrorist-financing activities are being carried on in the country, by its government or by persons resident/incorporated there, which pose a significant threat to the UK's national interests.
- The Treasury reasonably believes that the country is developing or producing nuclear or chemical, weapons, or doing anything to facilitate that, and poses a significant threat to the UK's national interests.

If a direction is made to an individual firm, it will be served upon them. However, it is not yet clear how orders that apply to specified types of firm or to the whole sector (which will require secondary legislation each time) will be publicised. It may or may not be via the sanctions mechanism or something similar – this issue is still being clarified with the Treasury.

Her Majesty's Treasury (HMT) Sanctions

The asset freezing unit of HMT publishes a consolidated list of financial sanctions targets listed by the United Nations (UN), the EU and the UK. This list includes all individuals and entities noted on all current sanctions lists. There are a number of statutory instruments relating to financial sanctions and terrorist financing. These measures apply to all firms regulated under the FSMA (rather than just to banks, on whom additional obligations are placed), and create a number of offences, including that of failing to disclose knowledge or suspicion that any person on the relevant HM Treasury sanctions list is, or has been, a customer of the firm.

Because terrorist groups can have links with other criminal activities, there is inevitably some overlap between anti-money laundering provisions and terrorist financing acts. However, there are two major difficulties when terrorist funds are compared with other money laundering activities:

1. Often, only quite small sums of money are required to commit terrorist acts.
2. If legitimate funds are used to fund terrorist activities, it is difficult to identify when the funds become terrorist funds.

Financial services firms need to be as careful in ensuring compliance with the anti-terrorist and terrorist-financing legislation (including the Terrorism Act 2000) as they do with the FCA rules on money laundering issues and the JMLSG Guidance Notes.

4.6 Bribery

Learning Objective

1.4.13 Understand the main offences set out in the Bribery Act 2010 and the penalties for committing the offences set out in that Act

The Bribery Act 2010 received Royal Assent in April 2010 and came into force on 1 July 2011.

Section 1 of the Act provides that a person is guilty of an offence where he, or someone acting on his behalf, offers, promises or gives a financial advantage to another person in either of two situations:

1. If he intends the advantage to bring about an improper performance of a relevant function or an activity by another person, or to reward such improper performance.
2. If he knows, or believes, that the acceptance of the advantage offered, promised or given in itself constitutes the improper performance of a relevant function or activity.

Section 2 provides the offence of being bribed. The offence arises when a person requests, agrees to receive or accepts a financial or other advantage in relation to the improper performance of a relevant function or activity.

Section 6 provides the separate offence of bribing a foreign public official (broadly, government officials and those working for international organisations).

Section 7 further provides that a commercial organisation is guilty of an offence if a person associated with it bribes another person, intending to obtain or retain business or a business advantage for the organisation. The organisation has a defence if it can show that it had in place adequate procedures designed to prevent bribery.

The types of relevant function or activity referred to above include all of the following:

- activities in connection with a business, trade or profession
- public functions
- activities performed in the course of employment
- any activity performed by or on behalf of a body of persons.

Improper performance is performance or non-performance which breaches a relevant expectation, ie, an expectation that the relevant activity or function will be performed from a position of trust.

An individual who is found guilty of an offence is liable on conviction in the Crown Court to imprisonment for a maximum term of ten years, or an unlimited fine, or both. Any other person found guilty will be liable to a fine.

In July 2011, the government published statutory guidance on steps companies can take to put in place adequate procedures, organised under six key principles:

1. **Proportionate procedures** – the action you take should be proportionate to the risks you face and the size of your business.
2. **Top-level commitment** – those at the top of an organisation are in the best position to ensure their organisation conducts business without bribery.
3. **Risk assessment** – think about the bribery risks you might face. For example, do some research into the markets you operate in and the people you do business with.
4. **Due diligence** – knowing exactly who you are dealing with can help to protect your organisation from taking on people who might be less than trustworthy.
5. **Communication** (including training) – communicating your policies and procedures to staff and to others who perform services for you.
6. **Monitoring and review** – the risks you face and the effectiveness of your procedures may change over time.

5. Insider Dealing

When a director of, or someone otherwise linked to, a listed company buys or sells shares in that company there is a possibility that they are committing a criminal act – insider dealing.

This is the case, for example, if that director or other linked person buys shares in the knowledge that the company's last six months of trade are better than the market expected (and that information has not yet been made publicly available). The person buying the shares has the benefit of this information because he is an insider to the company. Under the Criminal Justice Act (CJA) 1993 insider dealing is a criminal offence.

5.1 Inside Information and the Insider

Learning Objective

1.5.1 Understand the meaning of the terms inside information and insider (Criminal Justice Act 1993 (CJA 1993) S.52/56/57/58)

To be found guilty of insider dealing, a person must first be an insider who is in possession of inside information; and, secondly, commit one of three specific offences. The CJA defines both of these terms, as well as the offences that may be carried out.

Inside information is information which:

- relates to particular securities or to one or more particular issuers (ie, it is not so wide as to apply to securities or issuers of securities generally). It could, however, include information about the particular market or sector the issuer is active in
- is specific or precise
- has not been made public, and
- is price sensitive (ie, if it were made public, would be likely to have a significant effect on the price of any securities).

Some of these criteria may seem quite subjective; for example, what is **specific** or **precise**?

The CJA does give some assistance in interpretation; for example, it includes a (non-exhaustive) list of what made public means (from which we can work out when information has not been made public). For example, information becomes **public** when it is:

- published in accordance with the rules of a regulated market to inform investors (eg, a UK-listed company making an announcement through a regulated information service), or
- contained within records open to the public (eg, a new shareholding that is reflected in the company's register of shareholders), or
- it can be readily acquired by those likely to deal in securities to which the information relates, or securities of an issuer to which it relates.

This tells us that it need not be actually published – it just needs to be available to someone who exercises diligence or expertise in finding it (ie, you might have to look quite hard for it). Information may also be regarded as made public even if it has to be paid for.

Inside information is often referred to as unpublished price-sensitive information, and the securities which may be affected by it are referred to as price-affected securities.

A person in possession of price-sensitive information is an insider if he knows that it is inside information and that it has been knowingly acquired from an inside source.

He has obtained it from an inside source if he has got it:

- because he is an inside source himself (by being a director, employee or shareholder of an issuer of securities; and this need not necessarily be the company whose securities are the subject of the insider dealing), or
- because he has access to the information by virtue of his employment, office or profession (and, again, this need not necessarily be in relation to the company to which the information relates). An example might be the auditor, legal adviser or corporate finance adviser to a company, or
- directly or indirectly from a person who obtained it in one of these two ways. For example, a director's husband or wife will have information from an inside source if s/he sees confidential information at home about a takeover bid and then buys shares in the listed company which is the takeover target.

5.2 The Offences

Learning Objective

1.5.2 Understand the offences described in the Criminal Justice Act 1993 and the securities to which it applies (CJA 1993 S.54, Schedule 2)

1.5.3 Know the penalties for the criminal offence of insider dealing (CJA 1993 S.61(1))

A person commits the offence of insider dealing if they:

- deal in price-affected securities when in possession of inside information
- encourage someone else to deal in price-affected securities when in possession of inside information, or
- disclose inside information, other than in the proper performance of their employment, office or profession.

For a deal (ie, an acquisition or a disposal of price-affected securities) to be caught under the insider dealing legislation, it must take place on a regulated market, or through a professional intermediary – otherwise, the legislation does not apply to it.

These offences can be committed only by an individual (and, of course, only then by someone holding inside information as an insider); a company cannot commit the offence. However, by arranging for a company to deal, an individual could commit the offence of encouraging it to do so.

The offence of encouraging someone to deal need not result in an actual deal for the offence to have been committed (though it may be unlikely that the offence will come to light, if no deal results).

5.2.1 The Instruments

Only certain investment instruments are caught under the insider dealing legislation; they are, for the purposes of the CJA, those described as securities. (Note, you may find the term securities defined differently in different legislation.)

For the purpose of the CJA and insider dealing, securities are:

- shares
- debt securities (issued by a company or a public sector body)
- warrants
- depositary receipts
- options (to acquire or dispose of securities)

- futures (to acquire or dispose of securities), and
- CFDs (based on securities, interest rates or share indices).

You will see that this definition of securities does not embrace commodities or derivatives on commodities (such as options and futures on agricultural products, metals or energy products), nor foreign exchange (FX), or derivatives on FX, such as forward FX contracts. Nor does it include units or shares in OEICs – since these will not be price-sensitive or be affected in the same way as individual securities, the reason being that the price of the fund is determined by the prices of the underlying investments held.

5.2.2 The FCA's Prosecution Powers

The FCA has the power under the FSMA to prosecute certain criminal offences including insider dealing. In addition, the Secretary of State for Business, Innovation and Skills and the Crown Prosecution Service also have powers to prosecute insider dealing offences in England and Wales.

In addition to the criminal offences discussed above, since July 2005, the market abuse regime contains civil offences for insider dealing and market manipulation.

Insider dealing cases may be brought to a magistrates' court and then committed for trial by jury in a crown court, should they be considered to be of appropriate magnitude. A magistrates' court is permitted to impose a maximum fine of £5,000 and up to six months' imprisonment. The crown court can impose a higher sentence – an unlimited fine and a maximum of seven years' imprisonment.

5.3 The Defences

Learning Objective

1.5.4   Know the general and special defences available with regard to insider dealing (CJA 1993 S.53 and Schedule 1 paragraphs 1–5)

5.3.1 General Defences

The defences available to the defendant in an insider dealing case are as follows:

For the offence of **insider dealing**, or of **encouraging another to deal**, the defences are:

- the defendant did not expect the dealing to result in a profit (or avoid a loss) due to the information, or
- he believed, on reasonable grounds, that the information had been sufficiently widely disclosed to ensure none of those taking part in the dealing would be prejudiced by not having the information, or
- he would have acted in the same way regardless of being in possession the information.

For the offence of **disclosing only**, the defences are:

- he did not expect any person to deal, or
- although he may have expected a person to deal, he did not expect the dealing to result in a profit (or avoid a loss) due to the information.

5.3.2 Special Defences

There are further defences available to defendants in particular circumstances (special defences). These are for market makers, and in relation to market information and to price stabilisation activities.

Market Makers

As long as a market maker can show that he acted in good faith in the course of his business as a market maker, he will not be deemed guilty of insider dealing or encouraging another to deal. So, a market maker (or his employee) could have unpublished price-sensitive information as an insider and continue to make a market in that security.

A further defence is available if the market maker shows he was acting in connection with an acquisition or disposal where the price was under negotiation, and he acted in order to facilitate the deal. He must show that the information was market information arising directly out of the negotiations.

Market Information

Market information includes information such as the fact that the sale of a block of securities is under consideration or the price at which such a transaction is likely to be done. An insider is not guilty of dealing or encouraging others to deal if he can prove that the information he held was market information, and that it was reasonable for him to act as he did despite having the information at the time. Whether or not the action was reasonable depends on the content of the information and the circumstances within which the market maker acted.

Price Stabilisation

The FCA has a set of rules that allow the stabilisation of a security's price after a new issue in order to prevent too much volatility. These are known as the price stabilisation rules, and they provide a safe harbour for a number of activities, including insider dealing. As long as market makers can show that they are acting in conformity with these rules, they are not deemed to have undertaken insider dealing. The rules can be found in Chapter 2 of the FCA's sourcebook Market Conduct (MAR).

6.   The Financial Services Act 2012 Part 7

6.1   Misleading Statements and Impressions – The Offences

Learning Objective

1.6.1   Know the purpose, provisions, offences and defences of the Financial Services Act 2012 Part 7 in relation to misleading statements and impressions

---

Part 7, S.89–95 of the Financial Services Act 2012 Act repealed S.397 of FSMA and replaced the criminal offence relating to misleading statements and practices with the three new criminal offences, which are:

- making false or misleading statements (S.89)
- creating false or misleading impressions (S.90), and
- making false or misleading statements or creating false or misleading impressions in relation to specified benchmarks (S.91).

The first two offences, together largely replicate the now repealed FSMA S.397 offence. The misleading impressions offence, however, is now wider in scope and covers recklessly created misleading impressions as well as those created intentionally.

The new Section 91 offence has been introduced as a result of the recommendations made in the final report of the Wheatley Review of LIBOR (the only benchmark to which this new offence currently applies is LIBOR.)

For an offence to occur the offending behaviour must take place within the UK, or have an effect within the UK.

The sanctions are serious – under S.92, a person found guilty of a S.89–S.91 offence is liable to:

- six months' imprisonment and/or a maximum fine of £5,000 if the matter is tried in a magistrates' court (summary conviction)
- seven years' imprisonment and/or an unlimited fine if the matter is so serious that it is tried in a crown court.

Example

A stockbroker might tell a potential investor that the shares in XYZ PLC (a property developer) are very cheap because XYZ has just won a major contract to build a shopping centre in central London. If the information about the award of the contract to XYZ was false, the FCA could bring a criminal prosecution on the stockbroker under S.89 for making a false and misleading statement to persuade their client to purchase shares.

If the person has committed any of the actions above, he is guilty of an offence if he has made the statement, promise or forecast or has concealed the facts either for the purpose of inducing another person to enter into (or refrain from entering into) an agreement in relation to a regulated activity, or is reckless as to whether it may induce another person into such an agreement.

Section 89 will also apply to a person who creates a false or misleading impression of the market for, or the price of, an investment. An offence is committed if this is done in order to (or without sufficient care as to whether it will) induce another person to acquire, dispose of, underwrite, subscribe for or exercise rights in relating to those investments, or to refrain from doing any of these things.

For an offence to occur the offending behaviour must take place within the UK, or have an effect within the UK. There has to be intention, ie, the behaviour is done in order to induce another person to enter into a relevant agreement (ie, an agreement relating to regulated activity and specified investments) or exercise or refrain from exercising any rights conferred by specified investments in the UK.

Example

A firm of fund managers might let the market know that it is very keen to buy substantial quantities of shares in ABC PLC, when actually they hold a smaller quantity of shares in ABC that they plan to sell. The fund manager's expressions of interest in buying ABC shares might mislead participants in the market to pay more money for the shares in ABC that the fund manager anonymously sells. The fund manager is guilty under S.90.

6.2 Defences

The potential defences to a charge under S.89–S.92 are:

- The person reasonably believed that his act or conduct would not create an impression that was false or misleading.
- The person was acting in conformity with the price stabilisation rules of the FCA. These allow market participants, such as investment banks, to support the price of a new issue of securities for their clients, with the aim of preventing the market from being excessively volatile. The rules themselves require certain disclosures to investors considering investing in the stabilised securities and restrict the support operation to a particular period.
- The person was acting in conformity with the control of information rules of the FCA. These rules relate to statements, actions or forecasts being made on the basis of limited information. The firm may know the remainder of the information, but it rests behind so-called Chinese walls, and is not known to the relevant individual.
- The person was acting in conformity with certain EU provisions with regards to stabilising financial instruments.

7. Market Abuse

7.1 The Statutory Offence

Learning Objective

1.7.1 Know the statutory offences of market abuse (FSMA 2000, C.8 Part 8, S.118(2)-(8), S.123(1))

Market abuse is a civil offence under the FSMA at S.118. It relates to:

- behaviour (whether inaction or action)
- by a person, or a group of persons working together (not just authorised or approved persons),
- which occurs in relation to qualifying investments on a prescribed market
- that meets one or more of the following three conditions:
  1. It is based on information that is not generally available to those using the market and, if it were available, it would have an impact on the price.
  2. It is likely to give a false or misleading impression of the supply, demand or value of the investments concerned.
  3. It is likely to distort the market in the investments.

In all three cases, the behaviour is judged on the basis of what a regular user of the market would view as a failure to observe the standards of behaviour normally expected in the market, or what a **reasonable person** would consider appropriate.

Prescribed markets are those markets which are operated by an RIE – thus, it includes the LSE Main Market, the AIM Market and the ISDX Growth Market. Qualifying investments are those investments that are traded on prescribed markets, or where application has been made for trading on those markets.

The behaviour could amount to market abuse as long as it has an effect on investments traded on UK prescribed markets, regardless of where in the world the behaviour itself takes place. The examples given in Section 6.2 illustrate this.

From July 2016, the EU Market Abuse Regulation (MAR) will strengthen the existing UK market abuse framework by extending its scope to new markets, new platforms and new behaviours. It contains prohibitions for insider dealing and market manipulation, and provisions to prevent and detect these. MAR also applies to emission allowances and emission allowance market participants (EAMPs), and spot commodities are in scope in certain situations. MAR provisions that are dependent in MiFID II will apply from January 2017.

The new prohibitions of insider dealing and unlawful disclosure of inside information, and market manipulation, apply to the following:

a. Financial instruments admitted to trading on a regulated market or for which a request for admission to trading on a regulated market has been made.
b. Financial instruments traded on a multilateral trading facility (MTF), admitted to trading on an MTF, or for which a request for admission to trading on an MTF has been made.

c. Financial instruments traded on an organised trading facility (OTF).

d. Financial instruments not covered by point (a), (b) or (c), the price or value of which depends on or has an effect on the price or value of a financial instrument referred to in those points, including, but not limited to, credit default swaps and contracts for difference.

The Key Requirements

- **Inside information and disclosure** – the definition of inside information is broadly unchanged, but has been widened to capture inside information for spot commodity contracts. Issuers of securities admitted to trading only on an MTF or OTF are brought within the scope of the obligations for public disclosure of inside information. The obligation to disclose inside information has been extended to some EAMPs. Issuers and EAMPs must notify the regulator after delaying disclosure of inside information, and financial institutions must seek consent from the regulator prior to delaying disclosure due to financial stability concerns.

- **Insider dealing and unlawful disclosure** – it is clarified that the use of inside information to amend or cancel an order shall be considered to be insider dealing. It is also clarified that recommending or inducing another person to transact on the basis of inside information amounts to unlawful disclosure of inside information.

- **Market manipulation** – the manipulation offence has been extended to capture attempted manipulation. Benchmarks, and in some situations spot commodities, are now in scope of the manipulation offence. Examples of behaviours and activities that shall be considered as market manipulation are set out, eg, acting in collaboration to secure a dominant position over the supply or demand of a financial instrument, and certain algorithmic trading strategies which disrupt the functioning of a trading venue.

- **Market soundings** – introduces a framework for persons to make legitimate disclosures of inside information in the course of market soundings. Certain steps must be taken prior to conducting soundings and detailed record keeping requirements are imposed.

- **Buy-back programmes and stabilisation measures** – makes revisions to the existing framework for conducting buy-back programmes and stabilisation measures.

- **Accepted market practices (AMPs)** – continues to permit regulators to establish an accepted market practice which is subject to certain criteria and conditions.

- **Insider lists** – places an obligation on issuers and EAMPs to draw-up and maintain a list of all those persons working for them that have access to inside information. Issuers on SME growth markets will only be required to draw up a list when it is requested by the regulator.

- **Suspicious transaction and order reports (STORs)** – extends the existing obligation to report suspicious transaction reports to also include include suspicious orders. Trading venues are also caught by the obligation to submit STORs.

- **Managers' transactions** – persons discharging managerial responsibilities within issuers (PDMRs), and persons closely associated with them, must notify the issuer and the regulator of relevant personal transactions they undertake in the issuer's financial instruments. The issuer in turn must make that information public within three business days.

- **Investment recommendations** – continues to require persons producing or disseminating investment recommendations to ensure information is objectively presented, and to disclose any conflicts of interest.

- **Whistleblowing** – places requirements on regulators and firms to be able to receive whistleblowing notifications.

- **Regulators Powers** – new EEA minimum standards for regulators' investigatory and sanctioning powers. Powers must include fines of up to €5 million for individuals and 15% of firms' annual turnover.

7.2   The Seven Types of Market Abuse

Learning Objective

1.6.1   *know* the purpose, provisions, offences and defences of the Financial Services Act 2012 Part 7 in relation to misleading statements and impressions

The FSMA S.118 sets out the seven types of behaviour that constitute market abuse. These are:

1. **Insider dealing –** where an insider deals in, or attempts to deal in, a qualifying investment or a related investment on the basis of inside information. For market abuse purposes, an insider has inside information:
    a. as a result of his membership of the administrative, management or supervisory bodies of the issuer of the investment
    b. as a result of his holding in the capital of the issuer of the investment
    c. as a result of having access to the information through his employment, profession or duties
    d. as a result of criminal activities, or
    e. which he has obtained by other means and which he knows, or could reasonably be expected to know, is inside information.
2. **Improper disclosure –** where an insider discloses inside information to another person otherwise than in the proper course of the exercise of his employment, profession or duties.
3. **Misuse of information –** where behaviour is not covered by 1 above (insider dealing) or 2 above (improper disclosure) but is based on information that is not generally available to those using the market and which a regular user would regard as relevant and a failure to observe the standard of behaviour reasonably expected.
4. **Manipulating transactions –** where the behaviour consists of effecting transactions or orders to trade that are not for legitimate reasons and in conformity with accepted practices on the relevant market, and which:
    a. give, or are likely to give, a false or misleading impression as to the supply or demand for, or the price of, the qualifying investment, or
    b. secure the price of such investments at an abnormal or artificial level.
5. **Manipulating devices –** behaviour that consists of effecting transactions or orders to trade which employ fictitious devices or any other form of deception or contrivance.
6. **Dissemination –** where the behaviour consists of the dissemination of information by any means which gives, or is likely to give, a false or misleading impression as to a qualifying investment by a person who knew, or could reasonably be expected to have known, that the information was false or misleading.
7. **Misleading behaviour and distortion –** where behaviour which is not covered above by points 4 (manipulating transactions), 5 (manipulating devices) or 6 (dissemination):
    a. is likely to give a regular user a false or misleading impression as to the supply of, demand for, or price or value of, a qualifying investment, or
    b. is regarded by a regular user as behaviour likely to distort the market in such investments.

Items 3 and 7 were provisions (known as the sunset clauses) which were super-equivalent to the requirements of the MAD and were due to be repealed in December 2011, but, as has happened previously, these were kicked back again until the implementation of the Financial Services and Markets

Act 2000 (Market Abuse) Regulation 2014, effective 15 December 2014, that further extended the clause until 3 July 2016.

The following are practical examples of each of the seven types of market abuse, drawn from the FCA factsheet '*Why market abuse could cost you money*', published in June 2008.

Examples of Market Conduct Offences

Circumstances 1 and 2 – Insider Dealing and Improper Disclosure

An employee finds out that his company is about to become the target of a takeover bid. Before the information is made public, he buys shares in his company because he knows a takeover bid may be imminent. He then discloses the information to a friend. This behaviour creates an unfair marketplace because the person who sold the shares to the employee might not have done so if he had known of the potential takeover. The employee's friend also has this information and could profit unfairly from it.

Circumstance 3 – Misuse of Information

An employee learns that his company may lose a significant contract with its main customer. The employee then sells his shares, based on his assessment that it is reasonably certain the contract will be lost. This behaviour creates an unfair marketplace, as the person buying the shares from the employee might not have done so had he been aware of the information about the potential loss of the contract.

Circumstance 4 – Manipulating Transactions

A person buys a large number of a particular share near the end of the day, aiming to drive the stock price higher to improve the performance of their investment. The market price is pushed to an artificial level and investors get a false impression of the price of those shares and the value of any portfolio or fund that holds the stock. This could lead to people making the wrong investment decisions.

Circumstance 5 – Manipulating Devices

A person buys shares and then spreads misleading information with a view to increasing the price. This could give investors a false impression of the price of a share and lead them to make the wrong investment decisions.

Circumstance 6 – Dissemination

A person uses an internet bulletin board or chat room to post information about the takeover of a company. The person knows the information to be false or misleading. This could artificially raise or reduce the price of a share and lead to people making the wrong investment decisions.

Circumstance 7 – Distortion and Misleading Behaviour

An empty cargo ship that is used to transport a particular commodity is moved. This could create a false impression of changes in the supply of, or demand for, that commodity or the related futures contract. It could also artificially change the price of that commodity or the futures contract, and lead to people making the wrong investment decisions.

7.3 Defences and Penalties

Learning Objective

1.7.2 Know the due diligence defence (FSMA 2000, C.8 Part 8 s.123(2))

1.7.3 Know the penalties for market abuse

1.7.4 Understand the enforcement regime for market abuse (Market Conduct (MAR) 1.1.4-1.1.6, 1.2.20-1.2.21)

Market abuse is a civil offence, and therefore is not prosecuted through the criminal courts, and imprisonment is not a possible sanction. The burden of proof required for conviction is balance of probabilities.

Market abuse cases are investigated by the FCA, and heard by the RDC.

The FSMA gives the FCA the power to impose a sanction. These powers can be exercised if the FCA is satisfied that a person has engaged in market abuse, or if the person has taken (or refrained from taking) any action which required or encouraged another party to engage in behaviour that would amount to market abuse. The sanctions available are:

- withdrawal of approval or authorisation
- imposing an unlimited civil fine
- making a public statement that a person has engaged in market abuse
- applying to the court for an injunction to restrain threatened or continued market abuse, an injunction requiring a person to take steps to remedy market abuse or a freezing order
- applying to the court for a restitution order, and
- requiring the payment of compensation to victims of the abuse.

However, if there are reasonable grounds for the FCA to be satisfied that the person believed, on reasonable grounds, that the behaviour in question did not amount to market abuse, or that the person had taken all reasonable precautions and exercised all due diligence to avoid engaging in market abuse, the FCA cannot impose a penalty. This is referred to as the due diligence defence. In particular, the FCA will have regard to how far the person has complied with the provisions of the Code of Market Conduct.

7.4 The Regular Market User

As noted above, whether or not behaviour of types 3 and 7 amounts to market abuse depends on how a hypothetical reasonable regular user, familiar with the market in question, would view the behaviour. Unless a regular user feels that the behaviour falls below the standards expected on the market in question, it is not market abuse.

In assessing whether the behaviour falls below the standards expected, the following will be considered:

- The characteristics of the market, investments traded there and the users of that market.
- The rules and regulations of the market in question and any applicable laws (eg, if the behaviour occurred overseas, then compliance with the law overseas will be a consideration).
- The prevailing market mechanisms, practices and codes of conduct applicable to the market in question.

- The standards reasonably expected of the person in the light of their level of skill and knowledge (eg, the standards expected of a retail investor may differ from those expected of an institutional investor).
- The need for market users to conduct their affairs in a manner that does not compromise the fair and efficient operation of the market as a whole, or damage the interests of investors.

It is not essential for the person responsible for the behaviour in question to have intended to commit market abuse, although the regular user test may determine that market abuse has not occurred unless the intention of the person was to engage in market abuse.

7.5   Relationship with Other Legislation

The first two behaviour types that are potentially market abuse, namely:

1. insider dealing (and misuse of inside information), and
2. behaviour which is likely to give a false or misleading impression of the supply, demand or value of the investments concerned,

are, to an extent, also covered by the legislation relating to insider dealing (CJA, see Section 5) and the legislation relating to misleading statements and impressions (Part 7, S.89–95 of the Financial Services Act 2012, see Section 7).

There is some overlap with the insider dealing legislation under both these sections, but note that:

- both Section 89–95 of Part 7 of the Financial Services Act 2012 and the CJA provide for a criminal regime, whereas the FSMA market abuse regime provides for civil penalties and, consequently, a lower required standard of proof, and
- the CJA insider dealing regime applies to a more restricted range of investments, whereas the FSMA market abuse regime extends its insider dealing provision to other markets, such as commodities and energy.

As we have already noted, the FSMA market abuse regime complements the criminal regime for insider dealing and misleading statements and practices. There will be cases when a possible breach of both the criminal and civil law occurred and the FCA is required to assess whether it has sufficient evidence, and whether it is in the public interest, to commence criminal proceedings rather than impose civil sanctions for market abuse.

The FCA has stated that it is not its policy to impose a sanction for market abuse if a person is being prosecuted for insider dealing or misleading statements and practices. Similarly, it will not commence criminal proceedings if it has brought, or is seeking to bring, disciplinary proceedings for market abuse.

7.6   The Code of Market Conduct

Learning Objective

1.7.6   Know the status of the FCA's Code of Market Conduct (MAR 1)

The FCA is tasked under FSMA S.118 to prepare and issue a code containing such provisions as they consider will give appropriate guidance to those determining whether or not behaviour amounts to market abuse. This is called the Code of Market Conduct (MAR) and is a sourcebook in the business standards block of the FCA's Handbook.

The Code provides non-exhaustive guidance on what does and does not amount to market abuse and the factors which are taken into account in the determination of whether market abuse has occurred. FCA guidance is not legally binding on firms (in the same way as rules are) but the FCA will have regard to whether activity or (in this case) behaviour is in accordance with the guidance in investigating matters and reaching decisions.

7.7   Safe Harbours for Market Abuse

Learning Objective

1.7.5   Know statutory exceptions: Takeover Code, FCA Rules, buy-back and price stabilisation

1.7.7   Understand when price stabilisation is used (MAR 2.1.5)

There are certain **safe harbours** against a charge of market abuse, provided in the Code of Market Conduct. Safe harbours provide that if a person has complied with specific rules (the safe harbours) the behaviour in question is categorically not deemed to be market abuse.

7.7.1   FCA Rules

The FCA Handbook provides two areas where rules are provided in order to prevent market abuse:

- the rules relating to Chinese walls (covered in Chapter 2, Section 5.5 – located in the SYSC Sourcebook), and
- the disclosure rules relating to the timing, dissemination or availability, content and standard of care applicable to the announcement, communication and release of information for listed companies, in the disclosure and transparency rules and listing rules.

Providing that these rules are complied with, the action in question is not deemed to be market abuse.

7.7.2   Takeover Code

During the course of a takeover, both bidder and target have to comply with certain rules laid down in the Takeover Code. These are discussed further in Chapter 4.

There are no rules in the Takeover Code that permit or require a person to behave in a way that amounts to market abuse. Specifically, as long as any announcements, or disclosure of information conforms with the timing, dissemination and disclosure rules of the Takeover Code, is expressly permitted or required by such rules and conforms with the Takeover Code's relevant general principles, the action will not amount to market abuse.

7.7.3 Price Stabilisation

In an initial public offering (IPO), it is possible that the share price of the newly listed company will be very volatile for a period after the admission to listing. It is possible for the issuer's investment bank to take action in the market to stabilise the company's share price, through supporting the price of new issues of securities for a limited period after the issue by buying the relevant securities in the secondary market, or issuing new shares into the market to suppress price peaks.

This is in the interest of those investors having subscribed or purchased those relevant securities, and can contribute to greater confidence of investors and issuers in the financial markets. However, action of this kind, if not closely controlled, can fall within the definition of market abuse (market manipulation).

The Code of Market Conduct therefore includes buy-back and stabilisation rules. Price support activities carried out in accordance with the timing and procedures of these rules will not amount to market abuse. The rules extend to share buy-backs, as these are also an area where there is scope to commit market abuse.

7.8 Reporting of Suspicions

Learning Objective

1.7.8 Know the obligation to report suspicious transactions (SUP 15.10)

The supervision sourcebook (SUP) states that FCA-authorised firms and credit institutions that arrange or execute a transaction with or for a client in a qualifying investment, and which have reasonable grounds to suspect that the transaction may constitute market abuse, must notify the FCA of their suspicions without delay. Qualifying investments are those admitted to trading on a prescribed market (SUP 15.10.2).

Strictly, this obligation extends only to executed transactions and not to unexecuted orders – but a firm may bring an unexecuted suspicious order to the FCA's attention voluntarily. The provisions require that firms decide on a case-by-case basis whether there are reasonable grounds for suspecting that a transaction involves market abuse, taking into account the circumstances. Further, Principle 11 of the Principles for Businesses requires that a firm discloses to the FCA everything of which the FCA would reasonably expect notice, and many firms (or rather their employees) interpret this as giving them grounds to report suspicious unexecuted transactions as well.

7.9 Regulatory Update

7.9.1 Market Abuse

In April 2009, the EC launched a review into MAD as part of an action programme for reducing administrative burdens in the EU.

On 20 October 2011, the EC published its proposed revisions to the MAD in a draft regulation, which provides for:

- an extension to the scope of MAD to include additional financial instruments and markets, and covering financial instruments traded solely on MTFs and organised trading facilities (OTFs)
- a new definition of inside information for commodity derivatives and new powers for regulators to request information on spot commodity markets
- bringing emission allowances into the scope of the market abuse regime
- a new offence of attempting market manipulation
- broadening and clarifying the definition of market manipulation
- amendments to the disclosure requirements, and
- strengthening of the investigative powers of regulators.

The EC also published on 20 October 2011 a draft directive on criminal sanctions for insider dealing and market abuse. The draft directive proposed minimum rules on criminal offences and criminal sanctions for market abuse. These were agreed in early December 2012.

The Regulation brings the definition of financial instruments in MAD in line with the definition used in MiFID. MAD will apply to any financial instrument:

- admitted to trading on an MTF or OTF, irrespective of whether or not the behaviour or transaction actually takes place on that market, or
- whose value depends on the financial instruments traded on a regulated market, MTF or OTF (eg, OTC derivatives referenced to such financial instruments).

As a result, financial instruments which were outside the scope of MAD, such as credit default swaps, are therefore now caught.

To ensure that there is a level playing field, operators of regulated markets, MTFs and OTFs are required to ensure that they have mechanisms in place for preventing and detecting market manipulation and insider dealing.

The draft regulation and directive on criminal sanctions was passed to the European Parliament and the Council of the EU, which agreed the Commission's proposals in December 2012. The Regulation will apply two years after its entry into force (on which date MAD I will be repealed), and so member states had two years to transpose the directive into national law.

8.   The Markets in Financial Instruments Directive (MiFID)

Learning Objective

1.8.1   Know the purpose and scope of MiFID in relation to: the concept of passporting within the EEA; the categories of MiFID financial instruments; the responsibilities of the home and host state regulators

As a member of the EU, the UK plays a part in the attempt to create a single market across Europe for financial services. Primarily, this is achieved by the European Parliament issuing directives to the member states and their implementation into national legislation.

8.1   Introduction

The ISD was issued in 1993. Broadly, it specified that if a firm was authorised in one member state to provide investment services, this single authorisation enabled the firm to provide those investment services in other member states without requiring any further authorisation. This principle was, and still is, known as the passport.

The state providing authorisation is where the firm originates and is commonly referred to as the **home** state. States where the firm offers investment services outside its home state are known as **host** states.

The ISD was repealed and replaced by MiFID. MiFID provisions came into force in the UK on 1 November 2007.

One of the key aims of MiFID is to provide common investor protection rules across the EEA. Investor protection is ensured, inter alia, via the obligation to obtain the best possible result for the client, information disclosure requirements, client-specific rules on suitability and appropriateness and rules on inducements. As a general principle, MiFID places significant importance on the fiduciary duties of firms, so that MiFID established a general obligation for firms to act in the client's best interest, requiring them to put their client's interest ahead of the firm's interest.

8.2   The Purpose and Scope of MiFID

8.2.1   Passporting

MiFID was designed to support two key policy goals of the EU. These are:

*   extending the scope of the passport to include a wider range of services, and
*   removing a major hurdle to cross-border business, by applying host state rules to incoming passported firms.

8.2.2   MiFID versus Non-MiFID Firms

FCA-authorised firms may be classified as MiFID firms or non-MiFID firms. Broadly, a MiFID firm is one whose regular occupation or business is the provision to others of one or more MiFID services or activities, on a professional basis (with or without ancillary services), where the performance of one or more of these services or activities relates to MiFID financial instruments.

Non-MiFID firms are sometimes referred to as 'out-of-scope' firms, or as carrying on out-of-scope business. They include insurance undertakings, employee schemes, people administering their own assets, and any firms which do not provide investment services and/or perform investment activities.

8.2.3 Activities that can be Passported under MiFID

The activities that can be passported under MiFID are divided into core and ancillary investment services.

It should be noted that, whilst MiFID replaced the ISD, it did not replace any existing UK regulated activity. If a UK investment firm wishes to exercise passporting rights under MiFID, it must already have Part IV permission to conduct the equivalent UK regulated activity as shown in the table below.

Core Activities

MiFID activity	Broadly equivalent to the UK regulated activity
Receipt and transmission of orders in relation to one or more specified financial instruments	Arranging deals in investments
Execution of orders on behalf of clients	Dealing as principal Dealing as agent
Dealing on own account	Dealing as principal
Portfolio management	Managing investments
Investment advice	Advising on investments
Underwriting of financial instruments and/ or placing of financial instruments on a firm commitment basis	Dealing as principal Dealing as agent
Placing of financial instruments without a firm commitment basis	Dealing as principal Arranging deals in investment
Operation of MTFs	Operating an MTF, formerly known as an ATS

Ancillary Activities

The services on the following table cannot be passported in their own right – they can only be offered on a cross-border passported basis if they are being provided in conjunction with a core investment service from the previous table. The same principle applies for ancillary activities – UK firms must already have the relevant activity within their Part IV permission.

MiFID ancillary activity	Broadly equivalent to the UK-regulated activity
Safekeeping and administration of financial instruments for the account of clients, including custodianship. Also related services such as the management of cash and collateral	Safeguarding and administering investments Sending dematerialised instructions Agreeing to carry on regulated activities
Lending to investors to allow them to effect a transaction in one or more financial instruments where the lender is involved in the transaction	N/A
Advice to undertakings on capital structure industrial strategy and related matters; also advice/services relating to mergers and the purchase of undertakings	Dealing as principal Dealing as agent Arranging deals in investments Advising on investments Agreeing to carry on regulated activities
FX services (but only where these are connected with the provision of investment services)	Dealing as principal Dealing as agent Arranging deals in investments Advising on investments Agreeing to carry on regulated activities
Investment research and financial analysis, or other forms of general recommendation in relation to transactions in financial instruments	Advising on investments Agreeing to carry on regulated activities
Services in relation to underwriting	Arranging deals in investments Advising on investments Agreeing to carry on regulated activities
Investment services and activities, and ancillary services, related to the underlying assets of certain derivatives where these are connected to the provision of investment or ancillary services	Dealing as principal Dealing as agent Arranging deals in investments Advising on investments Operating an MTF Managing investments Agreeing to carry on regulated activities

8.2.4 Home State versus Host State Regulation

As mentioned earlier, the concept of passporting under MiFID relies on the concept of the co-operation of home state and host state regulators. In essence, the home state is where the firm carrying on activities is established; the host state is the state in which it is providing services as a guest. The home state authorises a firm by granting it permissions; and then those permissions can be passported into host states, as if the firm had gained authorisation in the host state.

The challenge under ISD was establishing which rules applied to business passported into a host state, as in most cases host state rules applied. This created huge difficulties for firms trying to conduct cross-border business in several countries, since, instead of relying on their own home rules being sufficient, they had to comply with the (often quite different) rulebooks of all those different states into which they were selling. Imagine, for example, the complexity of trying to arrange brochures or a website compliant with the rules of all the EU states.

MiFID tackled this hurdle to a single market in the following ways:

- It allows firms to carry on cross-border business from their home state solely on the basis of their home country rules.
- It harmonises these home country rules so that they are all sufficiently similar that an investor is, in theory, just as well protected under the rules of one EU member state as he is under the rules of another. There are common standards of investor protection.
- Host state conduct of business rules apply where a passported MiFID branch of a firm conducts business with host state residents.
- Home state rules apply where services are being provided to residents in another EEA member state.

For this reason, EU member states have been encouraged to use the MiFID terminology in their domestic rules as closely as possible.

8.2.5   Financial Instruments Covered by MiFID

MiFID applies only to activities in relation to a specified list of financial instruments. These are:

- transferable securities
- money market instruments
- units in collective investment undertakings (UCITS)
- derivatives relating to securities, currencies, interest rates or yields, or other financial indices or measures which may be settled physically or in cash
- commodity derivatives that are traded on a regulated market and/or an MTF even if they are physically settled
- OTC commodity derivatives with a cash-settled option other than on default or other termination event;
- other OTC commodity derivatives which are physically settled, which are not for commercial purposes, and which are similar to other derivatives in certain criteria
- credit derivatives
- financial CFDs, and
- derivatives relating to climatic variables, freight rates, emission allowances or inflation rates or other statistics, and certain other derivatives.

Therefore, when exercising passporting rights the firm must also specify the financial instruments that are to be included within the passport. These are broadly equivalent to some (but not all) of the specified investments that are within a UK firm's Part IV permission.

Financial instruments not covered by MiFID include:

- bank accounts, and
- FX (unless it relates to the provision of an investment activity or service, eg, buying/selling an option on FX).

8.2.6   Exemptions

If a firm falls within an exemption, MiFID will not apply to it. The exemptions are listed in Articles 2 and 3 of MiFID, and they include, inter alia:

- insurance undertakings (including reinsurers)
- group treasury activities (eg, the internal cash management activities of major companies)
- professional investors investing only for themselves
- collective investment undertakings and pension funds whether co-ordinated at community level or not, and the depositaries and managers of such undertakings (however the offering of transferable securities and UCITS in collective investment undertakings is covered – see Section 8.2.5)
- commodity producers and traders
- employee schemes (when dealing in the administration of employee-participation schemes)
- persons administering their own assets
- undertakings which do not provide investment services and/or perform investment activities
- incidental business in the course of a professional activity, which is regulated by legal or regulatory provisions or a code of ethics governing that profession (this exemption applies to DPBs such as accountants and lawyers).

Note the term **undertakings** is one that tends to be used in European drafting: in this context you can take it to be the equivalent of **firms**.

Article 3 exemption is available for firms that:

- only provide investment advice and receive/transmit orders
- do not hold client funds or securities
- only transmit orders to other MiFID firms and certain other institutions.

This exemption is widely used by financial advisory firms. If a firm is relying on the Article 3 exemption and wishes to exercise a MiFID passport, it must first apply to the FCA to vary its UK Part IV permission to remove the exemption.

8.2.7   Regulatory Developments – MiFID II

MiFID was implemented in most European member states in November 2007. Partly as a result of the financial crisis, the European Commission decided that MiFID: *'exhibits the need for targeted but ambitious improvements'*. On 20 October 2011, it published a proposed replacement directive (MiFID II). Implementation is scheduled for January 2017.

These measures include a large number of new measures mainly in four areas:

- extending MiFID regulation of investment firms and credit institutions
- tougher conduct of business and prudential requirements
- extending EU regulation of markets and trading venues
- increasing the powers of ESMA and national supervisors.

The proposal is a further large step in the direction of a single European rulebook for financial services. Many provisions are now included in a regulation rather than a directive, so that they are directly applicable in member states, and the Commission and ESMA have extensive powers to make detailed supplementary rules.

There will be even less scope than there is at present for member states to make their own rules, or even their own guidance. This centralisation also carries over into supervision, with highly significant new supervisory powers conferred on ESMA, for example, in relation to the imposition of derivatives position limits and product intervention.

Third-country investment firms ie, those incorporated outside the EU/EEA do not currently enjoy a MiFID passport. They must apply for separate authorisation in each member state (for services/cross-border business or to operate a local branch). The regulatory perimeter varies from one member state to another and different authorisation requirements apply.

Third-country firms will not be able to obtain authorisation to provide any MiFID services to retail clients unless they have established a branch within the EEA. Once authorised, the third-country firm branch will be free to provide services in/to other member states without the need to establish a local branch or branches. It will have the benefit of an EEA-wide services passport (ie, it will able to conduct services business in other member states and only need complete a simple notification process to the member state authority which has granted its EEA authorisation, similar to the current passport regime for EEA firms).

There will be new requirements on regulated markets regarding systems resilience, circuit breakers and electronic trading; these include a prohibition on giving direct electronic access to any firm that is not authorised under MiFID. Extensive new requirements will apply to firms engaged in algorithmic trading including the obligation to report to their supervisor on their trading strategy and parameters as well as its related and risk/compliance controls. Additional requirements apply to firms with direct electronic access to trading venues and general clearing members.

ESMA and competent authorities now have the power to ban certain financial products, activities or practices, where there is a threat to investor protection, or to the orderly functioning and integrity of the financial markets, or to the stability of the financial system.

Custody of a client's investments is to become a MiFID investment service, not merely an ancillary activity as it is now. This means that firms providing this service will be subject to MiFID requirements, and will be able to use the MiFID passport, even when this service is not provided in connection with other MiFID services/activities.

Corporate governance requirements will be imposed on non-bank investment firms, similar to those being imposed on banks under the CRD 4 proposals. Members of the governing body will be required to commit sufficient time to discharge their duties and there will be limits on the number of directorships they can take on at any one time. Other requirements cover the need for adequate collective knowledge and skills within the board, independence of mind, and requirements for diversity to be taken into account in making board appointments. In all these areas specific detailed requirements are to be spelt out by ESMA.

MiFID also requires that the board manage the firm in a manner that *'promotes the integrity of the market'* as well as the interests of its clients. This small provision looks like a significant change in approach and could have important implications depending on how it is applied.

The Commission has decided not to prohibit true execution-only business altogether, but the categories of financial instruments for which this is permissible are to be narrowed.

End of Chapter Questions

Think of an answer for each question and refer to the appropriate section for confirmation.

1. What is the status of an EU regulation and an EU directive?
    Answer reference: Section 1.1.1

2. What is the concept of better regulation as considered by the FCA?
    Answer reference: Section 1.1.6

3. What is the consequence of carrying out regulated activities when not authorised?
    Answer reference: Section 1.3

4. What defence is available under FSMA for the offence of carrying on regulated activities without being authorised or exempt?
    Answer reference: Section 1.3

5. What activities constitute designated investment business?
    Answer reference: Section 1.4

6. What is the FCA's new enhanced process called?
    Answer reference: Section 2.4.2

7. What are the five types of controlled function?
    Answer reference: Section 2.6.1

8. What does Section 165 of FSMA permit the FCA to do?
    Answer reference: Section 2.9

9. What are the regulatory enforcement measures available to the FCA?
    Answer reference: Section 2.10.5

10. What are a sell-out and a squeeze-out?
    Answer reference: Section 3.2.1

11. What are the main statutory rights of a shareholder?
    Answer reference: Section 3.6.1 – 3.6.5

12. What is a memorandum of association and what is its main purpose?
    Answer reference: Section 3.8.1

13. What are the main offences set out in POCA 2002 in relation to money laundering?
    Answer reference: Section 4.2

14. What are the penalties for the money laundering offences?
    Answer reference: Section 4.2.1

15. What is the offence of insider dealing and what financial instruments are caught by the insider dealing legislation?
     Answer reference: Sections 5.1, 5.2.1

16. State the general defences and special defences available with regard to insider dealing.
     Answer reference: Section 5.3.1, 5.3.2

17. What are the three types of conditions give rise to the offence of market abuse?
     Answer reference: Section 7.1

18. What is the link between market abuse and insider dealing?
     Answer reference: Section 7.5

19. What is the concept of passporting under MiFID?
     Answer reference: Section 8.2.1

20. What financial instruments are covered by MiFID?
     Answer reference: Section 8.2.5

The FCA Conduct of Business Sourcebook

This syllabus area will provide approximately 10 of the 50 examination questions

1. The Application and General Provisions of the FCA's Conduct of Business Sourcebook (COBS) to Corporate Finance Business

1.1 The Application of the Conduct of Business Sourcebook (COBS)

Learning Objective

2.1.1   Know the application of COBS to corporate finance business (COBS 1.1 (and Annex 1), COBS 18.3)

The Conduct of Business Sourcebook (COBS) is contained within the business standards block of the FCA Handbook. It came into force on 1 November 2007, replacing the old Conduct of Business rules (which were referred to as COB), and implementing the provisions of MiFID that relate to conduct of business. COBS provides detailed rules and guidance for firms on how they manage their day-to-day activities and interactions with clients.

The general application rule at COBS 1.1 states that firms are subject to the COBS rules if they carry on any of a range of activities (shown below at Section 1.1.1) from an establishment maintained by them or their appointed representative in the UK. This is the case whether or not a firm is subject to MiFID.

Some COBS rules are modified or disapplied for specific circumstances, eg, based on a firm's location or its activities.

1.1.1 Activities Subject to Conduct of Business Sourcebook (COBS)

The COBS rules apply when a firm is carrying out the following activities:

* accepting deposits (certain rules only)
* designated investment business
* long-term insurance business in relation to life policies, and
* activities relating to the above.

Annex 1 of COBS 1 sets out certain COBS rules which are disapplied for specific types of activity. For example, the following COBS rules are disapplied for firms carrying on eligible counterparty business (see Section 4.1.3).

* A large part of COBS 2 – the conduct of business obligations.
* Much of COBS 4 – communicating with clients (including financial promotions).
* COBS 6.1 – provision of information about the firm, its services and its remuneration.
* COBS 8 – client agreements.
* COBS 10 – appropriateness (for non-advised services).
* Certain parts of COBS 11 – best execution, client order handling and use of dealing commission.
* Parts of COBS 12 – labelling of non-independent research.
* COBS 14.3 – information relating to designated investments.
* COBS 16 – reporting requirements to clients.

1.1.2 The Impact of Location

The general application rule is modified depending on the firm's location and activities. For example:

- The rules in COBS that derive from MiFID apply to UK MiFID firms carrying on MiFID business from a UK establishment. They also apply to the MiFID business of a UK MiFID firm carried on from an establishment in another EEA state, but only if that business is not carried on within the territory of that state.
- The rules in COBS that derive from MiFID apply to an EEA MiFID investment firm doing MiFID business from an establishment in, and within the territory of, the UK.
- Rules on investment research and personal transactions apply on a home state basis.

See Chapter 1, Section 8 for a definition of MiFID and non-MiFID firms.

1.2 COBS Specialist Regimes – Corporate Finance

Pre-MiFID, the COB Sourcebook had only limited application for corporate finance business, reflecting the nature of the business and the general sophisticated nature of the customers in these markets, as well as the FCA's discretion to allow a concessionary regime.

However, the implementation of MiFID on 1 November 2007 reduced the ability of the FCA to grant concessions or modifications to those conduct of business rules required to implement MiFID. Those corporate finance firms which were carrying out MiFID business found themselves subject to the requirements of COBS, whereas those which were not carrying out MiFID business have the benefit of some exemptions from these rules.

Where some rules are disapplied for certain types of firm, these are set out at COBS 18.

In COBS 18.3 – corporate finance business – the FCA provides tables of the rules and provisions that do not apply or are not expected to be relevant in respect of corporate finance business carried on by a MiFID firm (ie, which is carrying on MiFID or equivalent third-country business).

For example:

- describing the breadth of advice when advising on investments (COBS 6.2)
- disclosing information about services, fees and commission in relation to packaged products (COBS 6.3)
- disclosure of charges, remuneration and commission (COBS 6.4)
- suitability reports (COBS 9.4)
- basic advice on stakeholder products (COBS 9.6)
- use of dealing commission (COBS 11.6)
- recording telephone conversations (COBS 11.8).

In relation to non-MiFID business (ie, corporate finance business carried on by a firm which is not MiFID or equivalent third-country business) the FCA provides a table of the provisions/rules that will apply to these firms. The list includes:

- acting honestly, fairly and professionally (COBS 2.1.1)
- inducements (COBS 2.3)
- agent as client and reliance on others (COBS 2.4)
- client categorisation (COBS 3)
- communicating to clients, including financial promotions (COBS 4, but excluding 4.5 to 4.11)
- personal account dealing (COBS 11.7)
- aspects of the Distance Marketing Directive in relation to distance contracts (COBS 5.1)
- e-commerce (COBS 5.2)
- investment research (COBS 12
- cancellation of a distance contract (COBS 15).

2. Rules Applying to all Firms Conducting Designated Investment Business

2.1 Rules Applying to Firms Conducting Designated Investment Business

Learning Objective

2.2.1 Know the requirement for a firm to act honestly, fairly and professionally in accordance with the best interests of its client (COBS 2.1)

The following requirements apply to all firms conducting designated investment business.

2.1.1 Acting Honestly, Fairly and Professionally

A firm must act honestly, fairly and professionally in accordance with the best interests of its client (the client's best interests rule). This rule applies in relation to designated investment business carried on:

- for a retail client, and
- in relation to MiFID or equivalent third-country business, for any other client.

Exclusion of Liability

A firm must not, in any communication relating to designated investment business, seek to:

- exclude or restrict, or
- rely on any exclusion or restriction of,

any duty or liability it may have to a client under the regulatory system.

2.2   Inducements

Learning Objective

2.2.2   Know the application and purpose of the rule on prohibition of inducements (COBS 2.3.1–2.3.9)

The rules on inducements apply to firms carrying on MiFID as well as non-MiFID designated investment business. The rules only apply to dealings with professional clients and retail clients; therefore, investment firms are not subject to the detailed inducement provisions when undertaking eligible counterparty business.

The inducements rules may be described as payments rules, as they prohibit any payment unless expressly permitted. In relation to MiFID business, firms are prohibited from paying or accepting any fees or commissions, or providing or receiving non-money benefits, other than:

- fees, commissions or non-monetary benefits paid to or by the client, or someone on his behalf (such as management fees), or
- proper fees which are necessary for the provision of the service (eg, custody costs, legal fees, settlement fees) and which cannot by their nature give rise to conflicts,
- fees, commissions or non-monetary benefits paid to/by a third party (or someone on their behalf) which are permissible only if:
    - they do not impair compliance with the firm's duty to act in the client's best interests
    - they are designed to enhance the quality of the service to the client, and
    - they are disclosed in accordance with set standards prior to the provisions of the service to the client.

Firms can satisfy their disclosure obligations under these rules if they:

- disclose the essential arrangements for such payments/benefits in summary form
- undertake to their client that further details will be disclosed on request, and
- do, in fact, give such details on request.

Firms must also keep full records of such payments/benefits made to other firms, for all MiFID business.

The inducements provisions do not apply in full for non-MiFID firms/business. In relation to third-party payments, these firms will have to comply only with the **does not impair** compliance test, the other two tests (disclosure and enhancement) being disapplied.

2.3 Reliance on Others

Learning Objective

2.2.3 Know the rules, guidance and evidential provisions regarding reliance on others (COBS 2.4.4–2.4.10)

If a firm carrying on MiFID business or ancillary activities (or, in the case of MiFID or equivalent third-country business, other ancillary services) receives an instruction to provide investment or ancillary services for a client through another firm, and that other firm is a MiFID firm or is an investment firm authorised in another EEA state, and subject to equivalent regulations, then the firm can rely on:

- information relayed about the client to it by the third-party firm, and
- recommendations that have been provided by the third-party firm.

The third party will be responsible for the information provided to the other firm, as well as for considering the appropriateness of the recommendations provided to the client. The firm that has received the instruction from the third party will be responsible for concluding the services or transaction based on this information or recommendations in accordance with the applicable regulatory requirements.

A firm receiving such information/details from a third-party firm in this way must establish that the third party providing written information is:

a. not connected with the firm, and
b. competent to provide the information.

A firm may only rely on information provided to it by a third-party, if this information is provided in writing.

For firms that are not MiFID investment firms, the FCA states that it will generally be reasonable for a firm to rely on information provided to it in writing by an unconnected authorised person or a professional firm, unless the firm is aware, or ought reasonably to be aware, of any fact that would give reasonable grounds to question the accuracy of that information.

3. The Financial Promotion Rules

3.1 The Financial Promotion Rules

Learning Objective

2.3.1 Know the application of the rules on communication to clients, including financial promotions and the firm's responsibilities for appointed representatives (COBS 4.1)

2.3.2 Know the implications of FSMA 2000, C.8, Part 2, S.21, the purpose of the financial promotion rules and the relationship with Principles 6 and 7 (2.1.1)

2.3.3 Know the rule on fair, clear and not misleading communications and the guidance on fair, clear and not misleading financial promotions (COBS 4.2)

2.3.4 Know the rule on identifying promotions as such (COBS 4.3)

2.3.5 Know the main exemptions to the financial promotion rules in the financial promotions order

3.1.1 The Application of the Financial Promotion Rules

A financial promotion is defined as: *'an invitation or an inducement to engage in investment activity, that is communicated in the course of business'*. The term therefore describes most forms and methods of marketing financial services and products. It covers traditional advertising, most website content, telephone sales campaigns and face-to-face meetings.

The rules in relation to financial promotions come from two main sources:

a. S.21 FSMA makes it an offence to issue a financial promotion, unless it is issued or approved by an authorised firm.
b. COBS 4 provides the financial promotion rules, which include standards and restrictions which relate to the financial promotions themselves.

The financial promotion rules apply to firms communicating with clients regarding their designated investment business and communicating or approving a financial promotion other than:

- for qualifying credit, a home purchase plan or a home reversion plan
- promotion for a non-investment insurance contract, or
- the promotion of an unregulated CIS which it is not permitted to approve.

The rules also apply to authorised professional firms in accordance with COBS 18 (Specialist Regimes), and include corporate finance firms in accordance with COBS 18.3.

In general, these rules apply to a firm which carries on business with, or communicates a financial promotion to, a client in the UK (including when this is done from an establishment overseas), except that they do not apply to communications made to persons inside the UK by EEA firms.

The majority of these rules do not apply when the client is an eligible counterparty, although Principle 7 (for communications not to be misleading) still applies.

Firms must also ensure that they comply with the provisions of COBS 4 when they communicate financial promotions via their appointed representatives. The FCA expects authorised firms to conduct thorough reviews of the suitability and conduct of their appointed representatives. The exemption from regulation that appointed representatives enjoy (Section 39 of FSMA and the FSMA (Appointed Representatives) Regulations 2001) comes at a price of imposing on the appointing firm the responsibility for vetting and monitoring, which the FCA would normally conduct itself.

The provisions that govern the appointment and monitoring of appointed representatives are in the FCA's Supervision Manual (Chapter 12). The principal provision is as SUP 12.3.2G, which states that: *'the firm is responsible, to the same extent as if it had expressly permitted it, for anything that the appointed representative does or omits to do, in carrying on the business for which the firm has accepted responsibility'.*

3.1.2   The Purpose of the Financial Promotion Rules

The purpose of the financial promotion rules is to ensure that financial promotions are identified as such, and that they are **fair, clear and not misleading**. The financial promotion rules are consistent with Principles 6 and 7 of the FCA's Principles for Businesses:

- **Principle 6** – a firm must pay due regard to the interests of its customers and treat them fairly.
- **Principle 7** – a firm must pay due regard to the information needs of its clients and communicate information to them in a way which is clear, fair and not misleading.

As stated above, Section 21 of the FSMA imposes a statutory restriction on the communication of financial promotions by unauthorised persons. An individual (including a firm) must not communicate a financial promotion unless:

- they are an authorised person, or
- the content of the financial promotion is approved by an authorised person

unless the financial promotion is subject to an exemption, as discussed further later.

The maximum penalty for a breach of Section 21 of the FSMA is two years in jail and/or an unlimited fine.

3.1.3   Fair, Clear and Not Misleading

There is an over-arching obligation for firms to ensure that all communications relating to designated investment business, including financial promotions, are fair, clear and not misleading.

The way in which this is achieved should be appropriate and proportionate and take account of the means of communication and what information the communication is intended to convey. So, for example, communications aimed at professional clients may not need to include all the same information as those aimed at retail clients.

In connection with financial promotions, firms should ensure that:

- those which deal with products or services where a client's capital may be at risk make this clear
- those quoting yields give a balanced impression of both the short-term and long-term prospects for the investment
- if an investment product is, or service charges are, complex, or if the firm may receive more than one element of remuneration, this is communicated fairly, clearly and in a manner which is not misleading and which takes into account the information needs of the recipients
- in cases where the communication names the FCA as the firm's regulator, any matters which it refers to that are not regulated by the FCA are clearly identified as not being FCA-regulated. (NB, a financial promotion does not have to include reference to the FCA)
- those relating to packaged or stakeholder products not produced by the firm itself give a fair, clear and non-misleading impression of the producer or manager of the product.

3.1.4 Identifying Promotions as Such

Firms must ensure that financial promotions which they communicate or approve, and which are addressed to clients, are clearly identifiable as such.

This rule does not apply to a third-party prospectus in respect of MiFID (or equivalent third-country) business. There are some exceptions in respect of non-MiFID business, including prospectus advertisements, image advertising, non-retail communicating and deposits.

3.1.5 Exemptions to the Financial Promotion Rules

The financial promotion order (FPO) provides certain exemptions from the requirements of the financial promotion rules, which are available to unauthorised persons (including those regulated by DPBs). These include the following:

- Sale of a body corporate (eg, an information memorandum in relation to a company sale).
- Offering qualifying credit to corporate entities.
- Promotions made only to investment professionals.
- Communications made by journalists (with some provisions).
- Communications by a government, central bank or financial market.
- Communications by a company to its shareholders and creditors.
- Prospectuses and supplementary prospectuses approved by the FCA.
- Prospectuses and supplementary prospectuses passported into the UK from another EEA member state.

As noted earlier in this manual, the FCA is permitted to ban misleading financial promotions, meaning that financial promotions can be removed immediately from the market or prevented from being used in the first place, without having to go through the lengthy enforcement process. This, together with the regulatory requirement to have customers placed at the heart of new products, means that active regulatory engagement is advisable.

The use of this new power is determined by the specific promotion and not used against a firm as a whole. It can be used on its own or before the FCA takes enforcement action against a firm.

The FCA will give a direction to an authorised firm to remove its own financial promotion or one it approves on behalf of an unauthorised firm, setting out the reasons for banning it. The next step is for firms to make representations to the FCA if they think that it is making the wrong decision.

The FCA will decide whether to confirm, amend or revoke its direction. If it is confirmed, it will publish it – along with a copy of the promotion and the reasons behind its decision.

3.2   Requirements for Financial Promotions

Learning Objective

2.3.6   Know the general rule in connection with communicating with retail clients (COBS 4.5); the rules on past, simulated past and future performance (COBS 4.6); and the rule on financial promotions containing offers or invitations (COBS 4.7)

2.3.7   Know the rules on unwritten promotions; the restriction on cold calling (COBS 4.8); and the rule in relation to financial promotions for overseas persons (COBS 4.9)

2.3.8   Know the requirement for approving financial promotions and the circumstances in which it is permissible to rely on another firm's confirmation of compliance (COBS 4.10)

3.2.1   Communicating with Retail Clients

The rules on communicating with retail clients apply to a wide range of communications on designated investment business and to all financial promotions other than:

- those in respect of qualifying credit, home purchase plans or home reversion plans
- those for non-investment insurance contracts (such as motor or home insurance)
- unregulated CISs which cannot be made by an authorised person (such as hedge funds and private equity funds).

The methods of communication covered include:

- direct offer financial promotions (these are promotions that make an offer to any person to enter into an agreement and include a form of response or specify the manner of responding)
- cold calls (unsolicited) and other unwritten promotions.

Firms must ensure that, if they provide information about designated investment business, or issue/approve a financial promotion that is likely to be received by a retail client, they adhere to certain rules. These rules state that:

- the firm's name is included on the communication
- the information is accurate and does not emphasise potential benefits without also giving fair and prominent indication of any relevant risks
- the information is sufficient for, and presented in a way likely to be understood by, the average member of the group at whom it is directed or by whom it is likely to be received
- the information does not disguise, diminish, or obscure important items, statements or warnings.

If comparisons are made, they must be meaningful and presented in a fair and balanced way. For MiFID business, the data sources for the comparisons must be cited, as must any key facts and assumptions used.

If tax treatment is mentioned, firms must explain that this depends on the individual circumstances of each client and that it may be subject to change. Information included in financial promotions must be consistent with that given in the course of carrying on business.

These rules are disapplied for third-party prospectuses and image advertising. For non-MiFID businesses they are also disapplied for excluded communications.

3.2.2   Past, Simulated Past and Future Performance

Past Performance

Firms must ensure that information, including indications of past performance, is such that:

- the past performance indication is not the most prominent feature
- it covers at least the immediately preceding five years (or the whole period that the investment has been offered/the financial index has been established/the service has been provided if this is less than five years); in any event, it must show complete 12-month periods
- reference periods and sources are clearly shown
- there is a clear and prominent warning that the data/figures refer to the past and that past performance is not a reliable indicator of future results
- if the figures are in a currency other than that of the EEA state in which the client is resident, that the currency is stated and there is a warning about the possible effects of currency fluctuations
- if the performance is cited gross, that the effect of commissions, fees and other charges is disclosed.

Simulated Past Performance

If firms give figures based on simulated (ie, notional, not having taken place in reality) past performance because the product or service does not have a track record, a firm must ensure that the simulated past performance figures:

- relate to an investment or financial index
- are based on actual past performance of one or more investments/indices which are the same as, or underlie, the investments being simulated
- meet the rules set out above on past performance (except for the statement that they relate to that investment's past performance, since they do not)
- contain a prominent warning that they relate to simulated past performance and that past performance is not a reliable indicator of future performance.

Future Performance

Firms must ensure that information containing an indication of the possible future performance of relevant business, a relevant investment, a structured deposit, or a financial index:

- is not based on, and does not refer to, simulated past performance
- is based on reasonable assumptions supported by objective data
- if it is based on gross performance, discloses the effects of commissions, fees or other charges
- contains a prominent warning that such forecasts are not reliable indicators of future performance.

3.2.3 Direct Offer or Invitations

Direct offer promotions (those making a direct offer or invitation, such as in a newspaper, trade magazine or mailed directly) must contain the following if they are likely to be received by a retail client:

- prescribed information about the firm and its services
- when relevant, prescribed information about the management of the client's investments
- prescribed information about the safekeeping of client investments and money
- prescribed information about costs and charges
- prescribed information about the nature and risks of any relevant designated investments including information about taxation, where relevant
- when an investment is the subject of a public offer, any prospectus published in accordance with the Prospectus Directive is available
- if a designated investment combines two or more investments or services, so as to result in greater risk than the risks associated with the components singly, an adequate description of those components and how that increase in risk arises
- if a designated investment incorporates a third-party guarantee, enough detail for the client to make a fair assessment of it.

The above need not be included, however, if the client would have to refer to another document containing that information in order to respond to the offer.

The offer should include a statement that the recipient should seek a personal recommendation if they are unsure about the suitability of the investment or service being promoted.

3.2.4 Unwritten Promotions, Cold Calling and Overseas Persons

Unwritten Promotions

A firm must not initiate an unwritten promotion to a particular person outside its premises, unless the individual doing so:

- does so at an appropriate time of day
- identifies himself and his firm at the outset and makes the reason for the contact clear
- gets clarification of whether the client would like to continue with the communication or terminate it (and does so if requested), and
- gives the client a contact point, if he arranges an appointment with him.

Cold Calling

Cold calling is the practice of authorised persons or exempt persons contacting people without a prior appointment with a view to communicating a financial promotion to them.

Firms must not cold call unless:

- the recipient has an existing client relationship with the firm and would envisage receiving such a call, or
- the call relates to a generally marketable packaged product which is neither a higher volatility fund, nor a life policy linked to such a fund, or
- it relates to a controlled activity relating to a limited range of investments, including deposits and readily realisable investments other than warrants or generally marketable non-geared packaged products.

Overseas Persons

Firms are not permitted to communicate or approve financial promotions for overseas firms, unless the promotion sets out which firm has approved/communicated it, and (if relevant) explains:

- that the rules for the protection of investors do not apply
- the extent that the UK compensation scheme arrangements will be available (and if they will not, that fact), and
- if the communicator wishes to do so, the details of any overseas compensation/deposit protection scheme applicable.

The firm must not communicate/approve the promotion unless it has no doubt that the overseas firm will deal with its UK retail clients honestly and reliably.

3.2.5   Approval of Financial Promotions

As mentioned above, it is an offence for an unauthorised person to communicate a financial promotion, unless the promotion is exempt (by virtue of the Financial Promotion Order) or it has been approved by an authorised firm.

Approving a financial promotion is a formal process set out in the FSMA and reflected in COBS 4.10 rules.

The COBS rules on approval of financial promotions complement requirements under SYSC. SYSC 3 and SYSC 4 require that a firm which:

- communicates with a client, in relation to designated investment business, or
- communicates or approves a financial promotion

puts in place systems and controls or policies and procedures in order to comply with the rules on financial promotions.

Approving a Financial Promotion

COBS states that, before an authorised firm approves a financial promotion for communication by an unauthorised person, it must confirm that it complies with the financial promotion rules. If, later, it becomes aware that the financial promotion no longer complies, it must withdraw its approval and notify anyone it knows to be relying on that approval as soon as is reasonably practicable. The rules for approving a financial promotion apply in the same way as though the firm was communicating the financial promotion itself.

Firms may not approve real-time financial promotions, that is, financial promotions to be made in the course of personal visits, telephone conversations or other interactive dialogue.

Authorised firms are restricted in the promotion of unregulated collective schemes, and so they may not approve a financial promotion relating to such a scheme unless they would have been able to legitimately promote it for themselves, namely, by way of an exemption or in compliance with certain FCA rules made for this purpose.

If a firm approves a financial promotion for which any of the financial promotion rules are disapplied, it must do so on the terms that its approval is limited to those circumstances. For example, if the approval is for communication to a professional client or eligible counterparty, the approval must state this limitation. If an unauthorised person communicates the promotion outside of the limited approval, they are committing an offence.

3.2.6 Firms Relying on Promotions Approved by Another Party

In relation to non-MiFID business only, a firm is not in breach of the rules if it communicates a financial promotion that has been produced by another party and:

- takes reasonable care to establish that another authorised firm has confirmed that the promotion complies with the rules
- takes reasonable care that it communicates it only to the type of recipient it was intended for at the time of the confirmation
- as far as it is (or should be) aware, the promotion is still fair, clear and not misleading, and has not been withdrawn by the other party.

4. Client Categorisation

4.1 Client Categorisation

Learning Objective

2.4.1 Understand client status (PRIN 1.2.1 – 1.2.3, Glossary, COBS 3), in particular: the application of the rules on client categorisation (COBS 3.1); the definition of 'client' (COBS 3.2); the nature of a corporate finance contact and a venture capital contact (COBS 3.2.1,3.2.2); the definitions of retail client (COBS 3.4); professional client (COBS 3.5) and eligible counterparty (COBS 3.6)

4.1.1 Application of the Client Categorisation Rules

A firm is required to categorise its clients if it is carrying on designated investment business.

MiFID laid down rules as to how client categorisation has to be carried out for MiFID business. For non-MiFID business, the FCA has used the same client categorisation terminology, but the rules on how the categories must be applied are modified in some cases.

If a firm provides a mix of MiFID and non-MiFID services, it must categorise clients in accordance with the MiFID requirements, unless the MiFID business is conducted separately from the non-MiFID business.

So, for example, if a firm advises a client on investing in a CIS (advice about which falls within the scope of MiFID) as compared with a life policy (which does not), it should use the MiFID client categorisation.

4.1.2 Definition of a Client

COBS defines a client as: *'someone to whom a firm provides, intends to provide, or has provided a service in the course of carrying on a regulated activity'*; and in the case of MiFID or equivalent third-country business, this includes anything which is an **ancillary service**. (These were covered in Chapter 1.)

The term includes potential clients and people acting as agent for another person. In addition, in relation to the financial promotion rules, it includes persons with whom the firm communicates, whether or not they are actually clients.

Clients of a firm's appointed representative or tied agent are also regarded as clients of the firm.

4.1.3 The Client Categories

Under COBS, clients may be categorised as:

- a retail client
- a professional client, or
- an eligible counterparty.

The classification determines the level of protection the client receives, with retail clients being afforded the most protections and eligible counterparties the least.

A **retail client** is any client who is not a professional client or an eligible counterparty. (Note that the term customer means both retail clients and professional clients.)

Professional clients may be either elective professional clients, or per se professional clients. An elective professional client is one who has chosen to be treated as such. This is discussed in more detail in Section 4.2.2 below.

Per se professional clients are those which fall into any of the following categories – unless they are an eligible counterparty, or are categorised differently under other specific provisions.

The categories are:

- Entities required to be authorised or regulated to operate in the financial markets, ie:
  - credit institutions
  - investment firms
  - any other authorised or regulated financial institutions
  - insurance companies
  - CISs or the management companies of such schemes
  - pension funds or the management companies of a pension funds
  - commodity or commodity derivatives dealers
  - local authorities
  - any other institutional investors.

- **Large undertakings** – companies whose balance sheet, turnover or own funds meet certain levels. Specifically:
  - for MiFID and equivalent third-country business, this means undertakings that meet any two of the following size requirements on a company basis:
    - a balance sheet total of €20 million
    - a net turnover of €40 million
    - own funds of €2 million.
  - For other (non-MiFID) business, large undertakings are:
    - companies whose called-up share capital or net assets are or have at any time in the past two years been at least £5 million, or currency equivalent (or any company whose holding companies/subsidiaries meet this test), or
    - companies which meet (or of which the holding companies/subsidiaries meet) any two of the following criteria:
      + a balance sheet total of €12.5 million
      + a net turnover of €25 million
      + an average of 250 employees during the year
    - partnerships or unincorporated associations whose net assets are, or have at any time in the past two years been, at least £5 million, or currency equivalent. In the case of limited partnerships, this should be calculated without deducting any loans owing to the partners
    - trustees of a trust (other than certain types of pension scheme dealt with in the next bullet point) which has or has at any time in the past two years had assets of at least £10 million
    - trustees of an occupational pension scheme or a small self-administered scheme, or the trustee/operator of a personal pension or stakeholder pension scheme, if the scheme has – or has at any time in the past two years – had:
      + at least 50 members, and
      + assets under management of at least £10 million
    - local authorities or public authorities.

The list of per se professional clients also includes:

- governments, certain public bodies, central banks, international/supranational institutions and similar, eg, the World Bank and the IMF, and
- institutional investors whose main business is investment in financial instruments.

The final category is **eligible counterparties (ECPs)**. COBS contains a list of the types of client which can be classified as ECPs.

The following are ECPs (per se), including non-EEA entities that are equivalent to any of the following, unless they are given a different categorisation under COBS 3:

- credit institutions
- investment firms
- other financial institutions authorised or regulated under the EC legislation or the national law of an EEA state (including regulated institutions in the securities, banking and insurance sectors)
- insurance companies
- CISs authorised under the UCITS Directive or their management companies
- pension funds or their management companies

- national governments or their corresponding offices, including public bodies that deal with the public debt
- central banks
- undertakings exempted from the application of MiFID under either Article 2(1)(k) (certain own account dealers in commodities or commodity derivatives) or Article 2(1)(l) (certain own account dealers that hedge positions using financial derivatives) of that directive
- supranational organisations (eg, World Bank or European Investment Bank).

You will note that the list above is very similar to the per se professional clients listed earlier in this section; however, the ECP category is narrower as it does not include large undertakings.

A client can only be categorised as an ECP for the following five types of business:

- executing orders; and/or
- dealing on own account; and/or
- receiving and transmitting orders
- ancillary services relating to the above activities
- arranging.

This means that if an ECP wants to engage in other types of business with a firm, such as investment management or investment advice, it will have to be classified by that firm as a per se professional client.

Many of the COBS rules do not apply when the client is an ECP; the result of this is that the ECP will not benefit from the protections afforded by these rules. Having said that, most ECPs are large firms who are very familiar with the financial markets, or are themselves large players in the financial markets and do not need such protections anyway. Some ECPs, however, would rather have more protections by voluntarily asking to opt-down a client category and be classified as a professional client.

4.2 Client Status

Learning Objective

2.4.2   Understand client status (PRIN 1.2.1–1.2.3, Glossary, COBS 3), in particular: when a person is acting as agent for another person (COBS 2.4.1–2.4.3); the rule on classifying elective professional clients (COBS 3.5.3–3.5.9); the rule on elective eligible counterparties (COBS 3.6.4–3.6.6); when is it necessary to provide clients with a higher level of protection (COBS 3.7); the requirement to provide notifications of client categorisation (COBS 3.3)

4.2.1   Agents

If a firm knows that someone to whom it is providing services (A) is acting as the agent of another person (B), then it should regard A as its client. The exception is when the firm has agreed in writing with A that it should treat B as its client instead.

There is a further exception if the involvement of A in the arrangement is mainly for the purpose of reducing the firm's duties to B: in this circumstance, B should be treated as the client in any case.

4.2.2 Elective Professional Clients

A retail client may be treated as an elective professional client if:

- the firm has assessed his (or its) expertise, experience and knowledge and believes he can make his own investment decisions and understands the risks involved (this is called the **qualitative test**), and for MiFID business
- any two of the following are true (this is called the **quantitative test**):
  - ○ the client carried out, on average, ten significantly sized transactions on the relevant market in each of the past four quarters
  - ○ the size of the client's financial portfolio exceeds €500,000 (defined as including cash deposits and financial instruments)
  - ○ the client works, or has worked, as a professional in the financial services sector for at least a year on a basis which required knowledge of the transactions envisaged.

The firm must follow certain procedures, including giving a clear written warning to the client of the lost protections; and the client must agree in writing to this. In particular, the client must state in writing to the firm that it wishes to be treated as a professional client either generally or in respect of a particular service or transaction or type of transaction or product.

For MiFID business, a client may be treated as an elective professional client if it meets both the qualitative test and the quantitative test. If a firm becomes aware that a client no longer fulfils the initial conditions for categorisation as an elective professional client, the firm must take appropriate action. If the appropriate action involves re-categorising the client as a retail client, the firm must notify that client of its new categorisation. It is up to the professional client to keep the firm up-to-date with their circumstances and notify the firm of anything that may affect their classification.

4.2.3 Elective Eligible Counterparties (ECPs)

A professional client may be treated as an elective ECP if it is a company and it is:

- a per se professional client (other than one which is only a professional client because it is an institutional investor), or
- it asks to be treated as such and is already an elective professional client (but only for the services for which it could be treated as a professional client), and
- it expressly agrees with the firm to be treated as an ECP.

4.2.4 Recategorising Clients and Providing Higher Levels of Protection

Firms must allow professional clients and ECPs to request recategorisation, so as to benefit from the higher protections afforded to retail clients or professional clients (as applicable).

In addition, firms can, at their own initiative as well as at the client's request:

- treat per se professional clients as retail clients, and
- treat per se ECPs as professional or retail clients.

Recategorisation may be carried out for a client:

- on a general basis, or
- on more specific terms, for example, in relation to a single transaction only.

A firm can classify a client under different client classifications for different financial instruments that they may trade/undertake transactions in. However, this would mean complex internal arrangements for firms, and this is why most firms will classify a client just once for all financial instruments that they may undertake transactions in.

A retail client is any client who is not a professional client or an eligible counterparty, and is afforded the maximum level of protection which reflects the perceived lack of specialist knowledge that other classifications of clients are deemed to have as they are assessed. (Note that the term customer means both retail clients and professional clients.)

4.2.5 Notifications of Client Classification

New clients must be notified of how the firm has classified them. They must also, before services are provided, be advised of their rights to request recategorisation, and of any limits in their protections that will arise from this.

4.2.6 Corporate Finance and Venture Capital Contacts

For most purposes, a corporate finance contact or a venture capital contact is not a client, because a firm does not provide a service to such a contact.

However, it will be considered to be a client for the purposes of the financial promotion rules. If the firm communicates or approves a financial promotion that is or is likely to be communicated to such a contact, it will have to treat this contact as a client, and will need to categorise it.

Communicating or approving a financial promotion that is or is likely to be communicated to such a contact is not MiFID or equivalent third-country business. In such circumstances, the non-MiFID client categorisations are relevant and, in categorising these contacts as elective professional clients, the quantitative test (see Section 4.2.2) does not need to be satisfied.

4.3 Policies, Procedures and Records

Learning Objective

2.4.3 Know the procedures and record-keeping requirements in relation to client categorisation (COBS 3.8)

Firms must implement appropriate written internal policies and procedures to categorise their clients. Firms must make a record of the form of each notice provided and each agreement entered into. This record must be made at the time that the standard form is first used and it must be retained for the relevant period after the firm ceases to carry on business with or for clients who were provided with that form.

The relevant periods are:

- five years in relation to MiFID or equivalent third-country business,
- three years in relation to non-MiFID business.

5. Conflicts of Interest (SYSC 10, PRIN 2.1)

5.1 Application and Purpose of the Conflicts of Interest Requirements

Learning Objective

2.5.1 Understand the concept of conflicts of interest and the application and purpose of the rules and procedures on conflicts of interest (SYSC 10.1)

The FCA requires that all UK-based firms properly identify and correctly manage actual and potential conflicts of interest that arise within all their business areas. Compliance with the FCA rules on conflicts of interest is one of the ways in which firms seek to ensure that customers are treated fairly and that conflicts of interest are identified and managed effectively.

The conflicts of interest rules are derived from MiFID, which requires firms to act honestly, fairly and professionally in accordance with the best interests of their clients. The conflicts of interest rules also reflect the FCA's Principles for Businesses.

The detailed rules on conflicts of interest are contained in SYSC. They apply both to common platform firms in respect of regulated business and of ancillary services which constitute MiFID business, as well as non-MiFID firms and businesses.

The rules require that firms take all reasonable steps to identify conflicts of interest between:

- the firm, including its managers, employees, appointed representatives/tied agents and parties connected by way of control and a client of the firm, and
- one client of the firm and another.

Firms under these obligations should, inter alia:

- maintain (and apply) effective organisational and administrative arrangements, designed to prevent conflicts of interest from adversely affecting the interests of their clients
- for those producing externally facing investment research, have appropriate information controls and barriers to stop information from these research activities flowing to the rest of the firm's business (for example, this may include Chinese walls/information barriers)
- where a specific conflict cannot be managed away, ensure that the general or specific nature of it is disclosed (as appropriate to the circumstances). Note that disclosure should be used only as a last resort;
- prepare, maintain and implement an effective conflicts policy

- provide retail clients and potential retail clients with a description of that policy, and
- keep records of those of its activities when a conflict has arisen.

Principle 8 of the Principles for Businesses states: *'a firm must manage conflicts of interest fairly, both between itself and its customers and between a customer and another client'*. Therefore, Principle 8 requires that authorised firms ensure that when conflicts of interest do materialise, they manage the conflicts to ensure that customers are treated fairly.

The requirements of the SYSC conflicts of interest provisions will only apply when a service is provided by a firm. The status of the client to whom the service is provided (as a retail client, professional client or eligible counterparty) is irrelevant for this purpose.

5.2 Types of Conflicts

Learning Objective

2.5.2 understand the circumstances in which conflicts of interest can arise and the types of conflicts particularly relevant to corporate finance (SYSC 10.1.3–10.1.5, 10.1.13–10.1.15)

Common-platform firms (ie, firms subject to either the CRD or MiFID), must take all reasonable steps to identify conflicts of interest that may arise in the course of the firm providing regulated activities or ancillary activities or providing ancillary services.

For the purpose of identifying the types of conflict of interest that arise, or may arise, in the course of the firm providing a service and whose existence may entail a material risk of damage to the interest of a client, firms must take into account, as a minimum, whether the firm, or a person directly or indirectly linked by control to the firm:

- is likely to make a financial gain, or avoid a financial loss, at the expense of the client
- has an interest in the outcome of a service provided to the client or of a transaction carried out on behalf of the client, which is different from the client's interest in that outcome
- has a financial or other incentive to favour the interest of another client or group of clients over the interest of the client
- carries on the same business as the client
- receives, or will receive, from a person other than the client an inducement in relation to a service provided to the client, in the form of monies, goods or services other than the standard commission or fee for that service.

The conflict of interest may arise if the firm, or person, carries on a regulated activity or ancillary activity or provides ancillary services or engages in other activities.

For non-common-platform firms (ie, those not subject to either the CRD or MiFID), the above requirements must be taken as being guidance rather than a rule, other than when the firm produces, or arranges the production of, investment research in accordance with COBS 12.2 (investment research) or produces or disseminates non-independent research in accordance with COBS 12.3 (non-independent research).

When a firm is undertaking the service of management of a securities offering, the firm's duty is to its corporate finance client (in many cases the corporate issuer or seller of the relevant securities), but its responsibilities to provide services to its investment clients are unchanged. This situation needs to be carefully controlled, to ensure that inside information in relation to the corporate finance client is not provided to investment clients, and that the pricing of the securities offer and the allocation of securities is not influenced by the interests of the firm's investment clients.

Measures that a firm might wish to consider in drawing up its conflicts of interest policy in relation to the management of an offering of securities include:

- at an early stage, agreeing with its corporate finance client relevant aspects of the offering process, such as the process the firm proposes to follow in order to determine what recommendations it will make about allocations for the offering:
  - how the target investor group will be identified
  - how recommendations on allocation and pricing will be prepared
  - whether the firm may place securities with its investment clients or with its own proprietary book, or with an associate, and how conflicts arising might be managed
- agreeing allocation and pricing objectives with the corporate finance client
- inviting the corporate finance client to participate actively in the allocation process
- making the initial recommendation for allocation to retail clients of the firm as a single block and not on a named basis
- having internal arrangements under which senior personnel responsible for providing services to retail clients make the initial allocation recommendations for allocation to retail clients of the firm, and
- disclosing to the issuer details of the allocations actually made.

5.3 Managing, Disclosing and Recording Conflicts

Learning Objective

2.5.3   Know the rules on managing, disclosing and recording conflicts of interest (SYSC 10.1.6–10.1.9)

5.3.1 Managing Conflicts

A common platform firm must maintain and operate effective organisational administrative arrangements to ensure that it is taking all reasonable steps to prevent conflicts of interest arising (as defined in SYSC 10.1.3) from constituting or giving rise to a material risk of damage to the interests of its clients. SYSC 10.1.3 was discussed in Section 5.2.

5.3.2 Disclosing Conflicts

When the arrangements that a firm puts in place to manage potential conflicts of interest are not sufficient to ensure, with reasonable confidence, that the risk of damage to the interest of a client will be prevented, the firm must clearly disclose the general nature and/or source of conflicts of interest to the client before undertaking business for/on behalf of the client.

Disclosure must be made in a durable medium and include sufficient detail, taking into account the nature of the client, to enable that client to take an informed decision with respect to the service in the context of which the conflict of interest arises. The FCA has defined durable medium as paper or any instrument which enables the recipient to store information addressed personally to them in a way accessible for future reference for a period of time adequate for the purposes of the information.

Common-platform firms should aim to identify and manage the conflicts of interest arising in relation to their various business lines, and when applicable, their group's activities, under a comprehensive conflicts of interest policy. The disclosure of conflicts of interest should not exempt firms from the obligation to maintain and operate effective organisational and administrative arrangements under SYSC 10.1.3 (as noted above in Section 5.3.1).

While disclosure of specific conflicts of interest is required under SYSC 10.1.8, an over-reliance on disclosure without adequate consideration as to how conflicts may appropriately be managed is not permitted.

Therefore, the disclosure of a conflict of interest should be undertaken as a last resort, if its internal controls (managing conflicts) do not satisfy the risk of material damage to the client's best interests.

5.3.3   Recording Conflicts

Common-platform firms must keep and regularly update a record of the kinds of services or activity carried out by or on behalf of the firm in which a conflict of interest entailing a material risk of damage to the interest of one or more clients has arisen or, in the case of an ongoing service or activity, may arise.

For non-common-platform firms, the above requirements must be taken as guidance rather than a rule, other than where the firm produces, or arranges the production of, investment research in accordance with COBS 12.2 (investment research), or produces or disseminates non-independent research in accordance with COBS 12.3 (non-independent research).

5.4   Conflicts of Interest Policies

Learning Objective

2.5.4   Understand the rule that requires a conflicts policy and the contents of the policy (SYSC 10.1.10–10.1.12)

Firms are required to have in place (and apply) an effective conflicts of interest policy, which is set out in writing and is appropriate to the size and organisation of the firm and the nature, scale and complexity of its business. The rules do not prescribe how the policy should be structured, so large and complex firms may have more detailed policies than smaller and simpler firms.

SYSC requires that the policy should be designed to ensure that all of a firm's relevant persons, who are engaged in activities which involve a conflict of interest with material risk of damage to client interests, carry on those activities with a level of independence. The policy should record the circumstances which constitute or may give rise to a conflict of interest, if they have been identified as having the potential to impact on the firm's business, and should detail how these are to be managed, specify the procedures that are to be followed and outline the measures adopted in order to manage such conflicts.

If a firm is a member of a group, the policy should take into account any potential conflicts arising from the structure/business activities of other members of that group.

The procedures and measures provided for must:

- be designed to ensure that relevant persons engaged in different business activities involving a conflict of interest of the kind specified above carry on those activities at a level of independence appropriate to the size and activities of the common-platform firm and of the group to which it belongs, and to the materiality of the risk of damage to the interests of clients
- include such of the following as are necessary and appropriate for the common-platform firm to ensure the requisite degree of independence:
  - effective procedures to prevent or control the exchange of information between relevant persons if the exchange of that information may harm the interests of one or more clients
  - the separate supervision of relevant persons whose principal functions involve carrying out activities and represent different interests that may conflict, including those of the firm
  - the removal of any direct link between the remuneration of relevant persons principally engaged in one activity and the remuneration of, or revenues generated by, another activity
  - measures to prevent or limit any person from exercising inappropriate influence over the way in which a relevant person carries out services or activities
  - measures to prevent or control the simultaneous or sequential involvement of a relevant person in separate services or activities if such involvement may impair the proper management of conflicts of interest.

If the adoption or the practice of one or more of those measures and procedures does not ensure the requisite level of independence, a common-platform firm must adopt such alternative or additional measures and procedures as are necessary and appropriate.

For non-common-platform firms, the above requirements must be taken as being guidance rather than a rule, other than when the firm produces, or arranges the production of, investment research in accordance with COBS 12.2 (investment research) or produces or disseminates non-independent research in accordance with COBS 12.3 (non-independent research).

5.5   Managing Conflicts of Interest

Learning Objective

2.5.5   Understand how to manage conflicts of interest to ensure the fair treatment of clients (SYSC 10.2) including, for example, information barriers

Chinese wall is the term given to arrangements made by a firm to manage conflicts of interest where information held by an employee in one part of the business must be withheld from (or, if this is not possible, at least not used by) the people working in another part of the business.

There is no requirement for a firm to have Chinese walls in place; they are just one example of how to manage conflicts of interest. However, SYSC requires that if a firm establishes and maintains a Chinese wall, it must:

- withhold or not use the information held, and

- for that purpose, permit its employees in one part of the business to withhold the information from those employed in another part of the business.

It need only do so to the extent that at least one of those parts of the business is carrying on regulated activities, or another activity carried on in connection with a regulated activity.

The requirement to maintain Chinese walls includes taking reasonable steps to ensure that these arrangements remain effective and are adequately monitored.

When a common-platform firm establishes and maintains a Chinese wall, it allows the persons on one side of the wall (eg, corporate finance) to withhold information from persons on the other side of the wall (eg, equity research/market-making arm) but only to the extent that one of the parts carries on regulated activities, ancillary activities or MiFID ancillary services.

The effect of the Chinese wall rule is that the corporate finance department may have plans for a company that will change the valuation of that company's shares. The equity research/market-making arm on the other side of the wall should have no knowledge of these plans; consequently the inability to pass this knowledge on to clients is not seen as a failure of duty to their clients.

A firm will not be guilty of the offences of market manipulation (Section 397 FSMA), market abuse (Section 118 FSMA) or be liable to a lawsuit under Section 150 FSMA when the failure arises from the operation of a Chinese wall.

Firms may use the following additional processes and procedures in order to manage conflicts of interest to ensure the fair treatment of clients (SYSC 10.2): information barriers such as reporting lines; remuneration structures; segregation of duties; policy of independence. The processes and procedures must meet the requirements set out in Section 5.4 above.

5.6 Conflicts of Interest in Relation to Investment Research and Research Recommendations

Learning Objective

2.5.6 Understand the rules on managing conflicts of interest in the context of investment research and research recommendations (COBS 12.1, 12.3, 12.3.1–12.3.4, 12.4.1)

In general, the conflicts management rules on the production and dissemination of investment research apply to all firms. The requirements for certain disclosures in connection with research recommendations are derived from the MAD.

5.6.1 Measures and Arrangements

If a common-platform firm produces investment research, it must implement all the measures for managing conflicts of interest set out in SYSC 10.1.11 in relation to the financial analysts involved in producing research, and other relevant persons, if their interests may conflict with those to whom it is disseminated. The SYSC rules prescribe the contents of a firm's conflicts of interest policy.

Firms must also ensure that they have in place arrangements designed to ensure that the following conditions are satisfied:

- Financial analysts and other relevant persons who know the likely timing/content of investment research which is not yet publicly available or available to clients and which cannot be inferred from information that is so available cannot undertake personal transactions, or trade for others, until the recipient of the investment research has had a reasonable opportunity to act on it. However, there are certain exceptions, such as the receipt of an instruction from an execution-only client or a market maker acting in good faith.
- In cases not covered by the above, they cannot undertake personal account transactions without prior approval from the firm's compliance or legal department and then only in exceptional circumstances.
- The firm and any person involved in the production of research must not accept inducements from those with a material interest in the subject matter of the research.
- They may not promise issuers favourable research coverage.
- Issuers, relevant persons other than financial analysts, or anyone else must not be allowed to review draft investment research which includes a recommendation or target price, other than to verify compliance with the firm's legal obligations.

A firm which disseminates investment research produced by another person to its clients is exempt from the above requirements if the following criteria are met:

- The person (firm) that produces the investment research is not a member of the group to which the firm belongs.
- The firm does not substantially alter the recommendation within the investment research.
- The firm does not present the investment research as having been produced by itself.
- The firm verifies itself that the producer of the investment research is itself subject to the requirements in COBS 12.2.3 and 12.2.5 (as noted above) in relation to the production of investment research, or has established a policy setting such requirements.

Some conflicts management rules are disapplied to the extent that a firm produces non-independent research labelled as a marketing communication.

5.6.2 Required Disclosures

If a firm produces investment research, it must make the following disclosure requirements in the context of conflicts of interest:

- All of its relationships and circumstances that may reasonably be expected to impair the objectivity of the research recommendation. When the disclosure would be disproportionate in relation to the length of the research recommendation, the firm must make clear and prominent reference to such a place where disclosures can be directly and easily accessed by the public.
- Major shareholdings that exist between it on the one hand and the relevant issuer (the subject of the investment research recommendation) on the other hand, including at least:
  - shareholdings exceeding 5% of the total issued share capital held by the firm or affiliated company
  - shareholdings exceeding 5% of the total issued share capital of the firm or any affiliated company held by the relevant issuer.

- Any other financial interests held by the firm or any affiliated company in relation to the relevant issuer which are significant in relation to the research recommendation.
- If applicable, a statement that the firm or any affiliated company is party to any other agreement with the relevant issues relating to the provision of investment banking services.
- In general terms, the effective organisational and administrative arrangements set up within the firm for the prevention of avoidance of conflicts of interest with respect to research recommendations, including information barriers.

Application of Conflicts of Interest to Non-Common-Platform Firms when Producing Investment Research or Non-Independent Research

The rules relating to:

- types of conflict – SYSC 10.1.4 (Section 5.2)
- records of conflicts – SYSC 10.1.6 (Section 5.3.3)
- conflicts of interest policies – SYSC 10.1.10 (Section 5.4).

also apply to a firm which is not a common-platform firm when it produces, or arranges for the production of, investment research that is intended or likely to be subsequently disseminated to clients of the firm or to the public in accordance with COBS 12.2 (investment research) and when it produces or disseminates non-independent research in accordance with COBS 12.3 (non-independent research).

6. Personal Account Dealing (COBS 11.7)

6.1 Personal Account Dealing Rules

Learning Objective

2.6.1 Understand the application and purpose of the personal account dealing rules and the restrictions on personal account dealing (COBS 11.7.1-11.7.3)

The personal account rules apply to employees who are relevant persons and involved in activities that could lead to conflicts of interest, or who could have access to inside information or other confidential client information. Relevant persons are directors, managers, partners, appointed representatives and those carrying out regulated activities.

Firms must have arrangements in place to prevent these employees from:

1. entering into a personal transaction that is contrary to the MAD; involves misuse or improper disclosure of confidential information, or conflicts with the firm's duties to a customer
2. improperly advising or procuring that anyone else enters into a transaction that (if it had been done by the employee himself) would have fallen foul of 1. above or of a **relevant provision**, or

3. improperly disclosing information or opinion, if they know or should know that the person to whom he has disclosed it is likely to enter into a transaction that (if it had been done by the employee himself) would have fallen foul of 1. above or of a relevant provision, or encouraging someone else to do so.

The relevant provisions are:

- the rules on personal account transactions undertaken by financial analysts contained elsewhere in COBS (ie, investment research – COBS 12.2)
- the rules on the misuse of information relating to pending client orders (which we will be looking at in Section 7.4 of this chapter).

Firms must keep records of all personal transactions notified to them, and of any authorisation or prohibition made in connection with them.

6.2 Compliance with, and Exceptions to, the Personal Account Dealing Rules

Learning Objective

2.6.2 Know the arrangements required to comply with the personal account dealing rules including the notification requirements and exceptions regarding personal account dealing (COBS 11.7.4-11.7.7)

The arrangements must ensure that the employees concerned are aware of the restrictions on personal transactions and of the firm's procedures in this regard. The arrangements must be such that the firm is informed promptly of any such personal transaction, either by notification of the transaction, or by some other procedure enabling the firm to identify it.

When outsourcing takes place, the arrangements must be such that the outsource firm maintains a record of personal transactions undertaken by any relevant person and provides it to the firm promptly on request.

The rules on personal account dealing are disapplied for:

- deals under a discretionary management service, if there is no prior communication between the portfolio manager and the relevant person (or any other person for whose account the transaction is being executed) about the deal
- deals in units/shares in certain classes of fund, if the relevant person (and any other person for whom the deals are effected) is not involved in the management of the fund
- personal transactions in life policies.

7.　Advising and Dealing (COBS 9 and COBS 11)

7.1　Application of the Rules on Suitability

The COBS rules on the suitability requirements apply when firms:

- make personal recommendations relating to designated investments
- manage investments.

There are specific rules relating to the provision of basic advice (personal recommendations on stakeholder products); firms may, if they choose, apply those rules instead of the more general rules on suitability when advising on stakeholder products.

For non-MiFID business, the rules only apply for:

- retail clients, or
- when the firm is managing the assets of an occupational, stakeholder or personal pension scheme.

7.2　The Requirement to Assess Suitability

The suitability rules exist to ensure that firms take reasonable steps to ensure that personal recommendations (or decisions to trade) are suitable for their clients' needs.

When a firm makes a personal recommendation or is managing investments, it should obtain the necessary information regarding the client's:

- knowledge and experience in the investment field relevant to the specific type of designated investment business
- financial situation, and
- investment objectives,

to enable it to make the recommendations, or take the decisions, which are suitable for the client.

A firm must provide a retail client with a suitability report if it makes a personal recommendation to the client, if the client:

- acquires a holding in, or sells all or part of a holding in:
  - a regulated CIS
  - an investment trust, in which the shares have been or are to be acquired through an investment trust savings scheme
  - an investment trust in which the shares are to be held in an ISA which has been promoted as the means for investing in one or more specific investment trusts, or

- buys, sells, surrenders, converts or cancels rights under, or suspends contributions to, a personal pension scheme or a stakeholder pension scheme, or
- elects to make income withdrawals or purchase a short-term annuity, or
- enters into a pension transfer or pension opt-out.

A firm must also provide a suitability report if it makes a personal recommendation in connection with a life assurance policy.

There are some exceptions to the requirement to provide a suitability report:

- when a firm, acting as investment manager for a retail client, makes a personal recommendation in connection with a regulated CIS
- when the client is habitually resident outside the EEA and is not present in the UK at the time of acknowledging consent to the proposal form to which the personal recommendation relates
- when the personal recommendation is made by a friendly society in connection with a small life policy sold by it, with a premium not exceeding £50 a year or (if payable weekly) £1 a week
- when the personal recommendation is to increase a regular premium to an existing contract, or
- if it is to invest additional single premiums or single contributions to an existing packaged product, to which a single premium or single contribution has previously been paid.

In terms of timing, a suitability report must be provided:

- in connection with a life policy, before the contract is concluded – unless the necessary information is provided orally, or cover is required immediately (in which case the report must be provided in a durable medium immediately after the contract is concluded), or
- in connection with a personal pension scheme or a stakeholder pension, when the cancellation rules apply, within 14 days of concluding the contract, or
- in any other case, when or as soon as possible after the transaction is effected or executed.

The suitability report must, at least, specify the client's demands and needs, explain any possible disadvantages of the transaction to the client and explain why the firm has concluded that the recommended transaction is suitable for the client – having due regard to the information provided by the client.

If the transaction is the sale of a life policy by telephone, and the only contact between the firm and client before the contract is concluded by telephone, then the suitability report must:

- comply with the Distance Marketing Directive (DMD) rules
- be provided immediately after conclusion of the contract, and
- be in a durable medium.

7.2.1   Information Required to Make a Suitability Assessment

To make a suitability assessment, a firm should establish, and take account of, the client's:

- knowledge of and experience in the investment relevant to the specific type of designated investment or service
- level of investment risk that he can bear financially and that is consistent with his investment objectives, and
- investment objectives.

In order to do so, a firm should gather enough information from its client to understand the essential facts about him. It must have a reasonable basis to believe that (bearing in mind its nature) the service or transaction:

- meets his investment objectives
- carries a level of investment risk that he can bear financially, and
- carries risks that he has the experience and knowledge to understand.

In terms of assessing the client's knowledge and experience, the firm should gather information on:

- the types of service/transaction/investment with which he is familiar
- the nature, volume, frequency and period of his involvement in such transactions/investments, and
- his level of education, profession or relevant former profession.

Firms must not discourage clients from providing this information (for example, because it would rule a particular transaction out and result in a loss of business to the firm). They are entitled to rely on the information the client provides, unless it is manifestly out of date, inaccurate or incomplete.

If a firm does not obtain the information it needs to assess suitability in this way, it must not make a personal recommendation to the client or take a decision to trade for him.

7.2.2   Assessing Suitability – Professional Clients

A firm is entitled to assume that a client classified as a professional client in respect of MiFID or equivalent third-country business, has the necessary experience and knowledge of the products, transactions or services concerned, and that the client is able financially to bear any related investment risks consistent with their investment objectives.

7.3   The Requirement for Best Execution

Learning Objective

2.7.2   Understand the requirement to provide best execution (COBS 11.1.6, 11.2.1, 11.2.6-11.2.7) and the rules on client order handling (COBS 11.3.1-11.3.6)

The rules on best execution apply to both MiFID and non-MiFID firms and business; however, there is an exemption from the requirements for firms acting in the capacity of an operator of a regulated collective scheme when purchasing or selling units/shares in that scheme.

The best execution rules under COBS require firms to execute orders on the terms that are most favourable to their client. Broadly, they apply if a firm owes contractual or agency obligations to its client and is acting on behalf of that client.

Specifically, they require that firms take all reasonable steps to obtain, when executing orders, the best possible result for their clients, taking into account the execution factors. These factors are price, costs, speed, likelihood of execution and settlement, size, nature and any other consideration relevant to the execution of an order. The relative importance of each factor will depend on the following criteria and characteristics:

- the client, including how he is categorised
- the client order
- the financial instruments involved, and
- the execution venues to which that order could be directed.

Best execution is not merely how to achieve the best price. Any of the other factors mentioned above should be considered and, depending on the criteria or characteristics, could be given precedence. For some transactions, for example, the likelihood of execution could be given precedence over the speed of execution. In other transactions, the direct and/or implicit execution costs of a particular venue could be so high as to be given precedence over the price of the instrument of this venue.

The obligation to take all reasonable steps to obtain the best possible results for clients applies to a firm which owes contractual or agency obligations to the client. The obligation to deliver the best possible result when executing client orders applies in relation to all types of financial instruments.

However, given the differences in market structures or the structure of financial instruments, it may be difficult to identify and apply procedures and a uniform standard of best execution that is effective and appropriate for all classes of instrument. Therefore, best execution obligations should be applied in a manner that takes into account all the different circumstances associated with the execution of orders related to particular types of financial instruments.

7.3.1 The Role of Price

For retail clients, firms must take account of the total consideration for the transaction, ie, the price of the financial instrument and the costs relating to execution, including all expenses directly related to it such as execution venue fees, clearing and settlement fees, and any fees paid to third parties.

7.3.2 Best Execution when there are Competing Execution Venues

If a firm can execute the client's order on more than one execution venue, the firm must take into account both its own costs and the costs of the relevant venues in assessing which will give the best outcome. Its own commissions should not allow it to discriminate unfairly between execution venues, and a firm should not charge a different commission or spread to clients for execution in different venues if that difference does not reflect actual differences in the cost to the firm of executing on those venues.

7.3.3 Client-Specific Instructions

Whenever a firm receives a specific instruction from a client, it must execute the order as instructed. It will be deemed to have satisfied its obligation to obtain the best possible result if it follows such specific instructions (even if an alternative means of executing the order would have given a better result).

Firms should not induce clients to instruct an order in a particular way, by expressly indicating or implicitly suggesting the content of the instruction to the client, when they know that any instruction to the client will have the likely effect of preventing it from obtaining the best possible result for the client.

7.4 Client Order Handling

Learning Objective

2.7.2 Understand the requirement to provide best execution (COBS 11.1.6, 11.2.1, 11.2.6–7) and the rules on client order handling (11.3.1–6)

Firms must apply procedures and arrangements which provide for the prompt, fair and expeditious execution of client orders, relative to the other orders or trading interests of the firm. (Note, you should see that this rule is also consistent with the need for firms to avoid conflicts of interest, if possible.)

In particular, these should allow comparable client orders to be executed in the order in which they are received.

Firms should ensure that:

- executed client orders are promptly and accurately recorded and allocated
- comparable orders are executed sequentially and promptly, unless this is impracticable or client interests require otherwise
- retail clients are informed of any material difficulty in the prompt execution of their order, promptly on the firm becoming aware of this
- when the firm is responsible for overseeing or arranging settlement, that the assets or money are delivered promptly and correctly.

Firms must not misuse information relating to client orders and must also take steps to prevent its abuse (eg, to profit by dealing for its own account).

End of Chapter Questions

Think of an answer for each question and refer to the appropriate section for confirmation.

1. When are some COBS rules modified or disapplied for specific circumstances?
    Answer reference: Section 1.1

2. What is the purpose of the FCA's corporate finance specialist regime?
    Answer reference: Section 1.1–1.2

3. When is a firm required to act honestly, fairly and professionally in accordance with the best interests of its client?
    Answer reference: Section 2.1.1

4. What is the purpose of the inducements provisions?
    Answer reference: Section 2.2

5. What is the purpose of the financial promotion rules?
    Answer reference: Section 3.1.2

6. What is the purpose of the client categorisation requirements?
    Answer reference: Section 4.1.3

7. How do the client categorisation rules apply when a person is acting as the agent of another person?
    Answer reference: Section 4.2.1

8. What is the purpose of providing a higher level of protection for clients?
    Answer reference: Section 4.2.4

9. What is a corporate finance contact?
    Answer reference: Section 4.2.6

10. What are the main conflicts of interest that will arise for a corporate finance firm?
    Answer reference: Section 5.2

11. What processes and procedures is a firm required to have in order to manage conflicts of interests?
    Answer reference: Section 5.5

12. What is the purpose of the personal account dealing rules?
    Answer reference: Section 6.1

13. When is a firm required to undertake a suitability assessment?
    Answer reference: Section 7.2

14. What is the purpose of the best execution requirements?
    Answer reference: Section 7.3

15. What is the purpose of the client order handling requirements?
    Answer reference: Section 7.4

Chapter Three

Corporate Governance and Business Ethics

This syllabus area will provide approximately 2 of the 50 examination questions

1. The UK Corporate Governance Code

Learning Objective

3.1.1 Understand the main principles of the UK Corporate Governance Code relating to: leadership, effectiveness, accountability, remuneration, relations with shareholders

1.1 History and Background of the UK Corporate Governance Code

'Corporate governance is the system by which companies are directed and controlled. Boards of directors are responsible for the governance of their companies. The shareholders' role in governance is to appoint the directors and the auditors and to satisfy themselves that an appropriate governance structure is in place. The responsibilities of the board include setting the company's strategic aims, providing the leadership to put them into effect, supervising the management of the business and reporting to shareholders on their stewardship. The board's actions are subject to laws, regulations and the shareholders in general meeting.' (Source: UK Corporate Governance Code).

Good governance should facilitate efficient, effective and entrepreneurial management that can deliver shareholder value over the longer term. The UK Corporate Governance Code (the Code) is published by the Financial Reporting Council (FRC) to support these outcomes and promote confidence in corporate reporting and governance.

The Code was originally derived from the recommendations of the Cadbury, Greenbury and Hampel reports in the 1990s, which considered corporate accountability and directors' remuneration. Further additions were made following the Higgs report on the role of NEDs and the Smith report on audit committees, creating the Combined Code on Corporate Governance. However, the financial crisis of 2008–09 triggered widespread criticism of governance systems, and in the UK Sir David Walker was asked to conduct a review into the governance of banks and other financial institutions. The FRC initiated a review of the Code alongside the Walker Review, so that corporate governance in listed companies generally could be evaluated at the same time.

The conclusions of the review were reported in late 2009, and a new edition of the Code was published, now under its new name of the UK Corporate Governance Code, and incorporating a number of the recommendations of the Walker Review. The main conclusions of the FRC's review were that more attention should be paid to following the spirit of the Code as well as the letter; and that the impact of shareholders in monitoring the Code could and should be enhanced by better interaction between the boards of listed companies and their shareholders. With this in mind, the FRC has also developed a Stewardship Code, addressed at the role of shareholders in corporate governance. This is discussed at the end of this chapter.

The UK Corporate Governance Code applies to accounting periods beginning on or after 29 June 2010, and to all companies with a premium listing of equity shares in the UK, regardless of whether they are incorporated in the UK or overseas.

1.2 Status and Structure of the UK Corporate Governance Code

Learning Objective

3.1.2 Understand the 'comply or explain' approach to corporate governance

The Code is not a rigid set of rules, and there is no legal obligation for compliance. Rather, it is a guide to the components of good board practice distilled from consultation and widespread experience over many years. It is structured as a set of main principles, supporting principles, and more detailed provisions.

The Code itself is not part of the Listing Rules. However, the Listing Rules (LR 9.8.6 (5–6)) require all companies with a premium listing (but not a standard listing, where compliance is voluntary) in the UK to include a corporate governance report in their annual report and accounts. Firstly, this must describe how the company has complied with the main principles of the Code. Secondly, it must show whether the company has or has not complied with the provisions, and the reasons for any non-compliance. The descriptions together should give shareholders a clear and comprehensive picture of a company's governance arrangements in relation to the Code as a criterion of good practice.

Although it is expected that companies will comply wholly or substantially with its main principles, it is recognised that non-compliance with specific provisions may be justified in particular circumstances if good governance can be achieved by other means. A condition of non-compliance is that the reasons for it should be explained to shareholders, who may wish to discuss the reasons with the company and whose voting intentions may be influenced as a result. The company must give shareholders a careful and clear explanation which shareholders should evaluate on its merits. In providing an explanation, the company should aim to illustrate how its actual practices are consistent with the principle to which the particular provision relates and contribute to good governance.

This **comply or explain** approach has been in operation since the Code's beginnings in 1992, and the flexibility it offers is valued by company boards and by investors in pursuing better corporate governance.

Smaller listed companies may judge that some of the provisions are disproportionate or less relevant in their case, and some of the provisions do not apply to companies below the FTSE 350. Moreover, the Code does not apply to companies quoted on AIM or the ISDX Growth Market. Such companies may nonetheless consider that it would be appropriate to adopt the approach in the Code and they are encouraged to do so. Externally, managed investment companies typically have a different board structure, which may affect the relevance of particular provisions; the Association of Investment Companies Corporate Governance Code and Guide can assist them in meeting their obligations under the Code. The Quoted Companies Alliance provides an alternative, simpler standard for those companies quoted on AIM or the ISDX Growth Market.

The Code is divided into five sections, as follows:

- **Leadership** – guidance on the structure of the board.
- **Effectiveness** – guidance on the procedures and processes of the board, and appointment and training of directors.
- **Accountability** – guidance on the responsibilities of the board, including corporate reporting, control and audit.
- **Remuneration** – guidance on remuneration for executive and non-executive directors.
- **Relations with Shareholders** – guidance on relationships with shareholders and the use of the AGM.

1.2.1 Leadership

The main principles under this section are:

- Every company should be headed by an effective board which is collectively responsible for the long-term success of the company.
- There should be a clear division of responsibility at the head of the company between the running of the board and the executive responsibility for the running of the company's business (ie, separation of the roles of chairman and chief executive).
- The chairman is responsible for leadership of the board and ensuring its effectiveness on all aspects of its role.
- As part of their role as members of a unitary board, NEDs should constructively challenge and help develop proposals on strategy.

Amongst the provisions in this section are requirements that a chairman should, on appointment, be independent, and that a chief executive should not go on to become chairman.

1.2.2 Effectiveness

The main principles under this section are:

- The board and its committees should have the appropriate balance of skills, experience, independence and knowledge of the company to enable them to discharge their respective duties and responsibilities effectively.
- There should be a formal, rigorous and transparent procedure for the appointment of new directors to the board.
- All directors should be able to allocate sufficient time to the company to discharge their responsibilities effectively.
- All directors should receive an induction programme on joining the board and should regularly update and refresh their skills and knowledge.
- The board should be supported in a timely manner with information in a form and of a quality appropriate to enable it to discharge its duties.
- The board should undertake a formal and rigorous annual evaluation of its own performance and that of its committees and individual directors.
- All directors should be submitted for re-election at regular intervals, subject to continued satisfactory performance.

Further provisions state that a board should include an appropriate combination of executive and non-executive directors, including independent NEDs. For companies in the FTSE 350, at least half of the board should comprise independent NEDs, and smaller companies should have at least two NEDs.

Additionally, the board should appoint a nomination committee, made up of a majority of independent NEDs, for board appointments. NEDs should be appointed for specified terms and generally not for more than six years. All directors of FTSE 350 companies should be subject to annual election by shareholders.

1.2.3 Accountability

The main principles under this section are:

- Financial and business reporting – the board should present a balanced and understandable assessment of the company's position and prospects.
- The board is responsible for determining the nature and extent of the significant risks it is willing to take in achieving its strategic objectives. The board should maintain sound risk management and internal control systems.
- The board should establish formal and transparent arrangements for considering how they should apply the corporate reporting and risk management and internal control principles and for maintaining an appropriate relationship with the company's auditor.

The key provisions here state that the board should, at least annually, conduct a review of the effectiveness of its risk management and control systems, and report that it has done so to its shareholders. It should establish an audit committee of at least three (smaller companies: two) independent NEDs, at least one of whom should have recent and relevant financial experience.

1.2.4 Remuneration

The main principles under this section are:

- Levels of remuneration should be sufficient to attract, retain and motivate directors of the quality required to run the company successfully, but a company should avoid paying more than is necessary for this purpose. A significant proportion of executive directors' remuneration should be structured so as to link rewards to corporate and individual performance.
- There should be a formal and transparent procedure for developing policy on executive remuneration and for fixing the remuneration packages of individual directors. No director should be involved in deciding his or her own remuneration.

The provisions require the establishment of a remuneration committee of at least three (smaller companies: two) independent NEDs. Shareholders should be invited to approve all new long-term incentive schemes and significant changes to existing schemes.

1.2.5   Relations with Shareholders

The main principles under this section are:

- There should be a dialogue with shareholders based on the mutual understanding of objectives. The board as a whole has responsibility for ensuring that a satisfactory dialogue with shareholders takes place.
- The board should use the AGM to communicate with investors and to encourage their participation.

The provisions state that the company should arrange for the notice of the AGM and related papers to be sent to shareholders at least 20 working days before the meeting (rather than the 21 calendar days required by the Companies Act 2006). The chairman should ensure that all directors are made aware of their major shareholders' issues and concerns, and arrange for the chairmen of the audit, remuneration and nomination committees to be available to answer questions at the AGM and for all directors to attend.

1.2.6   Regulatory Changes

When the UK Corporate Governance Code came into effect in June 2010 it included for the first time a supporting principle recognising the value of diversity in the boardroom. This states that *'the search for board candidates should be conducted, and appointments made, on merit, against objective criteria and with due regard for the benefits of diversity on the board, including gender'.*

The *2010 Female FTSE Board Report* published by Cranfield University, showed that women accounted for only 12.5% of all directors in FTSE 100 companies, and 7.8% in FTSE 250 companies. The Cranfield University study also found that there were no women on the boards of 21% of FTSE 100 companies, down from 25% in 2009, and that 52.4% of FTSE 250 companies had no women on the board.

Later in 2010 the government commissioned Lord Davies of Abersoch to undertake a review of gender diversity on the boards of listed companies (the **Davies Review**). The aim was to identify the barriers preventing more women from reaching the boardroom, and to make recommendations on how government and business could increase the proportion of women on boards.

The Report on the Davies Review was published in February 2011. Amongst other things, it recommended that the FRC should amend the UK Corporate Governance Code, so as to require premium listed companies to establish policies on boardroom diversity, including setting measurable objectives for implementing the policy, and should make an annual disclosure on the policy and progress made in achieving the objectives. The report argued that this was needed because *'enhanced corporate governance statements will allow companies to pay attention to, and consider what diversity means within their own organisations. Stakeholders, both investors and customers, will be able to make informed decisions about the diversity of the company and the performance of that company in addressing the diversity challenge'.*

Following this, the FRC launched a consultation on whether amendments to the Code were required to implement the recommendations of the Davies Report, and if so, what they should be and when they should come into effect. The consultation closed in July 2011.

In September 2012, the FRC published revised editions of both codes following consultation earlier in the year. The codes apply to reporting periods beginning on or after 1 October 2012.

The main changes to the UK Corporate Governance Code included that:

- boards should confirm that the annual report and accounts taken as a whole are fair, balanced and understandable
- audit committees should report more fully on their activities, and
- FTSE 350 companies should put the external audit contract out to tender at least every ten years.

The requirement for companies to report on their boardroom diversity policies, first announced in 2011, also came into effect. As with all existing provisions of the Code, these additions are subject to **comply or explain**.

The introductory section to the new Code identifies the sort of information that the FRC believes should be disclosed when companies choose to explain in order to help investors assess the appropriateness of the company's governance arrangements. This report contains case studies assessing the information provided where companies have chosen not to follow the Code's recommendations.

1.2.7   Regulatory Developments

The FRC stated that it would consult during 2013 on whether the sections of the Code dealing with the framework for making decisions on directors' remuneration needed to be updated, and would separately consult on revisions to its guidance on the issues to be considered when assessing whether the company is a going concern, and its guidance to directors on their responsibilities for risk and internal control. The consultation on remuneration issues will not take place until after the government's revised legislation on reporting and voting on remuneration has been finalised.

1.3   The UK Stewardship Code

Learning Objectives

3.2.1   Understand the principles of the UK Stewardship Code

Following the findings of the Walker Review, the FRC initiated consultation on a new Stewardship Code, which was published in final form in July 2010. The Code is aimed at institutional investors and operates alongside the UK Corporate Governance Code for listed companies.

The Code includes the following seven principles, which state that institutional investors should:

- publicly disclose their policy on how they will discharge their stewardship responsibilities
- have a robust policy on managing conflicts of interest in relation to stewardship and this policy should be publicly disclosed
- monitor their investee companies
- establish clear guidelines on when and how they will escalate their activities as a method of protecting and enhancing shareholder value
- be willing to act collectively with other investors where appropriate
- have a clear policy on voting and disclosure of voting activity
- report periodically on their stewardship and voting activities.

The purpose of the Code is to improve the quality of corporate governance through promoting better dialogue between shareholders and company boards, and more transparency about the way in which investors oversee the companies they own.

The new Stewardship Code, published in September 2012, has been more extensively revised than the UK Corporate Governance Code, although the seven principles of the Code are unchanged. The main changes to the Stewardship Code include:

- clarification of the respective responsibilities of asset managers and asset owners for stewardship, and for stewardship activities that they have chosen to outsource; and
- clearer reporting requirements, including on the policy on stock lending.

Compliance with the Stewardship Code is not mandatory for institutional investors. However, the FRC encourages them to disclose how far they have complied with it, and publishes on its website a list of those investors who have made such a disclosure, with links to the disclosure itself.

2. The Chartered Institute for Securities & Investment (CISI) Code of Conduct

Learning Objective

3.3.1 Know the Chartered Institute for Securities & Investment's Code of Conduct

3.3.2 Be able to apply the Code of Conduct to the provision of corporate finance advice

2.1 The CISI Code of Conduct

Certain approved persons may, as well as having to comply with the FCA Statements of Principle, also be members of the Chartered Institute for Securities & Investment (CISI). Membership of the CISI requires compliance with CISI's own Code of Conduct – this includes an obligation to meet a set of standards set out within the CISI's Principles. These principles impose an obligation on members to act in a manner which goes beyond mere compliance and which is consistent with the underlying values of the CISI.

A material breach of the Code of Conduct is incompatible with continuing membership of the CISI.

Members who find themselves in a position which might require them to act in a manner contrary to the principles are encouraged to do the following:

- discuss their concerns with their line manager
- seek advice from their internal compliance department
- approach their firm's non-executive directors or audit committee
- if unable to resolve their concerns and, having exhausted all internal avenues, contact the CISI for advice.

2.2 The CISI's Eight Principles

1. To act honestly and fairly at all times when dealing with clients, customers and counterparties and to be a good steward of their interests, taking into account the nature of the business relationship with each of them, the nature of the service to be provided to them and the individual mandates given by them.
2. To act with integrity in fulfilling the responsibilities of your appointment and to seek to avoid any acts, omissions or business practices which damage the reputation of your organisation or the financial services industry.
3. To observe applicable law, regulations and professional conduct standards when carrying out financial service activities, and to interpret and apply them to the best of your ability according to principles rooted in trust, honesty and integrity.
4. To observe the standards of market integrity, good practice and conduct required or expected of participants in markets when engaging in any form of market dealing.
5. To be alert to and manage fairly and effectively and to the best of your ability any relevant conflict of interest.
6. To attain and actively manage a level of professional competence appropriate to your responsibilities, to commit to continuing learning to ensure the currency of your knowledge, skills and expertise and to promote the development of others.
7. To decline to act in any matter about which you are not competent unless you have access to such advice and assistance as will enable you to carry out the work in a professional manner.
8. To strive to uphold the highest personal and professional standards.

The CISI has an established disciplinary process to consider infractions by members of its membership regulations and Code of Conduct. Many of these principles are echoed in the specific regulatory requirements for various aspects of corporate finance (and other) work. For example, Principle 5 (conflicts of interest) is also reflected in the SYSC requirements in relation to conflicts of interest (discussed in Chapter 2, Section 5) as well as the requirements of the AIM rules for nominated advisers (NOMADs), the requirements for sponsors under the FCA listing rules, and the requirements for Rule 3 advisers under the Takeover Code. In the same way, the provisions of Principle 6 relating to professional competence are elaborated on in the requirements for nomads and sponsors to have adequate experience and expertise for their roles.

End of Chapter Questions

Think of an answer for each question and refer to the appropriate section for confirmation.

1. What is the status and purpose of the UK Code on Corporate Governance?
    Answer reference: Sections 1.1, 1.2

2. Which firms are required to comply or explain with the UK Code on Corporate Governance?
    Answer reference: Sections 1.1 – 1.3

3. What is the responsibility of institutional shareholders in relation to the UK Code on Corporate Governance?
    Answer reference: Section 1.2.5

4. What are the main roles and responsibilities of the audit committee?
    Answer reference: Section 1.2.3

5. Who is responsible for setting overall remuneration and benefits for both executive directors and non-executive directors?
    Answer reference: Section 1.2.4

6. Which type of investor is the Stewardship Code aimed at?
    Answer reference: Section 1.3

7. What is the status and purpose of the CISI's Code of Conduct?
    Answer reference: Sections 2.1 – 2.2

8. How many principles are there in the CISI's Code of Conduct?
    Answer reference: Section 2.2

Chapter Four
Takeovers and Mergers

This syllabus area will provide approximately 8 of the 50 examination questions

1. Relevant Bodies

1.1 The Role of the Takeover Panel

Learning Objective

4.1.1 Understand the role of the Panel on Takeovers and Mergers (the Takeover Panel or PTM) in takeovers and mergers

1.1.1 The Takeover Panel (PTM)

The Panel on Takeovers and Mergers (PTM) is an independent body, established in 1968, whose main functions are to issue and administer the City Code on Takeovers and Mergers (the Takeover Code, the City Code or the Code) and to supervise and regulate takeovers and other matters to which the City Code applies in accordance with the rules set out in the City Code. It has been designated as the supervisory authority to carry out certain regulatory functions in relation to takeovers pursuant to the European Directive on Takeover Bids.

Its statutory functions are set out in and under Chapter 1 of Part 28 of the Companies Act 2006.

In all cases, the PTM's function is to ensure that shareholders of an offeree company are treated fairly and are not denied an opportunity to decide on the merits of a takeover, and that offeree shareholders of the same class are afforded equivalent treatment by a bidder (referred to in these rules as an offeror). The Code is not concerned with the financial or commercial advantages of a takeover, which it considers to be matters for the offeree company and its shareholders. Wider questions of public interest are dealt with by the BIS and the EC.

The PTM's role in takeovers is threefold:

* to provide advice and guidance on the application and interpretation of the relevant rules to offerors, offerees, advisers and, where relevant, market participants
* to monitor the progress of an actual or contemplated takeover bid, for breaches of compliance with the relevant rules
* to enforce the Code, through reaching decisions on issues arising or seeking enforcement through the courts.

Where necessary the PTM may impose sanctions, generally through private warnings, public censure and/or reference to other regulators as appropriate. It also has the power to cold-shoulder offenders, ie, ensure that the facilities of the market are withdrawn from them, with respect to takeover activity, for a period of time.

1.1.2 EU Takeovers Directive

The EU Takeovers Directive was implemented in the UK in 2006, by means of the introduction of statutory provisions in the Companies Act 2006, as well as amendments to the existing Code. It aims to create a level playing field throughout the EU to ensure fair and equal treatment for all shareholders during a takeover.

The Takeovers Directive requires all EU member states to provide a statutory basis for their domestic takeover regulation, which must be compliant with an EU-wide set of six general principles, set out in Article 3 of the Directive. These principles are incorporated into the Code, and are shown in Section 2.3 below. The Directive applies to takeover offers where the target (offeree) company is both registered in the EU and traded on an EU-regulated market.

It should be noted that the Code has a wider application than the Directive.

1.2 Other Relevant Bodies

Learning Objective

4.1.2 Understand the role of the UK and EU competition authorities and the Pensions Regulator in respect of takeovers and mergers

1.2.1 Competition Authorities

It is the role of the competition authorities to investigate the effect of a merger or acquisition on suppliers, customers and competitors in an industry, and establish whether the transaction should be permitted, blocked, or permitted only on certain conditions.

The UK merger control regime is established under the Competition Act 1998, together with the Enterprise Act 2002 which replaced a number of the provisions of the Competition Act, and in turn substantially updated again in the Enterprise and Regulatory Reform Act 2013, which saw the Office of Fair Trading and the Competition Commission replaced by the Competition and Markets Authority.

The EU competition regime was originally established under the 1957 Treaty of Rome, as variously amended over the years. The relevant sections of the Treaty are Articles 81–82, which in the UK are mirrored in provisions of the Competition Act. Specific provisions for investigations of mergers in the EC are provided under the European Community Merger Regulation (ECMR). These investigations are carried out by the Directorate General for Competition (a Directorate of the EC), often known as DG Comp.

1.2.2 The Competition and Markets Authority

The CMA promotes competition for the benefit of consumers, both within and outside the UK. Its aim is to make markets work well for consumers, business and the economy. The CMA came into effect on 1 April 2014 when it took over the functions of the Competition Commission (CC) and the Office of Fair Trading (OFT). It was established under the Enterprise and Regulatory Reform Act 2013.

Although it covers financial services, it is not solely a financial services body.

The CMA is independent and is responsible for:

- investigating mergers that could restrict competition
- conducting market studies and investigations in markets where there may be competition and consumer problems
- investigating where there may be breaches of UK or EU prohibitions against anti-competitive agreements and abuses of dominant positions
- bringing criminal proceedings against individuals who commit the cartel offence
- enforcing consumer protection legislation to tackle practices and market conditions that make it difficult for consumers to exercise choice
- co-operating with sector regulators and encouraging them to use their competition powers
- considering regulatory references and appeals.

The CMA responsibilities are supported by a range of powers which are based on legislation.

The five strategic aims of the CMA are:

- **delivering effective enforcement** – to deter wrongdoing, protect consumers and educate businesses
- **extending competition frontiers** – by using the markets regime to improve the way competition works, in particular within the regulated sectors
- **refocusing consumer protection** – working with its partners to promote compliance and understanding of the law, and empowering consumers to make informed choices
- **achieving professional excellence** – by managing every case efficiently, transparently and fairly, and ensuring all legal, economic and financial analysis is conducted to the highest international standards
- **developing integrated performance** – through ensuring that all staff are brought together from different professional backgrounds to form effective multi-disciplinary teams and provide a trusted competition adviser across government.

In setting up the CMA, by merging the CC and the OFT, the government wanted an organisation with a single powerful voice to advocate competition. The CMA works closely with the FCA..

1.2.3 The Competition Appeal Tribunal

The Competition Appeal Tribunal is an independent body established under the Enterprise Act. It hears appeals against decisions of the Competition and Markets Authority, or against fines imposed by them.

1.2.4 EU Merger Control: Directorate General (DG) Competition

When the conditions in either of the following tests are satisfied, a transaction is defined as a **concentration with a community dimension** (CCD) and the parties must make a mandatory notification of the transaction to the EC. A CCD must be cleared by the EC before it can proceed.

Test 1:

a. the combined worldwide turnover of all parties is greater than €5 billion, and
b. each of at least two merging parties realised an EU-wide turnover of over €250 million.

Test 2:

a. the combined worldwide turnover of all merging parties is greater than €2.5 billion, and
b. in at least three EU member states the merging parties have a combined turnover of greater than €100 million, and
c. in each of at least three of the EU member states included for the purpose of (b), the aggregate turnover of each of at least two of the undertakings concerned is more than €25 million, and
d. the aggregate Community-wide turnover of each of at least two of the undertakings concerned is more than €100 million.

However, in both cases, if each of the merging parties obtains more than two-thirds of its EU turnover only from one and the same member state, the transaction will fall under the jurisdiction of that member state's competition regulator.

The nationality of the parties concerned is irrelevant for the purposes of the ECMR.

Once the EC decides to initiate an investigation, any EU domestic regulator (including the OFT and CC) has no further jurisdiction, unless the EC decides to refer the merger back to a specific national regulator. Other non-EU regulators may of course be carrying out regional competition investigations at the same time.

DG competition investigates mergers in two stages:

- **Phase I investigation** – where DG competition determines whether to clear the transaction (possibly with conditions attached) or to initiate a full Phase II investigation; this takes 25 working days, with an automatic ten-day extension where parties submit proposals to remedies.
- **Phase II investigation** – which is a more detailed investigation, lasting 90 days with optional extensions of up to 125 days.

1.2.5   The Pensions Regulator

Another factor to consider during a takeover bid is whether the pension rights of current and future employees will be protected during and after the merger.

The Pensions Regulator is the regulatory body for work-based pension schemes in the UK. The Pensions Act 2004 gives the Regulator a set of specific objectives, which are to:

- protect the benefits of, or in respect of, members of occupational pension schemes
- reduce the risk of situations arising that may lead to claims for compensation from the Pension Protection Fund (PPF), and
- promote, and improve understanding of, the good administration of work-based pension schemes.

As part of its role, the regulator considers whether companies entering into transactions (including acquisitions or disposals) may weaken their financial position, to the detriment of a defined benefit pension scheme. Such a transaction would be classified as a Type A event. Companies contemplating transactions may (voluntarily) apply to the regulator in advance for clearance of a transaction. The six principles for good design and governance of workplace DC schemes are as follows:

- **Principle 1: Schemes are designed to be durable, fair and deliver good outcomes for members.** This principle covers the features necessary in a scheme to deliver good outcomes for members, including features such as the provision of a suitable default fund, transparent costs and charges, protected assets and sufficient protection for members against loss of their savings.
- **Principle 2: A comprehensive scheme governance framework is established at set-up, with clear accountabilities and responsibilities agreed and made transparent.** This includes identifying key activities which need to be carried out, and ensuring each of the activities has an 'owner' who has the necessary resources to carry out the activity.
- **Principle 3: Those who are accountable for scheme decisions and activity understand their duties and are fit and proper to carry them out.** This principle ensures that those who are given accountability or responsibility for a key governance task are able to carry this out. The principle will cover definitions of fitness and propriety for accountable parties and also conflicts of interest that may arise.
- **Principle 4: Schemes benefit from effective governance and monitoring through their full lifecycle.** This principle looks at the ongoing governance and running of the scheme, including the internal controls and monitoring needed to ensure that the scheme continues to meet its objectives, and continues to be run with the best interests of its membership in mind.
- **Principle 5: Schemes are well-administered with timely, accurate and comprehensive processes and records.** This principle is informed by our previous work on record keeping, looking specifically at the administration processes required in a DC scheme.
- **Principle 6: Communication to members is designed and delivered to ensure members are able to make informed decisions about their retirement savings.** This includes all communications to members during their time with the scheme – from joining through to making decisions about converting their pension pot into a retirement income, including promotion of the Open Market Option.

Where the Regulator considers that there is material cause for concern, it may issue a:

- **contribution notice** – whereby the company must make a payment into the pension scheme; this may be required if the regulator considers that the transaction has, as one of its main purposes, making a pension deficit less likely to be recovered
- **financial support direction** – whereby financial support arrangements must be made for the scheme; this may be required where the regulator considers that a company may be unable to fund its pension scheme, and believes that a connected person (for example, the parent company) should be made responsible for the scheme.

Otherwise, it may issue a clearance statement, which gives assurance that, based on the information provided, the regulator will not use its anti-avoidance powers to issue to the applicants either contribution notices or financial support directions.

1.2.6 The Role of Pension Fund Trustees

All UK occupational pension schemes are set up as trusts (rather than as companies) to ensure that the scheme assets are kept separate from those of the employer company. The scheme must appoint trustees to ensure that the scheme is run properly and that the interests of its members are protected. The trustees must act prudently, honestly, responsibly and impartially in the interests of scheme beneficiaries.

As part of their responsibilities, the trustees must consider whether the scheme employer is contemplating entering into a transaction of any kind which would be detrimental to the scheme, and whether they should require some action to be taken to protect the scheme (such as commitment to the reduction of a scheme deficit). If they consider that the employer is not proposing to seek clearance of a Type A event, they should consider notifying the regulator direct.

2. The Takeover Code

2.1 The Legal Nature and Purpose of the Takeover Code

Learning Objective

4.2.1 understand the legal nature and purpose of the Takeover Code (Section 2 of the Introduction)

4.2.2 understand the duty to consult the Takeover Panel (S.6(b) of the Introduction)

The Code is designed principally to ensure that shareholders are treated fairly and are not denied an opportunity to decide on the merits of a takeover, and that shareholders of the same class are afforded equivalent treatment by an offeror. The Code also provides an orderly framework within which takeovers are conducted. In addition, it is designed to promote, in conjunction with other regulatory regimes, the integrity of the financial markets.

The Code is based upon six general principles, which are essentially statements of standards of acceptable behaviour. These general principles mirror the general principles set out in Article 3 of the Takeover Directive. They are expressed in broad terms, and the Code does not define the precise extent of, or the limitations on, their application. They are applied in accordance with their spirit in order to achieve their underlying purpose.

In addition, the Code contains a series of 38 detailed rules, which operate alongside the general principles to ensure that the spirit of the Code is observed as well as the letter.

The provisions of the Companies Act 2006 give the PTM the legal power to regulate takeovers, and the right to seek enforcement of Code rules and compensation for disadvantaged shareholders in the Courts. Moreover, the Companies Act provides criminal sanctions for misleading or false statements in takeover documentation. Additionally, the FCA acts with the PTM to pursue cases of material Code breaches.

2.2 The Scope of the Takeover Code

Learning Objective

4.2.2   understand the duty to consult the Takeover Panel (S.6(b) of the Introduction)

4.2.3   know the companies, transactions and persons subject to the Takeover Code (Section 3 of the Introduction)

2.2.1   Companies

The Takeover Code applies to all offers to acquire control of the following:

- Companies registered in the UK, the Channel Islands or the Isle of Man that are traded on a regulated market or multilateral trading facility (MTF) (including AIM and ISDX Growth Market), in the UK, or any stock exchange in the Channel Islands or the Isle of Man.
- Plcs not traded on a regulated market, which are registered in the UK, Channel Islands or Isle of Man, but only if they have their place of central management and control within those jurisdictions.
- Private companies registered in the UK, the Channel Islands or the Isle of Man, but only if they have their place for central management and control within those jurisdictions, and if at any time during the previous ten years their securities have been admitted to the Official List, or if dealings and/or prices for their securities have been published on a regular basis for a continuous period of at least six months in the ten years prior to the relevant date.

If an offeree company is traded in one EEA member state, but incorporated in another, the Code provides for shared jurisdiction between the regulators of each state. Broadly, the regulator of the member state where the offeree company is incorporated will determine matters relating to the rights of shareholders or company law, and the regulator of the state where the offeree company is traded will determine matters relating to the dealings in and disclosures in relation to securities. The Code does not apply to OEICs.

2.2.2   Transactions

The Code is concerned with regulating changes of control, however effected, including by means of:

- takeover
- acquisition
- statutory merger
- scheme of arrangement.

It is also concerned with regulating other transactions. This includes:

- offers by a parent company for shares in a subsidiary
- dual holding company transactions
- new share issues
- share capital reorganisations
- offers to minority shareholders,

which have the objective or potential effect of obtaining or consolidating control of the relevant companies. In addition it regulates partial offers to shareholders for securities in the relevant companies.

Therefore, it does not apply to the acquisition of non-voting, non-equity capital unless these transactions are made alongside offers for control and required by Rule 15 (appropriate offer for convertibles).

2.2.3 Persons

The Code applies to a range of persons who participate in, are connected with or in any way seek to influence, intervene in or benefit from takeovers or other matters to which the Code applies.

This includes:

- parties to an offer (ie, offerors and offeree companies); and their shareholders of all kinds
- financial, legal and all other advisers
- directors or partners
- employees
- any other representatives of the above.

The Code applies in respect of acts or omissions of any person in connection with a takeover or any other matter to which the Code applies.

2.2.4 Recent Developments

The takeover by Kraft of Cadbury in early 2010 prompted widespread public and political concern as to whether the UK Takeover Code adequately protected UK companies from takeover by overseas offerors, and more widely whether the Code required amendment to reflect the challenges of recent years. Kraft's conduct during its bid for Cadbury was publicly criticised by the PTM, which concluded that certain statements of belief issued by Kraft were made without any reasonable basis.

Following the bid, the PTM announced a proposal to initiate a review of the Code, and published a consultation paper.

The two main themes of the consultation paper (CP) were whether:

- it is too easy for a hostile offeror to take control of an offeree company, or
- the outcomes of takeover bids, particularly hostile offers, are unduly influenced by the actions of short-term investors, such as hedge funds, who become interested in the offeree company shares only after the offer period commences.

The Panel's Code Committee published feedback in October 2010, concluding that amendments to the Code were required, to address the fact that offeree companies are disadvantaged under the existing regime. Following consultation on specific proposals, the following rule changes were introduced, with effect from 19 September 2011:

- A requirement for potential offerors to clarify their position within a specified period of time.
- Prohibition of deal protection measures and inducement fees, apart from certain limited exceptions.
- A requirement for both paper and cash offerors to provide the same level of financial information and information about their bid financing.

- A requirement for an offeror to provide greater detail on its intentions for the offeree company and its employees, and a requirement for an offeree board to provide more detail about its views on those intentions.
- A requirement for public disclosure of all bid-related fees.
- A clarification that offeree boards are not restricted in the factors that can be taken into account when providing their opinion on the offer and their recommendation to shareholders.
- Additional scope for employee representatives to make their views on the offer known.

In September 2013, the Code was extended to all companies registered in the UK, Channel Islands and Isle of Man whose shares are traded on any MTF or stock exchange in these jurisdictions. Prior to this the Code only applied where central management and control was also in these jurisdictions or where the shares were traded on a regulated market.

2.3   The Six General Principles

Learning Objective

4.2.4   Know the six General Principles

The six general principles mentioned earlier are:

1. All holders of the securities of an offeree company of the same class must be afforded equivalent treatment; moreover, if a person acquires control of a company, the other holders of securities must be protected.
2. The holders of the securities of an offeree company must have sufficient time and information to enable them to reach a properly informed decision on the bid; if it advises the holders of securities, the board of the offeree company must give its views on the effects of implementation of the bid on employment, conditions of employment and the locations of the company's places of business.
3. The board of an offeree company must act in the interests of the company as a whole and must not deny the holders of securities the opportunity to decide on the merits of the bid.
4. False markets must not be created in the securities of the offeree company, of the offeror company or of any other company concerned by the bid in such a way that the rise or fall of the prices of the securities becomes artificial and the normal functioning of the markets is distorted.
5. An offeror must announce a bid only after ensuring that it can fulfil in full any cash consideration, if such is offered, and after taking all reasonable measures to secure the implementation of any other type of consideration.
6. An offeree company must not be hindered in the conduct of its affairs for longer than is reasonable by a bid for its securities.

These are the essential guiding principles of the Code. If there is any doubt as to the application of a rule, then reference should always be made to the principles. A breach of a principle, even when in strict accordance with the rules, is deemed to be a breach of the Code itself.

The PTM applies the general principles in accordance with their spirit to achieve their underlying purpose.

2.4   Definitions

Learning Objective

4.2.5   Know the definitions of 'acting in concert', 'dealings', 'interests in securities' and 'relevant securities'

Takeover Code definitions are set out in full in the definitions section of the Code, available on the PTM website (www.thetakeoverpanel.org.uk). The following definitions are taken from this section, and are essential for an understanding of Code rules.

2.4.1   Acting in Concert

The definition of acting in concert is *'Persons who, pursuant to an agreement or understanding (whether formal or informal), co-operate to obtain or consolidate control (as defined below) of a company or to frustrate the successful outcome of an offer for a company'.*

Control in the context of the Code means an interest, or interests, in shares carrying in aggregate 30% or more of the voting rights of a company, irrespective of whether such interest or interests give de facto control.

The following persons will be presumed to be acting in concert with other persons in the same category unless the contrary is established (only the PTM can agree who is and who is not acting in concert, and any concert parties must be agreed by the PTM):

1. A company, its parent, subsidiaries and fellow subsidiaries, and their associated companies, and companies of which such companies are associated companies, all with each other (for this purpose ownership or control of 20% or more of the equity share capital of a company is regarded as the test of associated company status).
2. A company with any of its directors (together with their close relatives and related trusts).
3. A company with any of its pension funds and the pension funds of any company covered in (1.).
4. A fund manager (including an exempt fund manager) with any investment company, unit trust or other person whose investments such fund manager manages on a discretionary basis, in respect of the relevant investment accounts.
5. A connected adviser with its client and, if its client is acting in concert with an offeror or with the offeree company, with that offeror or with that offeree company respectively, in each case in respect of the interests in shares of that adviser and persons controlling, controlled by or under the same control as that adviser (except in the capacity of an exempt fund manager or an exempt principal trader).
6. Directors of a company which is subject to an offer or where the directors have reason to believe a bona fide offer for their company may be imminent.

Dealings and interests in securities held by members of concert parties are aggregated for the purposes of the Code. Thus, an offeror's shareholding in an offeree will be aggregated with that of its investment bank adviser, taking into account all interests held in all parts of that bank including the fund management arm, the market makers and the principal traders. This could impose significant restrictions on principal traders and fund managers in particular, whose activities are generally segregated from those of the corporate finance advisory arm and who have obligations to perform their roles as fund managers and market makers. If the PTM is satisfied that effective Chinese walls or other appropriate arrangements are in place, it may grant the fund managers and principal traders exempt status; this provides exemption from the obligation to aggregate interests in shares with those of the bank's corporate finance clients.

2.4.2 Dealings

Dealing includes the following:

- The acquisition or disposal of securities, or the right (whether conditional or absolute) to exercise or direct the exercise of the voting rights attaching to securities, or of general control of securities.
- The taking, granting, acquisition, disposal, entering into, closing out, termination, exercise (by either party) or variation of an option (including a traded option) in respect of any securities.
- Subscribing or agreeing to subscribe for securities.
- The exercise or conversion, whether in respect of new or existing securities, of any securities carrying conversion or subscription rights.
- The acquisition of, disposal of, entering into, closing out, exercise (by either party) of any rights under, or variation of, a derivative referenced, directly or indirectly, to securities.
- Entering into, terminating or varying the terms of any agreement to purchase or sell securities.
- Any other action resulting, or which may result, in an increase or decrease in the number of securities in which a person is interested or in respect of which they have a short position.

2.4.3 Interests in Securities

A person who has a long economic exposure, whether absolute or conditional, to changes in the prices of securities is treated as being interested in those securities. A short position in securities will not be treated as an interest in those securities.

In particular, a person will be treated as having an interest in securities if:

- They own them.
- They have the right (whether absolute or conditional) to exercise or direct the exercise of the voting rights attaching to them or have general control of them.
- By virtue of any agreement to purchase, option or derivative they a) have the right or option to acquire or call for the delivery, or b) are under an obligation to take delivery of them, whether the right, option or obligation is conditional or absolute and whether it is in-the-money or otherwise.
- They are party to any derivative a) whose value is determined by reference to their price and b) which results, or may result, in their having a long position in the security.
- In the case of Rule 5 only (see Section 2.8) he has received an irrevocable commitment in respect of them.

2.4.4 Relevant Securities

Relevant securities include:

- Securities of the offeree company for which an offer has been received or which carry voting rights.
- Equity share capital of the offeree company and an offeror.
- Securities of an offeror which carry substantially the same rights as any to be issued as consideration for the offer.
- Securities of the offeree company and an offeror carrying conversion or subscription rights into any of the foregoing.

2.5   Announcements

2.5.1   Secrecy

The most important rules governing the pre-bid environment relate to the secrecy of negotiations. The PTM is concerned to prevent leaks about potential bids that could result in the development of a false market in the securities of both the offeror and offeree companies.

Rule 2.1 of the Code emphasises the vital importance of absolute secrecy and security before an announcement, and states that all persons privy to price-sensitive information concerning an offer or possible offer must treat that information as secret and must only pass it to another person on a need-to-know basis, making them aware of the need for secrecy. Moreover, it is a requirement that advisers to bid parties should make their clients aware of the importance of this provision at the very beginning of discussions.

2.5.2   Offer Announcements

Rule 2.2 of the Code sets out the circumstances when an announcement is required, as follows:

- When a firm intention to make an offer is notified to the board of the offeree company.
- When, following an approach to the offeree board, there is rumour and speculation and an untoward movement in the share price of the offeree (broadly speaking, a 5% price increase in one day, or a 10% increase since the start of talks).
- When, before any approach to the offeree board, there is rumour and speculation about a possible offer, or an untoward movement in the share price of the offeree, and there are reasonable grounds for concluding that it is the potential offeror's actions which have led to the situation.
- When discussions regarding a possible offer are extended beyond a small number of parties (generally six) so that a leak becomes more likely.
- When a purchaser is being sought for shares carrying 30% or more of the voting rights of a company, and more than a restricted number of parties are to be approached.
- When a person or group of persons has acquired an interest in shares giving rise to an obligation to make a mandatory offer (this is discussed further in Section 2.8 below).

Until the offeree board has been approached, it is generally the potential offeror's responsibility to monitor the offeree's share price and make announcements where necessary. Once the offeree board has been approached, responsibility for such announcements passes to them.

If announcements are required under the Code, they must be made to the market through a regulatory information service (RIS) as well as to the other bid party (parties) and to the PTM.

An offer announcement may be a:

- firm announcement (of a firm intention to make an offer)
- talks announcement (stating that the offeree is in talks in relation to a possible offer)

- **no intention to bid** announcement (stating that a potential offeror will not in fact make a firm announcement for the next six months).

Each announcement has a particular significance.

- A firm announcement commits the offeror to making a formal offer in line with the timetable and other requirements of the Code.
- A talks, or possible offer, announcement must include the identity of the potential offeror, unless the approach has been unequivocally rejected. It does not, however, commit the potential offeror to making a formal offer. A talks announcement triggers the start of the offer period, during which certain provisions such as the Code share-dealing disclosure requirements apply. A list of companies in an offer period is found on the disclosure table on the PTM's website.
- A no intention to bid announcement is usually triggered by a put up or shut up requirement. Under Rule 2.6, a potential offeror who has been identified must, by no later than 17.00 on the 28th calendar day following the start of the offer period, put up or shut up: that is either, announce a formal offer on that day, or confirm that they have no intention to make an offer, or, together with the offeree company, seek an extension to the deadline. If a no bid announcement has been made, that offeror (together with its concert parties) is generally prohibited from announcing a bid for that offeree for the next six months.

Under Rule 2.7, a company should only make a firm announcement after careful and responsible consideration, as this announcement will commit the offeror to make its offer. The following details must be included in the announcement:

- the terms of the bid, including any conditions or pre-conditions to which the offer is subject;
- the identity of the offeror
- details of any relevant agreements entered into by the offeror, relating to circumstances in which it might seek to invoke a condition or pre-condition of the offer
- details of any concert party arrangements
- details of any deal-related agreements which have been permitted by the PTM
- a summary of the provisions of Rule 8 (which requires holders of 1% or more of the offeree's or a cash offeror's securities to announce their positions and dealings in these securities during the offer period) confirmation from a financial adviser that any cash element of the cash offer can be fulfilled
- a list of required documents published on a website with the address of that website.

2.5.3   Other Announcements

Once an offeree company has announced the fact of an approach from a potential offeror, it enters an offer period. At this time it must (under Rule 2.10) announce, as soon as possible and in any event by 09.00 on the next business day, details and numbers of all classes of its relevant securities in issue. The same information must be disclosed by a named offeror, by 09.00 on the day following its being named as a potential offeror, unless it has stated that its offer is likely to be solely in cash.

Certain dealings may give rise to an obligation to amend or increase an existing offer (eg, when the offeror or its concert parties acquire shares in the market above the offer price during the offer period). In this case, Rule 7.1 requires the offeror to announce an increased or amended offer without delay.

Rule 17.1 requires an offeror to announce the level of acceptances received for the offer. An announcement must be made by no later than 08.00 on the business day following the day on which the offer is due to expire, or the day on which the offer becomes unconditional with regard to acceptances, or when it is revised or extended. It must specify the total number of offeree shares for which acceptances have been received, and details of those relevant securities in which the offeror and its concert parties are interested, as well as the percentage of the offeree shares represented by these figures.

2.6   Independent Advice

Learning Objective

4.2.7   Know Rule 3 – Independent Advice

Under Rule 3, the board of the offeree company must obtain competent independent advice on any offer, and the substance of such advice must be made known to all its shareholders.

Likewise, the board of the offeror must also obtain competent independent advice on any offer when the offer being made is a reverse takeover or when the directors are faced with a conflict of interest. Again the substance of such advice must be made known to all its shareholders.

The PTM will not regard as an appropriate person to give independent advice any person who is in the same group as the financial or other professional adviser (including a corporate broker) to an offeror, or who has a significant interest in or financial connection with either an offeror or the offeree company of such a kind as to create a conflict of interest.

2.7   Prohibited Dealings

Learning Objective

4.2.8   Know Rule 4 – Prohibited Dealings

As mentioned above, following a talks announcement, an offeree company enters an offer period. This is defined as the period between the announcement of a proposed or possible offer, until the first closing date or (if later) the date the offer becomes unconditional as to acceptances or lapses. During the offer period, the dealing disclosures described below at Section 2.10.1 apply, as well as the following prohibitions on certain dealings.

Under Rule 4, the following dealing restrictions apply during an offer period:

- Dealings on the basis of inside information about a proposed offer are prohibited, except where securities are acquired by the offeror.
- The offeror and any persons acting in concert with it are not permitted to sell any securities in the offeree company except with the prior consent of the PTM and following 24 hours' public notice that such sales might be made. The PTM will not give consent for sales if a mandatory offer under Rule 9 is being made.

- The offeror and its concert parties may not acquire shares in the offeree through an anonymous order book system or otherwise, unless it can be shown that the purchase is not from an exempt principal trader connected with the offeror.
- No financial adviser or corporate broker to the offeree, or any member of their group, may deal in offeree securities.
- The offeror and offeree and their concert parties must not enter into or unwind any stock lending agreements in relation to offeree shares, without the Panel's approval.
- An exempt principal trader connected with either the offeror or offeree must not carry out any dealings with the purpose of assisting the offeror or the offeree company.

2.8 Timing Restrictions on Acquisitions

Learning Objective

4.2.9 Know Rule 5 – Timing Restrictions on Acquisitions

Rule 5 aims to prevent a person obtaining control, or consolidating control, over a company, except in a number of acceptable circumstances. The basic rule states that a person (in aggregate with its concert parties) is interested in shares carrying 30% or more of the voting rights, but they don't already hold 50% or more.

In addition, when a person (in aggregate with their concert parties) already holds an interest in shares carrying between 30% and 50% of the voting rights in a company, they may not acquire an interest in any further shares in that company. This is referred to as consolidating control.

In general, a breach of Rule 5 gives rise to an obligation under Rule 9 to make a mandatory offer for all the remaining shares of the company.

There are a number of exemptions to Rule 5, whereby it is permissible to acquire or consolidate control. However, even if an acquirer takes advantage of an exemption, this may in some cases still trigger a mandatory offer.

The exemptions are when:

- a person already holds shares carrying more than 50% of the voting rights, since they already have legal control
- control arises as the result of an issue of new shares, and a vote of independent shareholders (ie, excluding the acquirer of shares) approves the acquisition of control (a whitewash)
- the acquisition of shares or interests in shares is from a single shareholder and it is the only purchase in a seven-day period; although, when such an acquisition is made, no subsequent acquisitions are permitted unless the following conditions apply:
  - when the acquisition is immediately before a firm announcement to make an offer, and either the offer or the acquisition itself will be recommended by the offeree board and the acquisition is conditional on the offer being made
  - when the acquisition is immediately after a firm announcement to make an offer or during an offer, and either the acquisition is made with offeree board approval, or the offer or a competing offer has been recommended by the offeree board, or the first closing date of that or a competing offer has passed, or the offer is unconditional in all respects
  - when the acquisition of shares has arisen through the acceptance of an offer.

2.9   Offer Consideration and Cash Offers

Learning Objective

4.2.10   Know Rules 6, 11 – Minimum Level and Nature of Consideration to be Offered

The offer for an offeree company may be in the form of cash, shares or loan stock, or a mixture of cash and/or shares and/or loan stock. Shareholders may be offered a single structure, a choice of consideration options, or a mix and match alternative. In most cases, the offeror has discretion as to the form and amount of any payment consideration offered (subject to General Principle 1 which states that all holders of the securities of an offeree company of the same class must be afforded equivalent treatment).

However, in some circumstances the offeror may face restrictions which impose a minimum level of consideration, or require him to include a full cash alternative to all shareholders in his offer. These restrictions will arise when the offeror has acquired interests in offeree securities prior to making his offer, and are as follows:

- Under Rule 6, where the offeror (or its concert parties) have acquired any interests in the shares of the offeree company during the three months prior to the start of the offer period, or between the start of the offer period and a firm announcement, then the minimum price to be offered by the offeror is the highest price that they have paid to acquire offeree shares during that period (ie, it shall not be on less favourable terms).
- If the offeror or his concert parties purchase shares in the offeree at a price higher than the offer price during the offer period, the offeror must increase their offer to the highest price paid for these shares, and offer a full cash alternative if this is not already provided.
- Under Rule 11, if the offeror or his concert parties have purchased 10% or more of the voting shares in the offeree for cash during the offer period or in the 12 months beforehand, then the offer must be at least at the highest price paid by the offeror for offeree shares in that period, and must be in cash or with a full cash alternative available to all shareholders.

2.10   Disclosure of Dealings and Interests

Learning Objective

4.2.11   Know Rules 8, 24.4, 25.4 – Disclosure of Dealings and Interests

2.10.1 Disclosure of Dealings

During the offer period, certain dealings in relevant securities must be publicly disclosed under Rule 8.

The definitions of dealings and relevant securities are shown at Sections 2.4.2 and 2.4.4 earlier.

The following disclosures must be made:

Public Disclosure

Public disclosure is a disclosure to the market through an RIS, copied to the PTM and the bid parties. It must be made in respect of:

- any dealings in relevant securities by the offeror, offeree or their associates on their own account or on behalf of discretionary clients
- any dealings by persons with interests in securities representing 1% or more of the voting rights of offeror or offeree
- any dealings by an exempt fund manager connected to either of the bid parties
- summary of total acquisitions and disposals by exempt principal traders (such as market makers), with highest and lowest prices.

Private Disclosure

Private disclosure is a disclosure made to the PTM and the bid parties only. It must be made in respect of:

- any dealings in relevant securities on behalf of discretionary investment clients by an exempt fund manager, associated with the offeror and/or offeree
- any dealings by the bid parties or their concert parties on behalf of non-discretionary clients.

All disclosures must be made without delay, and at the latest by 12.00 on the next business day following the dealing (T+1), (15.30 for disclosures by 1% shareholders not connected to the bid parties).

2.10.2 Disclosure of Interests

Opening Position Disclosures

At the commencement of the offer period, Rule 8 provides that certain parties must provide opening position disclosures. These are announcements containing details of interests or short positions in, or rights to subscribe for, any relevant securities of a party to the offer, if the person concerned has such a position. An opening position disclosure is required to be made after the commencement of the offer period and, if later, after the announcement that first identifies an offeror.

They must be made by:

- the offeree company
- the offeror (after its identity is first publicly disclosed), and
- any person that is interested in 1% or more of any class of relevant securities of any party to the offer.

Opening position disclosures must be made within ten business days of the start of the offer period.

Disclosures in the Offer Document

Under Rule 24.4 the offer document must disclose details of the offeror's interests in, or rights to subscribe to, relevant securities in the offeree company, specifying the nature of the interest or rights concerned. Similarly, it must also disclose details of any short positions, including any short positions under a derivative; any agreement to sell or any delivery obligation or right to require another person to purchase or take delivery must also be stated. If there are no interests or short positions to be disclosed, then this fact should be stated.

If the offeror and/or its concert parties have dealt in relevant offeree securities during the period starting 12 months prior to the offer period and ending with the latest practicable date prior to the publication of the offer document, the details of such dealings, including dates, must be stated. Again, where no such dealings have taken place this also must be stated.

This will include details of the dealings of the following persons, deemed to be concert parties:

- Directors of the offeree company.
- Any company which is an associate of the offeree company.
- Any pension fund of the offeree company or of a company which is an associate of the offeree company.
- Any employee benefit trust of the offeree company or of a company which is an associate of the offeree company.
- Any connected adviser to the offeree company or to a company which is an associate of the offeree company.
- Any person controlling, controlled by or under the same control as any connected adviser.
- Any person which has an arrangement of the kind referred to in Rule 8 (indemnity or option arrangements).

Disclosures in the Defence Document

Similarly, Rule 25.4 provides that the offeree's first major defence document must also include certain details of interests and dealings. It must include details of any relevant offeror securities in which the offeree company or any of its directors has an interest or rights to subscribe, with details of these; also details of any short position, agreements to sell or delivery obligations. It must also show details of any interests in or rights or short positions over offeree company securities held by the offeree company, its directors or its concert parties.

This document must also show whether the offeree directors intend, in respect of their own beneficial shareholdings, to accept the offer or reject it.

2.11   The Mandatory Offer

Learning Objective

4.2.12   Know Rules 9, 37 and Appendix 1 – the Mandatory Offer, Redemption or Purchase by a Company of its own securities and 'Whitewashes'

2.11.1 Mandatory Offers

If a person (acting alone or in concert with others) takes their interest in a company to an aggregate level of 30% or more of the voting rights, they are required to make a mandatory offer to acquire the shares of all remaining shareholders, under Rule 9 of the Code.

Under the terms of a mandatory offer, much of the offeror's discretion to impose conditions is removed and the following rules apply:

- The minimum price of a mandatory offer is the highest price at which the offeror purchased shares in the offeree company within the last 12 months.
- The offer must be for cash or have a full cash alternative available for all offeree shareholders.
- The offer must remain open after the offer has become or has been declared unconditional as to acceptances for at least 14 days after it would otherwise have expired.
- The mandatory offer may only be subject to two conditions: regulatory clearances where required, and an acceptance threshold of a simple majority (over 50%). No other conditions are allowed.

It is possible for a mandatory offer to be triggered deliberately or inadvertently. In the latter case, the PTM may consider granting a Rule 9 waiver – ie, a waiver from the obligation to make a mandatory offer.

Rule 37 specifically considers the situation of a shareholder whose interest in the securities of a company is increased not through his own purchases, but by a share buy-back or other reduction in capital. Generally, the PTM will waive the obligation to make a mandatory offer in these circumstances, provided a **whitewash** procedure is carried out and that independent shareholders agree to no mandatory offer being made. However, if the shareholder acquired interests in shares in the knowledge of the proposed buy-back, the PTM will generally not grant a waiver.

2.12 Conditions and Pre-conditions

Learning Objective

4.2.13 Know Rule 13 – Conditions and Pre-conditions

It is normal for an offer to be made subject to conditions, such as:

- the reaching of an acceptance threshold (such as 90%, whereupon a squeeze-out is permitted, or 75% which allows a scheme of arrangement to be approved)
- offeror shareholder approval
- regulatory approval, including OFT clearance or EC Phase I clearance
- other bid-specific conditions.

The minimum acceptance threshold allowed under the Code is a level which gives legal control, ie, 50% plus one vote (a simple majority). However, unless the offer is a mandatory offer, the offeror may select an alternative higher acceptance threshold, while reserving the right to reduce the acceptance threshold to the Code minimum in due course.

It is also possible that an offeror may announce a pre-condition to their launching of a formal takeover offer; for example, he may announce that a bid will be made once industry regulator approval has been granted.

Rule 13 states that an offer must not normally be subject to conditions or pre-conditions which depend solely on subjective judgements by the directors of the offeror or offeree. The PTM may be prepared to accept an element of subjectivity in certain circumstances if it is not practicable to specify all the factors on which satisfaction of a particular condition or pre-condition may depend, especially in cases involving official authorisations or regulatory clearances.

Generally, it is acceptable to include a condition that the bid is conditional on its not being referred to the CC or EC Phase II investigation, when applicable.

2.13 Information

Learning Objective

4.2.14   Know Rules 19, 20 – Information

Rule 19 states that each document or advertisement published, or statement made, during the course of an offer must be prepared with the highest standards of care and accuracy and must be adequately and fairly presented. This is irrespective of whether it is published by the party directly or by an adviser on its behalf.

Each document or advertisement published in connection with an offer by, or on behalf of, the offeror or the offeree company, must state that the directors accept responsibility for the information contained in the document.

Directors must take care not to omit important information or to give misleading impressions to the market to create uncertainty.

If an offeror or an offeree company, or any person on its behalf:

- sends a document or information in relation to an offer to shareholders, persons with information rights or other relevant persons in accordance with Rule 19.8 (publication of documents, announcements and information), or
- publishes an announcement (whether related to the offer or not) by sending it to an RIS

the offeror or offeree must, as soon as possible and in any event by no later than midday on the following business day, ensure that a copy is published on its website.

2.13.1 Equality of Information

Rule 20 provides that information about parties to an offer must be made equally available to all offeree company shareholders and persons with information rights, as nearly as possible, at the same time and in the same manner. In particular, care must be taken when having discussions with institutional shareholders, giving analyst briefings or making statements at shareholder meetings, to ensure that no new information is disclosed which is not available to all shareholders. A representative of the broker or financial adviser to the relevant bid party must attend all such meetings, and confirm in writing to the PTM no later than 12.00 (midday) on the following business day that no material new information was forthcoming and no significant new opinions were expressed at the meeting.

Furthermore, any information provided to one offeror or potential offeror, whether named or unnamed, must on request be given equally and promptly to any other bona fide offeror or potential offeror, even if that other offeror is less welcome.

2.13.2 Independent Directors in a Management Buy-out

If the offer or potential offer is a management buy-out, the offeror is typically a private equity investment vehicle working in concert with the executive management of the offeree company, who is therefore not able to provide independent advice to their shareholders. The offeree must establish that there are sufficient independent directors to fulfil the requirement under Rule 3 to provide shareholders with a recommendation as to whether to accept the offer or not. The directors of the offeree must also furnish these independent directors or their advisers with all information which has been furnished by the bidding party to external providers or potential providers of finance (whether equity or debt) for the buy-out.

2.14 Restrictions on Frustrating Action

Learning Objective

4.2.15 Know Rule 21 – Restrictions on Frustrating Action

From the date that the offeree company's board has reason to believe that a bona fide offer might be imminent, the board must not, without the approval of the shareholders in a GM:

- take any action which might result in any offer or possible offer being frustrated or in shareholders being denied the opportunity to decide on its merits
- issue any authorised but unissued shares or transfer or sell, or agree to transfer or sell, any shares out of treasury
- issue or grant options in respect of unissued shares
- create or issue any securities carrying rights of conversion into or subscription for shares
- sell, dispose of or acquire, or agree to sell, dispose or acquire assets of a material amount
- enter into contracts otherwise than in the ordinary course of business.

Additionally, with effect from 19 September 2011, under Rule 21.2 an offeree, offeror, and any person acting in concert with them is prohibited from entering into any inducement agreement or other offer-related agreement (such as a break fee or exclusivity agreement) without the Panel's consent.

More widely, they must not take any action which would frustrate the ability of shareholders to accept an offer, without the approval of the shareholders.

2.14.1 Defences Available to the Offeree Company

If the directors of the offeree company view the offer as hostile, the following courses of action are available to them as part of their defence:

- publish a defence document, including profit forecasts and/or arguments as to why the bid itself, or the terms of it, are not in the best interest of the shareholders
- lobby for referral to the CC (or if relevant, the EC)
- seek an alternative purchaser on more favourable terms (a **white knight**).

2.15   Profit Forecasts

Learning Objective

4.2.16   Know Rule 28 – Profit Forecasts and Quantified Financial Benefits Statements

One particularly problematic area for regulators arises when the offeree company wishes to include profit forecasts in its defence document. Given the difficulties of verifying forecasts, there is considerable scope for misuse and, accordingly, the Code contains provisions on profit forecasts. A profit forecast must be compiled with due care and consideration by the directors, whose sole responsibility it is; the financial advisers must satisfy themselves that the forecast has been prepared in this manner by the directors.

Rule 28 of the Code states that when a profit forecast is included in a Code document, it must be reported on both by the auditors to the company making the statement, and by their financial advisers, and these reports must be included in the document concerned. There must be full disclosure of the assumptions underlying the profit forecast, and the reports must be accompanied by a statement that those making them have given and not withdrawn their consent to publication in the document.

2.16   Timing and Revision

Learning Objective

4.2.17   Know Rules 31–35 – Timing and Revision

Once a firm announcement of an offer has been made, the process becomes subject to a formal bid timetable, with a number of specific deadlines to be met. In outline, an offer must be open for a minimum of 21 days, and a maximum of 60 days. All deadlines shown are based on calendar days.

Announcement Day

Once a bid has been announced, the offeror has 28 days in which to post the offer document, giving full details of its offer, to offeree shareholders, and to make this available to offeree employees.

Day 0 – Posting Day

The posting day is the day on which the offer document is posted to the offeree's shareholders and must be no later than 28 days from the firm announcement date. This counts as day 0 for the entire timetable.

Day 14 – The First Defence Document

In a recommended offer, the offer document includes a letter by the offeree chairman to the offeree shareholders, setting out a recommendation that shareholders accept the offer, and including the Rule 3 adviser's opinion. In a hostile bid, however, the offeree board does not co-operate on the production of the offer document, but instead must post a defence document to all shareholders by the fourteenth day after the posting day, ie, day 14. The defence document contains the directors' response to the offer document, recommending shareholders to reject the offer and explaining the reasons why.

Day 21 – The First Closing Day

An initial offer must be open for at least 21 days following the date on which the offer document is published.

On day 21, the offeror counts the number of acceptances received from the offeree's shareholders, and determines whether the offer is unconditional with regard to acceptances (ie, the acceptance threshold has been met) and, if not, whether he will extend or amend the offer.

- There is no obligation to extend the offer if the acceptance condition has not been satisfied by the first or any subsequent closing date.
- If the company has reached its specified acceptance level, the offer must remain open for another 14 days, to allow the remaining shareholders to accept the offer.
- If the offeror improves its offer at any time the revised bid must remain open for acceptances for at least 14 days following posting of the revised offer.

Day 39 – Last Defence Documents

The offeree board is not permitted, unless with the consent of the PTM, to announce any new information or disclose any material new opinions, after day 39 (being 21 days before the final deadline of day 60).

Day 42 – Right of Withdrawal

If the offer has not been declared unconditional with regard to acceptances by day 42 (21 days after the first closing day) any shareholder who had accepted the original bid may now withdraw their acceptance.

Day 46 – Last Offer Amendment

The offeror company may amend its offer up to day 46 – 14 days before the final deadline or day 60 – should they wish to do so. Following this date the offeror must not buy shares in the market at above the offer price (as this would trigger a revised offer).

Day 60 – The Final Day

A bid can remain open for up to 60 days. However, if by day 60 the offer is not unconditional with regard to acceptances then the bid must lapse, unless an exemption is provided by the PTM.

At day 60 the offeror must state the total number of acceptances received, together with its own holdings and irrevocable commitments held. If a bid lapses, the offeror is generally not permitted to launch another offer for the offeree company for 12 months from that date.

If, however, the offer is referred to the CC for a detailed investigation, then the bid will lapse (ie, end). If the bid is then cleared by the CC, the offeror has 21 days to decide whether to launch a new offer. In a mandatory offer, the offeror will not have this flexibility but will be obliged to launch a new bid.

The Post-Bid Environment

Any offer declared unconditional as to acceptances must remain open for acceptance by the remaining shareholders for at least a further 14 days after that date. The offeror then has a maximum of 21 days from the date the offer goes unconditional to acceptances to fulfil any other outstanding conditions.

2.17   Schemes of Arrangement

Learning Objective

4.2.18   Know Appendix 7 – Schemes of Arrangement

A scheme of arrangement is an alternative method of launching a takeover bid that is usually used for an agreed bid. The existing shareholders of the offeree company agree to have their shares replaced with some other securities, such as shares in the bidding company, or redeemed for cash.

The specific details of the procedures required are set out in the Companies Act 2006, and this was explained in more detail in Section 3.1 of Chapter 1. The main contrast with a **normal** contractual offer is that shareholders are not asked to accept an offer, but to vote on proposals for a reconstruction of the company, which will have the effect of transferring it into new ownership.

The PTM requires that the same principles and many of the same provisions of the Code apply whether it is a contractual offer or a scheme of arrangement. There are, however, additional specific rules, which include:

* A scheme of arrangement cannot be used for a mandatory bid without the Panel's consent.
* 21 calendar days' notice is required for shareholder meetings to consider the scheme, and notice must be given of any revisions to the scheme at least 14 days before a meeting.
* The results of the meeting(s) must be announced by 08:00 on the next business day, including full details of the votes for and against the scheme.

If the offeror wants to switch from a contractual offer to a scheme of arrangement (or vice versa) then the Panel's consent is required. The PTM will determine any new timetable arrangements. If an offeror wishes to propose a scheme of arrangement without the offeree company's board consent, the PTM must be consulted first.

End of Chapter Questions

Think of an answer for each question and refer to the appropriate section for confirmation.

1.   What is the scope and purpose of the Takeover Panel?
     Answer reference: Section 1.1.1

2.   What is the purpose of the Takeover Code and the Competition Commission?
     Answer reference: Section 1.1.1

3.   How might the Pensions Regulator be involved in a takeover bid?
     Answer reference: Section 1.2.5

4.   What type of companies does the Takeover Code apply to and what transactions are caught by the Code?
     Answer reference: Sections 2.2.1, 2.2.2

5.   What are the six General Principles of the Takeover Code?
     Answer reference: Section 2.3

6.   How would acting in concert apply to an investment bank that undertakes market making as well as providing asset management and corporate finance advice?
     Answer reference: Section 2.4.1

7.   What is the definition of interests in securities?
     Answer reference: Section 2.4.3

8.   During an offer period, is the offeror or any connected party permitted to sell any securities in the target company?
     Answer reference: Section 2.7

9.   What are the requirements on disclosure of dealings in an offer period?
     Answer reference: Section 2.10.1

10. Who is responsible for the information contained in an offer document?
     Answer reference: Section 2.10.2

11. When would a mandatory offer be required?
     Answer reference: Section 2.11

12. Is the target company permitted to provide information selectively in a hostile bid situation?
     Answer reference: Section 2.13.1

13. What are the main bid defences available to a target company?
     Answer reference: Section 2.14

14. What is the significance of the posting day of the offer document to the target company's shareholders?
    Answer reference: Section 2.16.1

15. When is the offeror company not permitted to increase or amend its offer for the target company?
    Answer reference: Section 2.16

Chapter Five
Prospectuses

This syllabus area will provide approximately 3 of the 50 examination questions

1. Prospectus Rules

1.1 The Requirement to Produce a Prospectus

Learning Objective

5.1.1 Understand when a prospectus approved by the FCA in accordance with the Prospectus Rules (PR) will be required

5.1.2 Know which offers to the public are exempt and when an admission of shares to a regulated market is exempt (PR 1.2)

The FSA implemented the Prospectus Directive in the UK in July 2005 primarily through the introduction of the prospectus rules, located within the rules block of the handbook. In addition, relevant new provisions of FSMA were introduced. The Directive applies to all companies when issuing transferable securities within the EU.

Broadly, the prospectus rules require the issue of a prospectus whenever there is either:

1. an offer of transferable securities to the public in the UK, or
2. a request for the admission to trading of transferable securities on a regulated market in the UK

unless an exemption applies.

This means that the rules apply whenever a company is seeking admission to listing, or when a company which is already trading issues new securities which will be listed or offered to the public. A prospectus is not required for admission to AIM or the ISDX Growth Market unless it is a public offer (raising more than €5 million from 150 or more non-qualified investors in any EU member state), with an Admission Document being produced instead.

The purpose of a prospectus is to give potential investors a complete, accurate and up-to-date understanding of the issuer, including its history, management, structure, finances, operations and prospects. The rules set out the form, contents and approval requirements for prospectuses.

1.1.1 When is a Prospectus Required?

The Prospectus Directive, implemented via the FCA prospectus rules, requires a prospectus to be issued whenever transferable securities are offered to the public, or admitted to trading on a regulated market. This applies to both primary and secondary offerings of securities with a value of €5 million or more. (This threshold was increased from €2.5 million on 31 July 2011.) There are, however, certain exceptions to this requirement.

1.1.2 Exemptions

A prospectus may not be required in certain circumstances, in particular:

- when an offer is made only to qualified investors, or to fewer than 150 persons per EU member state, excluding qualified investors; this is referred to as the private placement exemption
- for offers for securities with a total consideration of less than €5.0 million, calculated over a 12-month period
- for units/shares issued by an OEIC
- for a bonus or capitalisation issue
- for non-equity securities issued by EEA government authorities and central banks (for example, gilts or Treasury stock issued by the DMO on behalf of HMT)
- for issues of non-transferable securities
- for issues of money market instruments with maturities of less than 12 months
- for the exercise of conversion rights or warrants, when this represents less than 10% of the issued share capital
- for shares issued in place of shares already listed, so long as the nominal value in total does not increase as a result, eg, a share split or consolidation
- with small issues of securities, which will not increase the class of securities in issue by 10% or more, or by more than €100,000 consideration over a year
- with issues of wholesale securities, ie, if the minimum subscription or denomination of the securities is €100,000. This will only realistically apply to corporate bond issues, and
- for securities already admitted to trading on one regulated market, which will not require a prospectus to seek admission to trading on additional markets, providing that they have a minimum trading history of more than 18 months.

Qualified Investors

Qualified investors comprise:

- firms which are authorised to operate in the capital markets (including investment firms, governments, supra-national organisations and local authorities)
- large companies
- small- and medium-sized companies, which have self-certified themselves as being qualified investors, and
- private individuals who have self-certified themselves as being sufficiently knowledgeable, experienced and wealthy to be qualified investors.

Example 1

XYZ plc is proposing to seek admission to the AIM market. Its nominated adviser tells it that, if it floats through a placing of shares to institutional investors, it can produce an admission document (instead of a prospectus). If, instead, it makes an offer to retail investors, it must produce a prospectus (to be approved by the FCA, and compliant with the prospectus rules).

This will also be the case if XYZ subsequently raises additional capital, through a rights issue; this is because it cannot limit this offer of shares to less than 150 persons, or to qualified investors, and cannot take advantage of the exemption for non-regulated markets, or it is raising less than €5 million in any 12-month period.

Example 2

ABC plc is now considering floating on the LSE main market. It hopes that floating by way of an introduction will avoid the need for a prospectus. However, its advisers inform ABC that as the main market is a regulated market, a prospectus is required. If instead they had elected to float on AIM, no prospectus would have been required.

1.2 Interaction of the Prospectus and the Financial Promotion Rules

Learning Objective

5.1.3 Understand the interaction between the Prospectus Rules and the Financial Promotion regime (COBS 4)

Whenever a company is considering a primary or secondary offering of shares, it must consider whether a prospectus is required. As set out in Section 1.1 above, there is a wide range of exemptions available, and if the company can benefit from one or more of these exemptions, then it need not produce a prospectus. In particular, if a company is seeking admission to AIM but does not market its shares widely, it may take advantage of the private placement exemption which is often considered to be a very significant advantage in terms of time, expense and complexity.

However, there are some advantages in producing a prospectus. A prospectus which has been approved by the FCA in accordance with the provisions of FSMA and the prospectus rules may be distributed widely, without restriction in the UK. In addition, a prospectus approved by the FCA may be **passported** to allow it to be used by one or more other EU member states.

When a company has determined that no prospectus is required for its share offering, it must still consider whether it has any obligations under the Financial Promotions regime, and in particular the requirements under Section 21 FSMA and COBS 4, which were discussed earlier in Chapter 2, at Section 3.1. This is because a share offering constitutes a financial promotion unless it is done through a prospectus or under one of the other exemptions in the financial promotions rules.

The FPO provides a very large number of exemptions from the requirement to comply with Section 21 and COBS 4. The exemption which is relevant to prospectuses is found at Article 70, which provides (inter alia) that the financial promotions restriction does not apply to any non-real time communication which is included in a prospectus or supplementary prospectus approved in accordance with the prospectus rules, or any other document required or permitted to be published by listing rules or prospectus rules. A further exemption which is relevant for this chapter is found at Article 19, whereby a communication which is only made to investment professionals, high net worth individuals and sophisticated investors is also outside the scope of the regime.

In summary, a company which is offering transferable securities to the public may have to produce and have approved a prospectus. If exemptions are available from this requirement under the Prospectus Rules, then it must still consider whether exemptions are available under the FPO; otherwise, its offering document must comply with the restrictions of Section 21 FSMA.

The FPO provides a wide number of exemptions to the requirements of Section 21 of the FSMA.

1.3 Prospectus Requirements

Learning Objective

5.1.4 understand the requirement to prepare, have approved (PR 3.1.7,3.1.8) and publish (PR 3.1.10) a prospectus (PR 3.1.1, 3.1.3)

1.3.1 Responsibility for Preparation of a Prospectus

One of the adviser's main obligations is co-ordinating the preparation of the prospectus in connection with an offering. However, the primary responsibility for the contents of a prospectus lies with the directors of the issuer. To this end, they are required to make a statement in the prospectus acknowledging their responsibility. In addition, they must also confirm to the FCA, by signed letter, that the prospectus contains all relevant information that they know or should have been aware of as the directors of the company.

1.3.2 Approval of the Prospectus

A prospectus must not be published, advertised or circulated until it has been approved by the competent authority. In the UK this is the FCA acting in accordance with its powers under FSMA 2000 Part 6 (see Chapter 6, Section 1.1.1). The FCA is also the UK's competent authority for the purpose of the Prospectus Directive. To obtain approval, the sponsor (for premium listings) or other adviser (for standard listings) must provide the FCA with certain stipulated information at least ten clear business days before the approval is granted (20 days for new issuers or in complicated cases); the information is known as the ten-day documents, and the main items include:

- draft prospectus and cover, and copies of all documents referred to within them
- request for authorisation to omit information normally required under the rules
- application forms to acquire or subscribe for shares
- copies of documents containing information to be incorporated by reference in the prospectus
- checklists cross-referencing the draft prospectus contents to the requirements of the prospectus requirements (PR)
- copies of the board resolution allotting the securities (or confirmation it will be provided within three days of approval)
- the sponsor's declaration on an application for listing (for a premium listing only)
- details of a contact available to answer questions, available 07.00 to 18.00.

In order to obtain final approval, the sponsor or adviser must provide the FCA with the information listed above in final form, including the final version of the prospectus, together with the relevant fee and Form A (Application for Approval of a Prospectus).

1.3.3 Contents of the Prospectus

The prospectus must contain all information necessary to enable investors to make an informed assessment of the assets and liabilities, financial position, profits and losses, and prospects of the issuer of the transferable securities and of any guarantor; and the rights attaching to the transferable securities.

This necessary information must be presented in a form which is comprehensible and easy to analyse, and be prepared having regard to the particular nature of the transferable securities and their issuer.

There are three parts to the prospectus:

- **Summary** containing a summary of key information, including the risk factors.
- **Registration document** containing general information about the issue and the issuer.
- **Securities note** containing detailed information about the equity or non-equity securities being offered.

Each part may be produced and approved by the FCA separately as a tripartite prospectus. More commonly, it may be prepared and approved as a single document.

The full contents of the registration document and securities note are specified in detail in the prospectus rules, and vary according to the type of securities being issued (eg, debt or equity), and the nature of the issuing company (eg, bank or investment company).

Summary

The summary must, briefly and in non-technical language, convey the essential characteristics of and risks associated with the issuer, any guarantor and the transferable securities to which the prospectus relates. It should be no longer than 2,500 words, unless more are required to convey the key features of the company.

Other than this, there are no details in the rules as to the contents of the summary. It is down to the issuer, the person offering the securities or the person seeking admission to listing to determine on its own what should be included.

The summary must also contain warnings to the effect that:

- it should be read as an introduction to the prospectus
- any decision to invest in the transferable securities should be based on consideration of the prospectus as a whole by the investor
- when a claim relating to the information contained in a prospectus is brought before a court, the plaintiff investor may, under the national legislation of the EEA states, have to bear the costs of translating the prospectus before the legal proceedings are initiated, and
- civil liability attaches to those persons who are responsible for the summary, including any translation of the summary, but only if the summary is misleading, inaccurate or inconsistent when read together with the other parts of the prospectus.

1.3.4 Supplementary Prospectus

It may be the case that, subsequent to approval of the prospectus, there is a significant change in the company's state of affairs. If this is the case, then a supplementary prospectus should be published giving details of the change or new matter that has arisen. This must be submitted to the FCA for approval as soon as practicable.

1.3.5 Publishing the Prospectus

After a prospectus is approved by the FCA, it must be filed with the FCA and made available to the public, as soon as practicable, and in any case at a reasonable time in advance of, and at the latest at the beginning of, the offer or the admission to trading of the transferable securities involved.

In the case of an offer of a class of shares not already admitted to trading that is to be admitted to trading for the first time, the prospectus must be made available to the public at least six working days before the end of the offer.

A prospectus is deemed to be made available to the public for the purposes of the rules (PR 3.2.1 to PR 3.2.3) when published either:

- by insertion in one or more newspapers circulated throughout, or widely circulated in, the EEA states in which the offer is made or the admission to trading is sought
- in a printed form to be made available, free of charge, to the public at the offices of the regulated market on which the transferable securities are being admitted to trading, or at the registered office of the issuer and at the offices of the financial intermediaries placing or selling the transferable securities, including paying agents
- in an electronic form on the issuer's website and, if applicable, on the website of the financial intermediaries placing or selling the transferable securities, including paying agents, or
- in an electronic form on the website of the regulated market where the admission to trading is sought. In the case of the FCA, this is the national storage mechanism.

The text and the format of the prospectus made available to the public must, at all times, be identical to the original version approved by the FCA.

If the prospectus is made available by publication in electronic form, a paper copy must nevertheless be provided to any investor on request and free of charge, by the issuer or their financial advisers.

End of Chapter Questions

Think of an answer for each question and refer to the appropriate section for confirmation.

1. When is a prospectus required?
   Answer reference: Section 1.1.1

2. A company is seeking admission for new shares to a regulated market. In what circumstances is it exempt from the obligation to produce a prospectus?
   Answer reference: Section 1.1.2

3. Is a prospectus required for the issue of gilts?
   Answer reference: Section 1.1.2

4. Is the issue of shares in a UK-authorised OEIC subject to the requirement for a prospectus?
   Answer reference: Section 1.1.2

5. What is the interaction between the Prospectus Rules and the financial promotions regime?
   Answer reference: Section 1.2

6. What is the financial promotions restriction?
   Answer reference: Section 1.2

7. Who is responsible for the preparation of a prospectus?
   Answer reference: Section 1.3.1

8. When is a summary needed for a prospectus?
   Answer reference: Section 1.3.3

9. What are the requirements in relation to publishing a prospectus?
   Answer reference: Section 1.3.5

Equity Capital Markets

This syllabus area will provide approximately 7 of the 50 examination questions

1. The Regulation of UK Equity Capital Markets

1.1 The FCA and its Role as the Lead Regulator

Learning Objective

6.1.1 Understand the FCA's role as the competent authority in the UK in the form of the United Kingdom Listing Authority (UKLA) and the purpose of the listing rules (LR) and the disclosure transparency rules (DTR)

6.1.3 understand the key differences between premium listing and standard listing

1.1.1 The Financial Conduct Authority (FCA)

Part VI of the FSMA provides that the FCA is designated as the competent authority in respect of UK regulated markets. Its duties and powers as competent authority are set out in FSMA Part 4A; these include maintaining the official list (the list of companies whose securities are admitted to trading on the main market or professional securities market of the LSE or the ISDX Main Board), approving prospectuses, admitting companies to the official list, and regulating listed companies. As part of this it is required to provide, maintain and enforce the rules that govern listed companies, found in the FCA Handbook.

The LSE is a listed company whose object is to run a marketplace in securities. It should be noted that it has no monopoly powers over the running of the marketplace, and other operators may, and do, compete against it; ISDX, for example, provides a regulated market (the ISDX Main Board) for listed securities (see Section 1.2.1).

The FCA regulates the LSE and has granted it the status of an RIE. The LSE operates two principal levels of entry into the equity market, namely, the official list (main market) and its junior market, AIM, together with two specialist markets: the professional securities market and the specialist fund market. As stated above, the FCA regulates listed companies (those which are quoted on the main market or professional securities market). However, the LSE regulates those companies which are quoted on the AIM market, as well as writing and enforcing the AIM rules and regulating AIM advisers. More detail on the AIM market will be found below in Section 2.1.

The LSE's rules govern secondary market trading in the shares of both listed and AIM companies by shareholders and intermediaries.

1.1.2 The FCA Rules

The FCA (through its UK Listing Authority (UKLA) department) determines which companies are eligible to join the official list, and writes and enforces the FCA Rules which apply to these companies. These rules were significantly amended from 2005 onwards to comply with the provisions of the Prospectus Directive, the MAD and the Transparency Obligations Directive. The format of these rules follows the FCA Handbook structure, with rules and guidance shown in a single text.

These rules are divided into three sourcebooks.

- **The listing rules (LR)** comprise general rules for listed companies, including the provisions for listing, over-arching listing principles and continuing obligations.
- **The disclosure and transparency rules (DTR)** provide rules and guidance for the dissemination of price-sensitive, and other, information, notifications of interests in shares, and corporate governance provisions.
- **The prospectus rules (PR)** consolidate all rules on prospectuses, including the content and form of prospectuses, the procedures for their approval, and exemptions from the requirement for a prospectus. Certain requirements, such as those listing the required contents of prospectuses are directly reproduced from the Prospectus Directive.

It should be noted that, although in general all of these rules apply to premium listed companies, some of these rules also have a wider application. In particular:

- **The LRs** apply widely to issuers with a premium listing, but only certain elements apply for issuers with a standard listing (described further below) and specialist issuers.
- **The DTRs** contain elements which are required by the MAD and therefore apply to issuers on prescribed markets, as well as regulated markets. They apply in general to listed companies, with certain elements also applying to AIM and ISDX Growth Market quoted companies.
- **The prospectus rules (PRs)** apply to all companies, both public and private, seeking to offer shares to the public or gain admission to trading on a UK regulated market. Chapter 5 provides more detail on the prospectus rules.

As a reminder, a prescribed market is any market operated by an RIE.

In 2012, the then regulator, the FSA, published proposals to amend the listing rules. The main changes proposed were:

- Scope of sponsor service (LR8.2.1).
- Related party transactions (LR8.2.1R).
- Roles and responsibilities of sponsors (LR8.3.1).
- Conflicts of interest (LR8.3.7 and LR8.7.12).
- Responsibilities of issuers (LR8.5.6R).
- Document retention (LR8.6.16AR).
- Sponsor notifications (LR8.7.8 and LR8.7.21AG).

The changes came into effect on 16 May 2014.

1.1.3 Premium and Standard Listing

The relevant European directives require certain minimum standards for issuers on regulated markets, while in general UK regulated markets have historically imposed more stringent, super-equivalent obligations and standards on issuers.

In 2008, the then regulator (the FSA) initiated a wholesale review of the UK listing regime, in order to address a lack of clarity in the market concerning the distinction between listing alternatives available in the main market, AIM and ISDX. Until 2010, the FSA allowed overseas, debt or GDR issuers to comply only with directive-minimum provisions, but required stricter standards for all UK equity issuers.

Its stated goals at the time were to:

- *'ensure that all market participants have a clearer understanding of what the Listing Regime represents and how it relates to other capital market offerings such as ISDX Growth Market and the London Stock Exchange's AIM*
- *devise a robust segmentation of the listing regime, offering competition and choice, which will be long-standing in the face of further market evolution*
- *recognise that the market particularly values the 'premium brand' of primary listing and therefore improvements to labelling should underpin that value, and*
- *ensure that we position the listing regime in a manner which continues to deliver confidence for all market participants in the capital raising process.'*

Following the review, with effect from April 2010, the listing rules have provided two tiers of listing for all main market companies, whether UK- or overseas-registered. These are:

- **Premium listing** is available for those issuers prepared to meet UK super-equivalent standards. It is available for equities issued by commercial companies, together with those equity securities issued by closed-ended investment companies (CEICs) and OEICs.
- **Standard listing** requires issuers to comply only with EU-minimum standards. It is available for both UK and overseas commercial equity issuers, as well as issuers of GDRs, debt, securitised derivatives, and miscellaneous securities. It is not available for CEICs or OEICs.

The listing rules set out generic requirements for all issuers, with additional requirements for premium issuers and their advisers. The main differences between the requirements for premium and standard listing, together with a comparison for AIM companies, are summarised in the table at the end of this chapter.

1.1.4   The Listing Rules

The Listing Rules set out the standards expected of listed issuers, and specific procedures to be followed. Their content is as follows:

- details of the FCA's enforcement regime
- the requirements for listing for all securities together with the super-equivalent provisions for premium listing
- the listing principles (see Section 1.3)
- the procedures for application for admission to listing, including secondary offerings
- requirements for sponsors, including criteria for approval, when required, and obligations
- certain continuing obligations for companies and directors, including corporate governance requirements
- requirements for shareholder approval of significant and related party transactions
- contents of circulars to shareholders, and financial information in circulars
- requirements for share buy-backs
- specific requirements for CEICs, OEICs, and issuers of debt, GDRs, and other non-equity securities.

1.1.5 The Disclosure and Transparency Rules (DTRs)

The aim of the DTRs is, in part, to implement those requirements of the MAD, and the Transparency Obligations Directive that apply to quoted companies in the UK, with a view to ensuring transparency for shareholders. In particular, they contain:

- provisions relating to the disclosure and control of inside information by issuers
- requirements to disclose transactions by persons discharging managerial responsibilities (PDMRs) and their related parties
- periodic financial reporting, including the timing and content of annual and interim accounts, and interim management statements
- vote-holder and issuer notifications (disclosure of substantial shareholdings)
- continuing obligations and access to information
- corporate governance requirements, including the requirement for an audit committee and corporate governance statements.

The DTRs are expected to be revised under the MAD 2 revisions (see Section 1.1.2).

1.2 Regulated Markets, Recognised Investment Exchanges (RIEs) and Multilateral Trading Facilities (MTFs)

Learning Objective

6.1.2 Understand the differences between a regulated market, a Recognised Investment Exchange (RIEs) and a Multilateral Trading Facility (MTFs)

It is important to understand the concepts of RIEs, regulated markets and MTFs. In summary:

- under MiFID, entities that offer multilateral trading for financial instruments (such as an order book), must be organised as either a regulated market or an MTF, with slightly different standards applying to each
- regulated markets are those which comply with the requirements for regulated markets under MiFID
- MTFs are those markets which are not designated as regulated markets
- an RIE is a firm which operates one or more of these markets and meets the standards required by the FCA to be an RIE.

These three types of entity are discussed in more detail in Sections 1.2.1–1.2.3.

1.2.1 Regulated Markets

The FCA glossary defines a regulated market as:

'A multilateral system operated and/or managed by a market operator, which brings together or facilitates the bringing together of multiple third-party buying and selling interests in financial instruments – in the system and in accordance with its non-discretionary rules – in a way that results in a contract, in respect of the financial instruments admitted to trading under its rules and/or systems, and which is authorised and functions regularly and in accordance with the provisions of Title III of the Markets in Financial Instruments Directive (MiFID)'.

The FCA is responsible, by virtue of Article 47 of MiFID, for maintaining the list of regulated markets for which they are the home member state. A market may ask to be added to the list of regulated markets if it satisfies the requirements set out in Title III of MiFID.

At the time of writing, the regulated markets were:

1. London Stock Exchange PLC (LSE).
2. LIFFE Administration and Management.
3. ICE Futures Europe.
4. London Metal Exchange Ltd (LME).
5. ICAP Securities & Derivatives Exchange Ltd (ISDX).
6. BATS Trading Ltd.
7. CME Europe Ltd.
8. Euronext UK Markets Ltd.

Note that the main market of the LSE is a regulated market; as such it must be regulated by the FCA in its role as competent authority for regulated markets. The AIM market is not a regulated market; it is an MTF, which is also designated as an exchange-regulated market or a prescribed market. It is regulated by its operator, the LSE, rather than the competent authority. The ISDX Growth Market is also an exchange-regulated market, regulated by ISDX.

1.2.2 Recognised Investment Exchanges (RIEs)

RIEs were described earlier in Chapter 1 (Section 1.2.6). As a reminder, an RIE is an investment exchange which is considered by the FCA to be fit and proper to act as such, and which, although it is subject to FCA supervision and oversight, is not required to be authorised.

The LSE is an RIE; as such it operates both a regulated market (main market) and an MTF (AIM). Any MTF operated by a UK RIE is described as a prescribed market under the FSMA.

1.2.3 Multilateral Trading Facilities (MTFs)

MTFs were also described in detail in Chapter 1 (Section 1.2.10). As a reminder, they are defined as any system that *'brings together multiple parties (eg, retail investors or other investment firms) that are interested in buying and selling financial instruments and enables them to do so. These systems can be operated by an investment firm or a market operator. Instruments may include shares, bonds and derivatives. This is done within the MTF operators' system'*. Examples include firms such as Chi-X and Turquoise.

Secondary market trading in AIM and main market shares may take place on both RIEs and MTFs.

1.3 Listing Principles

Learning Objective

6.1.4 Know the requirements to be admitted to the High Growth Segment (HGS)

6.1.5 Understand the Listing Principles (LR 7) including the guidance on Listing Principle 2 with regards to procedures, systems and controls (LR 7.2.2)

The Listing Rules Chapter 7 (LR7) contains six high-level listing principles which underpin the listing rules and are enforceable by the FCA in the same way as the rules. These apply only to issuers with a premium listing, in respect of all their obligations arising from the LRs and the DTRs.

The purpose of the principles is to ensure that premium issuers pay due regard to the fundamental role they play in maintaining market confidence and enabling fair and orderly markets, and to assist them in identifying their obligations and responsibilities under the LRs and the DTRs.

1.3.1 The Principles

The six listing principles are:

- **Principle 1** – a listed company must take reasonable steps to enable its directors to understand their responsibilities and obligations as directors.
- **Principle 2** – a listed company must take reasonable steps to establish and maintain adequate procedures, systems and controls to enable it to comply with its obligations.
- **Principle 3** – a listed company must act with integrity towards holders and potential holders of its listed equity shares.
- **Principle 4** – a listed company must communicate information to holders and potential holders of its listed equity shares in such a way as to avoid the creation or continuation of a false market in such listed equity shares.
- **Principle 5** – a listed company must ensure that it treats all holders of the same class of its listed equity shares that are in the same position equally in respect of the rights attaching to such listed equity shares.
- **Principle 6** – a listed company must deal with the FCA in an open and co-operative manner.

1.3.2 Procedures, Systems and Controls

LR7 provides specific guidance on Principle 2, which is intended to ensure that primary issuers have adequate procedures, systems and controls to enable them to comply with their various obligations under the LRs and the DTRs.

In particular, primary issuers should have adequate procedures, systems and controls in order to:

- ensure that they can properly identify obligations concerning significant transactions and related third-party transactions and information which requires disclosure under the LRs or DTRs in a timely manner, and
- ensure that any information identified above is properly considered by the directors and that such a consideration encompasses whether the information should be disclosed.

1.3.3 The High Growth Segment

The High Growth Segment (HGS) is a new segment of the Main Market, designed to assist mid-sized European and UK companies that require access to capital and a public platform to continue their growth.

HGS is for high growth businesses seeking access to the Main Market due to their size and stage of development but that at the point of IPO are not able to meet all the requirements for being on the FCA's Official List.

HGS has EU Regulated Market status to ensure a framework appropriate for larger companies, whereas AIM is not an EU Regulated Market, to allow for a market framework suitable for smaller companies.

What type of company can access HGS?

HGS is for the equity shares of UK and European trading businesses that can demonstrate significant growth in revenues and a longer term aspiration to join the Premium segment of the Main Market.

Specific eligibility criteria include:

- incorporation in an EEA state
- equity shares only
- revenue generating business with historic revenue growth of 20% (CAGR) over a 3-year period;
- minimum free float of 10% with a value of at least £30 million (majority of the £30 million must be raised at admission)
- a Key Adviser (who must be a UKLA approved Sponsor) to be retained at admission and for specific matters including notifiable transactions.

What is the regulatory status of HGS?

As noted, HGS has EU Regulated Market status, but sits outside the UK's Listing Regime. HGS companies would therefore be subject to London Stock Exchange's HGS Rulebook and existing Admission and Disclosure Standards. In addition, as a Regulated Market under the EU FSAP the relevant directives (including the Prospectus Directive, Transparency Directive and the Market Abuse Directive) apply.

A company transitioning from HGS to premium listing would remain on the same EU Regulated Market (the Main Market) but would need to apply for admission to the premium listing category of the Official List in accordance with Listing Rule 3. It would therefore have to meet the eligibility requirements for premium listed companies set out in the Listing Rules. An eligibility letter from a sponsor (setting out how the company satisfies Listing Rule 2 and Listing Rule 6) would also be required. A new prospectus may or may not be required, depending on the specific circumstances of the company. For example, if a company is undertaking a fundraising at the time of transition, the requirement to produce a prospectus may be triggered.

The HGS rules provide an exemption from seeking shareholder approval for cancellation from the segment where a concurrent application is made for admission to the premium segment.

In order to be admitted to HGS, companies must:

- Produce an EU Prospectus, approved by UK's Financial Conduct Authority (FCA) or other EEA competent authority.
- Appoint a Key Adviser, who plays a similar role to a Listing Sponsor, in relation to admission.
- Demonstrate eligibility for the segment, as set out under the HGS Rulebook, and compliance with the London Stock Exchange's HGS Rulebook and the Admission & Disclosure Standards.
- Be approved for admission by London Stock Exchange's Admissions Review Committee.
- On-going requirements as set out in the HGS Rulebook, include:
  - rules around significant transactions and website disclosure
  - requirement to consult a Key Adviser to specific events such as notifiable transactions.
- EU FSAP directives as applicable to Regulated Markets, including the Transparency Directive.
- An annual statement of what corporate governance code has been adopted and to what extent.

1.4   Listing Requirements

Learning Objective

6.1.6   Understand the key requirements for listing (LR 2.2)

The requirements for admission to the official list are contained in the LRs and are separated into those which apply to all issuers, and those which are specific to premium issuers.

The requirements for all securities to be listed (both premium and standard) are:

- Applicants must be duly incorporated in accordance with the law of their place of incorporation, and operate in accordance with their constitution.
- Securities must be duly authorised, conform with the law of the country of incorporation, and have any necessary statutory or other consents.
- Where any securities of a particular class are admitted to listing, all the existing securities and further issues of securities of that class must be admitted to listing.
- Securities must be admitted to trading on an RIE.
- Securities must be freely transferable.
- Shares must be fully paid up and free from liens and any other restrictions on the right of transfer.
- The expected market value of all securities issued by the company, and to be listed, must be at least £700,000 for shares and £200,000 for debt securities. (There are exceptions where the amount of debt securities is not fixed, and also if securities of the same class are already listed).
- A prospectus for the sale or admission to listing of the securities must be approved by the FCA and published in accordance with the prospectus rules.
- If another EEA state is the home member state for the securities, the competent authority of that home state (ie, the national regulator) must supply the FCA with a certificate of approval (a **passport**), a copy of the prospectus as approved and, if applicable, a translation of the summary of the prospectus.
- Convertible securities may be admitted to listing only if the securities into which they are convertible are already, or will become at the time, listed securities or securities listed on a regulated, regularly operating, recognised open market.
- At least 25% of the shares must be available for public trading, ie, not be held by directors or significant shareholders (5%+). This is known as free float.

A premium issuer is subject to additional requirements. The provisions below apply to commercial companies; investment companies, mineral companies and scientific research-based companies are subject to variations on these rules.

- The issuer must have published consolidated, independently audited accounts covering at least three years, with the latest accounts being no more than six months old at the date of its prospectus.
- At least 75% of the applicant's business must be supported by this three-year earning record, and it must carry on an independent business as its main activity and have controlled the majority of its assets for at least three years.
- The issuer must make a clean working capital statement, ie, show that it has sufficient working capital for the next 12 months.

1.5 Disclosure and Transparency

Learning Objective

6.1.7   Understand an issuer's obligation to disclose inside information (DTR 2.2)

6.1.8   Understand when an issuer may delay the public disclosure of inside information (DTR 2.5)

6.1.9   Understand how an issuer must control access to inside information including the requirement to draw up insider lists (DTR 2.6, 2.8)

1.5.1   Continuing Obligations

The continuing obligations for both standard and premium listed companies are contained in part within the listing rules and in part in the DTRs. They govern the conduct of directors of listed companies and the disclosure of information necessary to protect investors, maintain an orderly market and ensure that investors are treated fairly. In addition, the DTRs contain over-arching requirements which relate to the timely and accurate dissemination of inside information.

1.5.2   The Requirement to Disclose Inside Information

This reinforces Part 7, Section 95 of the FSA 2012 Act repealed Section 397 of FSMA and replaced the criminal offence relating to misleading statements and practices with three new criminal offences.

The offences are:

- making false or misleading statements (Section 89)
- creating false or misleading impressions (Section 90), and
- making false or misleading statements or creating false or misleading impressions in relation to specified benchmarks (Section 91).

The first two offences together largely replicate the now-repealed FSMA Section 397 offence. The misleading impressions offence, however, is now wider in scope and covers recklessly created misleading impressions as well as those created intentionally.

Chapter 9 of the LRs sets out a number of specific disclosures which an issuer must make. These relate, in particular, to new issues or redemptions or securities; to corporate actions such as dividends, rights issues or bonus issues; and to changes to the company's name, registered office or directors.

The central requirement is set out at DTR 2.2, which provides that a premium or standard issuer must make a public disclosure, through an RIS (described further later in this section), of any inside information which directly concerns it, and that this disclosure should be made as soon as possible.

Inside information is defined as information which is:

- specific to the issuer or its securities
- not in the public domain
- precise, and
- price-sensitive with regard to the issuer's securities.

In determining whether the information is price-sensitive, the issuer should apply the **reasonable investor** test, whereby he considers whether the information would be used by a reasonable investor as the basis of his investment decisions, and would thereby have a significant effect on the price of the issuer's securities.

Examples of inside information which could require disclosure include:

- changes in expectations of the company's profits, including major new contracts or losses
- material transactions, including acquisitions, disposals or joint ventures
- appointment or resignation of senior management
- changes to the financial stability of the company (such as withdrawal of lending facilities). Such disclosures must be made without delay, unless the provisions at Section 1.5.3 below apply.

Such disclosures must be made without delay, unless the provisions at Section 1.5.3 below apply.

A fundamental requirement of the inside information regime is the equal treatment of shareholders, who are entitled to receive inside information in the same way and at the same time. To achieve this, all regulatory disclosures required must be disclosed to the market through an RIS as soon as possible, prior to being disclosed to third parties.

An RIS is a firm that has been approved by the FCA to disseminate regulatory announcements to the market on behalf of listed companies. All listed companies must retain at least one RIS, and only regulatory announcements must be made through this mechanism. Once an announcement is sent to the RIS, the company's disclosure obligation is met. The RIS is then required to release the announcement to the markets through its links with secondary information providers such as data providers, newswires and the news media.

A company that provides inside information via an RIS must also make the information available on its own website by the close of the business day following the day of the RIS announcement. A company must ensure that such inside information is notified to an RIS before, or simultaneously with, publication of such information on its own website; it must not post inside information on its website before announcing it to the market.

In addition, the company must take reasonable care, without prejudice to its obligations in the UK under the FCA's LRs, to ensure that the disclosure of inside information to the public is synchronised as closely as possible in all jurisdictions where it has securities listed on a regulated market.

1.5.3 Delaying Disclosure of Inside Information

DTR 2.5 provides that an issuer may, under its own responsibility, delay the public disclosure of inside information, so as not to prejudice its legitimate interests, providing that:

- such omission will not be likely to mislead the public
- any person receiving the information owes the issuer a duty of confidentiality, regardless of whether such duty is based on law, regulations, articles of association or contract, and
- the issuer is able to ensure the confidentiality of that information.

Delaying disclosure of inside information will not always mislead the public, although a developing situation should be monitored so that if circumstances change an immediate disclosure can be made. Investors understand that some information – such as discussions regarding an acquisition – must be kept confidential until developments are at a stage when an announcement can be made without prejudicing the legitimate interests of the company.

1.5.4 Secrecy and Confidentiality

Following on from this, the DTR further provides a requirement for issuers to control undisclosed inside information in such a way as to prevent leaks. This particularly relates to developments or matters in the course of negotiation, when (apart from advisers) there must be no selective dissemination of information, and such matters that are in the course of negotiation must be kept confidential.

DTR guidance provides, however, that an issuer may disclose inside information selectively to persons owing it a duty of confidentiality, providing that they are validly involved in the matter which is the subject of the inside information. As well as relevant employees of the issuer, this may include, for example, its:

- advisers, and the advisers of any other party to the negotiations
- major shareholders
- bankers
- counterparties in negotiations
- potential underwriters
- employee representatives or trade unions
- government, statutory or regulatory authorities;
- credit rating agencies.

It may not always be appropriate to disclose inside information to all or any of these parties.

In any other circumstance, where inside information has been inadvertently or intentionally selectively disclosed, it must be disclosed to the market, via an RIS, as soon as possible.

1.5.5 Control of Inside Information

Companies must establish effective arrangements to deny access to inside information to persons other than those who require it for the exercise of their functions within the company. A company must have measures in place that enable public disclosure to be made via an RIS as soon as possible, in case they are unable to ensure the confidentiality of the relevant inside information. This ties in with the requirements of general principle 2, discussed in Section 1.3.2 above.

If an issuer is relying on the rules on delaying disclosure of inside information, as noted above, it should prepare a holding announcement to be disclosed in the event of an actual or likely breach of confidence.

1.5.6   Insider Lists

As part of the control of inside information, a premium or standard issuer must ensure that it, and persons acting on its behalf or on its account, draw up a list of those persons working for them, whether under a contract of employment or otherwise, who have access to inside information relating directly or indirectly to the issuer, whether on a regular or occasional basis. This applies to all staff, irrespective of their seniority or employment status.

This must be readily available to provide to the FCA on request.

Every insider list must contain the following information:

- the identity of each person having access to inside information
- the reason why such person is on the insider list
- the date on which the insider list was created and updated.

An insider list must be promptly updated:

- when there is a change in the reason why a person is already on the list
- when any person who is not already on the list is provided with access to inside information
- to indicate the date on which a person already on the list no longer has access to inside information.

Companies must also ensure that every insider list prepared by it, or by persons acting on its account or on its behalf, is kept for at least five years from the date on which it is drawn up or updated, whichever is the latest. The company, and not its advisers or agents, is ultimately responsible for the maintenance of insider lists.

Further, the company must include on the list the names of its principal contacts at any other firm or company acting on its behalf or on its account with whom it has had direct contact and who also has access to inside information about it. The issuer must contractually require such third parties to also maintain insider lists, detailing all those who both work on that issuer's business and have access to inside information on that issuer.

Companies must take the necessary measures to ensure that their employees with access to inside information acknowledge the legal and regulatory duties entailed (including dealing restrictions in relation to the issuer's financial instruments) and are aware of the sanctions attaching to the misuse or improper circulation of such information, with particular reference to market abuse and insider dealing.

1.6   The Sponsor's Role

Learning Objective

6.1.10   Understand: the requirement for a company with a premium listing to appoint a sponsor (LR 8.2); the role of a sponsor generally; the role of a sponsor on a transaction (LR 8.3, 8.4)

1.6.1   When a Sponsor Must be Appointed

A company with, or applying for, a premium listing of its equities must appoint a sponsor to advise it on certain transactions. There is no requirement for the sponsor to be an LSE member firm, but it must be a firm approved as a sponsor by the FCA as having adequate experience, skills and resources to advise issuers in the UK equity markets.

There is no ongoing requirement for a company to maintain the services of a sponsor firm, outside of the transactions shown below. No sponsor is required for a standard listed company.

Under Rule 8.2 of the LRs, a premium issuer must appoint a sponsor to advise it when it:

- makes an application for admission of equity shares which requires the production of a prospectus or where the prospectus is passported by another competent authority
- is required to produce a Class 1 circular, a circular in relation to a reconstruction or refinancing or a circular for a share buyback including a working capital statement
- applies to transfer its listing category from a standard listing to a premium listing, or
- is required to do so by the FCA because it appears to the FCA that there is or may be a breach of the LRs or DTRs.

If an issuer is considering entering into a transaction which might be a Class 1 or related party transaction, it must seek the advice of a firm which is approved as a sponsor firm, in order to establish its obligations under the LRs or DTRs. These transactions are discussed in more detail in Section 1.9.

1.6.2   Duties of Sponsors

Chapter 8 of the LRs sets out the requirements for sponsors, including high-level principles. The principles for sponsors are:

- A sponsor must, in relation to a sponsor service, act with due care and skill.
- Where a sponsor provides guidance to a listed company, it must be satisfied that the directors of the listed company understand their responsibilities and obligations under the LRs and the DTRs.
- It must deal with the FCA in an open and co-operative way and deal with all enquiries raised by the FCA promptly at all times and whether acting on sponsor services or not.
- It must disclose to the FCA in a timely manner when it has knowledge relating to the sponsor or the issuer which concerns non-compliance with the LRs and the DTRs.
- It must take all reasonable steps to identify conflicts of interest that could adversely affect its ability to perform its function properly in accordance with its role as a sponsor.
- It must put in place and maintain effective organisational and administrative arrangements that ensure conflicts of interest do not adversely affect its ability to perform its function properly in accordance with its role as a sponsor. If the sponsor is not reasonably satisfied that its arrangements will ensure that a conflict of interest will not adversely affect its ability to perform its functions properly, then it must decline to provide sponsor services on the transaction.

If a company appoints more than one sponsor to provide sponsor services in relation to a transaction, then the appointment does not relieve either of the appointed sponsors of their obligations. Each sponsor will be responsible for complying with the duties and obligations in relation to the transaction.

1.6.3 Role of a Sponsor on Transactions

In general, where a sponsor is appointed, it is required to liaise with the FCA, to submit all documents required to the FCA, and to submit the application for listing or circular to the FCA on behalf of its client.

In compliance with the principles set out above, it must also submit a conflicts declaration to the FCA. This confirms to the FCA that it has taken all steps to ensure that any conflicts of interest are being managed in such a way that it is not prevented from carrying out its responsibilities.

In addition, the sponsor has specific responsibilities, depending on whether it is advising an issuer on an initial listing, a secondary offering of securities, or a material transaction.

1.6.4 New Applications for Listing and Further Issues of Securities

In relation to an initial offering of shares, a sponsor must only submit to the FCA an application for admission to listing on behalf of an applicant when it has come to a reasonable opinion, after having made due and careful enquiry, that the:

- applicant has satisfied all requirements of the LRs relevant to an application for admission to listing
- applicant has satisfied all applicable requirements set out in the prospectus rules (unless the home member state of the applicant is not, or will not be, the UK)
- directors of the applicant have established procedures which enable the applicant to comply with the LRs and the DTRs on an ongoing basis
- directors of the applicant have established procedures which provide a reasonable basis for them to make proper judgements, on an ongoing basis, as to the financial position and prospects of the applicant and its group
- directors of the applicant have a reasonable basis on which to make the working capital statement required.

A sponsor must complete a sponsor's declaration, confirming the above, at the time of an application for listing as well as a shareholder statement or pricing statement. These must be submitted to the FCA on the day that the FCA is to consider the application for approval of the prospectus.

1.6.5 Class 1 Circulars, Share Buy-Backs and Refinancings

In relation to the publication of circulars, a sponsor must submit to the FCA an application for approval of a circular only when it has come to a reasonable opinion, after having made due and careful enquiry, that:

- the applicant has satisfied all requirements of the LRs relevant to the production of the circular
- the transaction will not have an adverse impact on the issuer's ability to comply with the LRs or DTRs, and
- the directors of the applicant have a reasonable basis on which to make the working capital statement required.

1.7 Bringing Securities to Listing

Learning Objective

6.1.11 Understand the main methods of bringing a company's shares to listing and the differences between them, eg, introduction, offer for sale, offer for subscription, placing, rights issue, open offer and vendor consideration placing

1.7.1 Primary Offerings

An IPO is also referred to as a flotation, and is the first time that a company offers shares to the public through a stock exchange.

There are five main methods for a new applicant to bring their securities to listing for the first time. They are referred to as primary offerings, and are:

- offer for sale
- offer for subscription
- intermediaries offer
- placing
- introduction.

An introduction does not involve an offer of shares for sale; rather, it merely allows a company's existing shareholders to trade their shares on a stock exchange. The other four methods are known as marketing operations, as the company offers shares for sale and must take steps to market them effectively.

Offer for Sale

In an offer for sale, the company offers shares for sale to the institutional investors and the retail public. These shares may have involved a new issue of shares by the company, for on-sale in the IPO, or they may be shares being sold by the company's existing shareholders, seeking a realisation of their investment. Either way, the offer itself is co-ordinated by the company's investment bank.

In most cases, the company will enter into agreements with underwriters whereby the underwriters undertake to acquire any unsold shares at the full offer price. Although this adds to the costs, it guarantees the issuer the full proceeds of the offer, and reduces the risk posed by volatile market conditions.

In the 1980s, many of the UK privatisations were offers for sale, when a broker acted on behalf of the government to sell stakes in privatised companies such as British Gas and BP back to taxpayers.

Offer for Subscription

An offer for subscription involves the company issuing new shares in response to applications for shares. The difference between this and an offer for sale is that the shares themselves are not physically in existence until applications have been received from investors, who become **subscribers** for the shares.

Offers for subscriptions are commonly used in fundraisings by investment companies. In addition, there are tax benefits available for investors in unlisted companies (in particular, AIM and ISDX Growth Market companies) which are only available on a subscription for shares and placings of newly issued shares.

As with an offer for sale, offers for subscription are likely to be underwritten.

Intermediaries Offer

An intermediary offer is similar to an offer of subscription, except an intermediary such as a bank or stockbroker acts as a conduit to gather investors from among its clients. Intermediary offers may or may not be underwritten.

Placing

This is the quickest and cheapest and most certain route open to a company to raise new funds. A company arranges for its investment bank to place blocks of new or existing securities with the bank's investor client base and other institutional contacts. This is sometimes referred to as selective marketing, as the new securities are not offered to the wider community of institutional investors. This reduces the cost and time required for marketing the issue, and may avoid underwriting costs.

A placing may be used in either a primary or a secondary offering, and may be used as a stand-alone route to an IPO or alongside an offer for sale, offer for subscription and/or an intermediaries offer to widen the number of potential investors.

Introduction

This method does not involve an issue of new shares. Instead, shares which are already widely held are admitted to listing. An introduction is only available to an issuer when the shares are already of such amount and are so widely held that their marketability can be assured once they are listed. For example, it might be used by a company which has an overseas listing, and is seeking a secondary listing in the UK; or when a company is already admitted to AIM and is now seeking a **move up** to the main market.

1.7.2 Secondary Offerings

An existing issuer may seek to raise additional equity capital through one of the following methods, all of which are referred to as secondary offerings:

- rights issue
- secondary placing
- open offer
- vendor consideration placing.

These are all discussed further below in this section.

When considering secondary offerings, we must take pre-emption rights into account (these were discussed earlier in Chapter 1, Section 3.2.2). As a reminder, companies listed in the UK are required to have pre-emption rights in their articles of association. These require a company which seeks to issue new shares in exchange for cash, to offer these shares in the first instance to its existing shareholders in proportion to their existing shareholdings.

Rights Issue

A rights issue is a transaction where a company offers all its existing shareholders the opportunity to buy further shares in that company in accordance with their pre-emption rights. In a rights issue, shareholders are offered shares pro-rata to their existing holding, at a discount to the existing market price. For example, in a 1 for 5 rights issue, shareholders are sent a transferable provisional allotment letter setting out their entitlement to buy one new share for every five that they currently hold. Shareholders may take up their entitlement and buy the shares; they may reject the offer; or they may sell their entitlement to third parties, at a price reflecting the level of the discount, by selling the provisional allotment letter.

In most cases, the company enters into underwriting agreements with their investment bank, which guarantee that they receive the money that they require from the rights issue. If, however, the shares are offered at a deep discount to the pre-offer share price, there may be no requirement for underwriting, or the fee will be relatively low.

Open Offer

An open offer is also a pre-emptive offer to existing shareholders to subscribe or purchase further shares in proportion to their existing shareholdings. However, unlike a rights issue, an open offer does not give shareholders a right to sell their entitlement to new shares, and the maximum price discount permissible (for listed companies) is 10%. As a result it is seen to be less attractive to shareholders than a rights issue, and may have a lower chance of being successful. It is therefore common practice to combine an open offer with a placing, designed in effect to underwrite the open offer by ensuring that the company has also identified institutional investors who are committed to taking up any unsold shares. An open offer also has a slightly shorter timescale, and is a quicker method of raising money for the issuer than a rights issue.

Vendor Consideration Placing

A vendor consideration placing (or vendor placing) is a way of raising a relatively small sum of money to finance an acquisition. It involves the issue of new shares to the vendor of the acquisition target as consideration for the acquisition, with a pre-arranged placing of these consideration shares in order to convert them into cash for the vendor. It is most easily explained using an illustration, as follows:

Example

Company A plc plans to acquire a small company, B Ltd and wants to use its own shares as consideration. However, the shareholders of B Ltd (the vendors) only wish to accept cash and refuse to take the shares in A plc as payment.

A plc is considering how to raise the cash. It has no cash and no debt capacity. The cost and time involved in a pre-emptive issue of shares to raise cash would be disproportionate to the size of the transaction. A placing to raise the cash will require shareholder approval for the disapplication of pre-emption rights – again, expensive and time-consuming. It decides on a vendor placing, and the acquisition will take the following form:

A plc issues new shares to the vendors of B Ltd in consideration for the shares in B Ltd. It has agreed in advance with its investment bank that these new shares will immediately be placed, on behalf of the vendors, with institutional and other investors. The placing realises cash that can be paid to the vendors, who are now effectively receiving cash consideration.

This issue of shares has been made in exchange for the B Ltd shares, and not in exchange for cash, so that it does not breach the pre-emption right rules.

1.8 Vote Holder and Notification Rules

Learning Objective

6.1.12 Understand the vote holder and issuer notification rules (DTR 5)

1.8.1 Notification of the Acquisition or Disposal of Major Shareholdings

Under DTR Chapter 5, a person must notify an issuer when the percentage of its voting rights that it holds either as a shareholder or directly or indirectly through other financial instruments reaches certain thresholds. The requirement could arise either as a result of the person's acquisition or disposal of shares or financial instruments; or as a result of events changing the breakdown of voting rights (such as a new share issue or redemption of shares). Note that disclosure is required in respect of indirect holdings; this is discussed in Section 1.8.2 below.

The thresholds depend on the identity of the issuer, as follows:

- If the issuer is listed and incorporated in the UK, disclosure is needed if the percentage reaches, exceeds or falls below 3% and each 1% thereafter up to 100%.
- In respect of a non-UK issuer, the thresholds requiring disclosure are 5%, 10%, 15%, 20%, 25%, 30%, 50% and 75%. These thresholds also apply to a UK issuer if the shareholder is a regulated discretionary investment manager or regulated CIS.

The following exceptions to the disclosure requirements apply:

- Shares held by a **custodian** (or nominee) in its capacity, whether operating from an establishment in the UK or elsewhere, providing that such a person can only exercise voting rights attached to such shares under instructions given in writing or by electronic means by the ultimate underlying beneficial owners.
- Shares held by an authorised **market maker** acting only in that capacity, if the threshold for disclosure is 10% and each percentage point thereafter.
- Shares held by a **credit institution or investment firm** providing that they are held within the trading book, and that they do not use the voting rights to intervene in the management of the underlying company; here the threshold for disclosure is 5% and each percentage point thereafter.
- Shares held by a **collateral taker** under a collateral transaction which involves the outright transfer of securities providing that the collateral taker does not declare any intention of exercising (and does not exercise) the voting rights attached to such shares.
- Shares provided by a borrower under a **stock lending** agreement providing that such shares (or equivalent) are on-lent or otherwise disposed of by the borrower by not later than close of business on the next trading day, or the borrower does not declare any intention of exercising (and does not exercise) the voting rights attaching to the shares.

1.8.2   Acquisition or Disposal of Major Proportions of Voting Rights

A person is an indirect holder of shares for the purpose of the applicable definition of shareholder to the extent that he is entitled to acquire, dispose of or exercise voting rights in any of the following cases or a combination of them:

a. Voting rights held by a third party with whom that person has concluded an agreement, which obliges them to adopt, by concerted exercise of the voting rights they hold, a lasting common policy towards the management of the issuer in question.

b. Voting rights held by a third party under an agreement concluded with that person providing for the temporary transfer for consideration of the voting rights in question.

c. Voting rights attaching to shares which are lodged as collateral with that person providing that person controls the voting rights and declares their intention of exercising them.

d. Voting rights attaching to shares in which that person has the life interest.

e. Voting rights which are held, or may be exercised, within the meaning of points (a) to (d) or, in cases (f) and (h), by a person undertaking investment management, or by a management company, or by an undertaking controlled by that person.

f. Voting rights attaching to shares deposited with that person which the person can exercise at its discretion in the absence of specific instructions from the shareholders.

g. Voting rights held by a third party in his own name on behalf of that person.

h. Voting rights which that person may exercise as a proxy when that person can exercise the voting rights at his discretion in the absence of specific instructions from the shareholders.

1.8.3   Qualifying Financial Instruments

The notifications in Section 1.8.1 above apply to any qualifying financial instruments held by a person, directly or indirectly, unless the financial instruments are held by a person who is a client-serving intermediary acting in a client-serving capacity, who is appropriately authorised under MiFID or the Banking Consolidation Directive (BCD) (the EU directive on credit institutions).

Qualifying financial instruments include:

*   transferable securities (including shares)
*   options, futures, swaps, contracts for difference and any other derivative contracts, providing:
    *   that they provide an entitlement to acquire, on the holder's own initiative alone, under a formal agreement, shares of the issuer which are already issued and to which voting rights are attached, and
    *   that the instrument holder will enjoy, on maturity, either the unconditional right or the discretion to acquire the underlying shares, under a formal, legally binding agreement.

1.8.4 Disclosures by Issuers

Under DTR 5.6, in order to enable vote-holders to establish their percentage holding, the issuer must update the market with changes to its total voting rights (TVR).

At the end of each calendar month during which it has increased or decreased its share capital, an issuer must disclose through an RIS:

a. the total amount of voting rights and capital in respect of each class of share which it issues, and
b. the total number of voting rights attaching to the issuer's shares which are held in treasury.

However, when during the calendar month there is an increase or decrease in total voting rights of 10% or more (for example, due to a rights issue or share buy-back) this must be announced immediately and no later than the close of business on the business day following the change of TVR.

1.8.5 Aggregation of Holdings

A person making the required notification must do so by reference to each of the following:

- the aggregate of all voting rights which the person holds as shareholder and as the direct or indirect holder of qualifying financial instruments and financial instruments with similar economic effects
- the aggregate of all voting rights held as direct or indirect shareholder (disregarding for this purpose holdings of financial instruments)
- the aggregate of all voting rights held as a result of direct and indirect holdings of qualifying financial instruments
- the aggregate of all voting rights deemed to be held as a result of direct and indirect holdings of financial instruments having similar economic effects to (but not including) qualifying financial instruments.

1.8.6 Procedures for the Notification and Disclosure of Major Holdings

The disclosure of major holdings must be made to the issuer of the underlying shares, as well as to the competent authority (the FCA, for UK companies). It must be made as soon as possible, but no later than two trading days after the vote-holder becomes aware of their holding (extended to four trading days for holders in non-UK issuers).

The notification must include:

- the resulting situation in terms of voting rights
- the chain of controlled undertakings through which voting rights are effectively held, if applicable
- the date on which the threshold was reached or crossed
- the identity of the shareholder, even if that shareholder is not entitled to exercise voting rights under certain specific conditions and of the person entitled to exercise voting rights on behalf of that shareholder.

A notification of voting rights arising from the holding of financial instruments must include the following information:

- the resulting situation in terms of voting rights
- if applicable, the chain of controlled undertakings through which financial instruments are effectively held
- the date on which the threshold was reached or crossed
- for instruments with an exercise period, an indication of the date or time period in which shares will or can be acquired, if applicable
- date of maturity or expiration of the instrument
- identity of the holder
- name of the underlying issuer.

1.9 Classifying Transactions

Learning Objective

6.1.13 Understand the class tests for proposed transactions entered into by companies with a premium listing (LR 10.2.2, 10.2.3)

If a premium listed company enters into a transaction of a non-revenue nature, outside the normal course of business, it is required to establish whether it is sufficiently material to require shareholder approval or specific disclosure. The transaction might be an acquisition, a disposal, or a purchase or sale of a capital asset such as a property, or it could include other contracts such as indemnities or break fees. These requirements do not apply to standard listed companies.

1.9.1 The Class Tests

To establish the materiality of a transaction, the size of the asset or business being acquired or disposed of is compared to the size of the listed company, using four **class tests**. These are:

- **gross assets test** – a division of the gross assets of the transaction target by the gross assets of the listed company, with gross assets defined as the total current assets plus the total non-current assets
- **profits test** – a division of the attributable profits of the transaction target by the profits of the listed company, with profits defined as profit after all deductions except taxation
- **consideration test** – a division of the total consideration paid or received for the target, by the market capitalisation of the listed company on the last business day before the announcement of the transaction
- **gross capital test** – a division of the gross capital of the transaction target by the gross capital of the listed company. Gross capital for the listed company is defined as its market capitalisation plus its net debt; gross capital for the target is defined as sum of the consideration, the value of any shares or debt not being acquired, any other non-current liabilities and the total of any excess of current liabilities over current assets.

Applying each test will result in the calculation of a percentage, and the highest percentage calculated will determine the class of transaction, and so the action required by the listed company.

- **Class 3 transaction** – a transaction in which all percentage ratios are less than 5%. In a Class 3 transaction, there is no requirement to disclose the transaction to the market, unless:
  a. new shares are to be issued in connection with the transaction, or
  b. a press release is issued.
- **Class 2 transaction** – a transaction in which any percentage ratio is 5% or more, but each is less than 25%. In this case, the listed company must disclose the transaction to the market, as soon as it is agreed, with full details of the transaction.
- **Class 1 transaction** – a transaction in which any percentage ratio is 25% or more. This requires shareholder approval through the passing of an ordinary resolution at a GM. The notice for the GM must be contained in a circular to shareholders, which must be approved by the FCA.
- **Reverse takeover** – a transaction consisting of an acquisition by a listed company of a business, an unlisted company or assets in which any percentage ratio is 100% or more or which would result in a fundamental change in the business or in a change in the board or voting control of the listed company. This transaction will also require shareholder approval, as for a Class 1 transaction. However, given the size of the transaction it is likely that the consideration will include the issue of new shares; when considering the application for admission to listing for these new shares, the FCA will generally treat this as a new listing, and thus requires a prospectus.

Note that a sponsor must be appointed to advise on a Class 1 transaction or reverse takeover, and to assist with the preparation and approval of the circular. If an issuer is in any doubt as to whether a transaction is a Class 1 transaction or reverse takeover, it is required to appoint a firm which is approved as a sponsor, to advise it on the matter.

Example

Builder plc, a premium issuer, has a market capitalisation of £1 billion, gross assets of £500 million, attributable profits of £200 million and gross capital of £1.2 billion.

Builder is proposing to acquire House Ltd for a consideration of £200 million. House has attributable profits of £20 million, gross capital of £250 million and gross assets of £150 million.

	Builder	House	
	£m	£m	%
Consideration	1,000	200	20
Gross assets	500	150	30
Profit	200	20	10
Gross capital	1,200	250	21

As the gross assets test generates a percentage ratio of 30%, the acquisition is classified as a Class 1 transaction and requires shareholder approval.

2. Rules Specific to the Alternative Investment Market (AIM)

2.1 The AIM Market

Learning Objective

6.2.1 Understand the status of AIM as an 'exchange-regulated market' and a prescribed market

AIM was first established by the LSE in 1995. It was originally intended to be a junior market providing light-touch regulation for smaller businesses. Over the years a wide range of businesses, including early stage and venture capital-backed, as well as more established companies from the UK and overseas, have joined AIM, seeking access to growth capital.

AIM is classified as an exchange-regulated market, whereas the main market is classified as an EU-regulated market. This means that the AIM does not meet the requirements to be a regulated market under MiFID and is not regulated by the FCA in its capacity as a competent authority for regulated markets. Instead it is regulated by its owner and operator, which is the LSE in its capacity as an RIE under Part XVIII of FSMA 2000. AIM therefore falls within the definition of a prescribed market under FSMA 2000 and is subject to the UK market abuse regime. Under the directives that form the EU's FSAP, AIM is not a regulated market but instead falls within the classification of an MTF as defined under MiFID and a prescribed market and exchange regulated market by the FCA.

Companies wishing to list on AIM apply to the LSE itself, which decides who joins this junior market.

2.2 Admission Requirements for the AIM Market

Learning Objective

6.2.2 Know the criteria for admission to AIM

For a company to be admitted to trading on AIM it must be incorporated as a plc (or the equivalent if incorporated overseas). Its shares must be freely transferable. However, there is no minimum free float, no minimum trading history and no minimum market value of the shares.

It must normally publish an admission document (or prospectus), which must be available publicly, free of charge, for at least one month from the admission of the applicant's securities to AIM.

At least ten business days before its expected admission to AIM, the applicant must provide the LSE with the following information in the form of a pre-admission announcement:

- its name
- its country of incorporation
- its registered office address and, if different, its trading address
- the website address at which the information required by AIM rule 26 will be available
- a brief description of its business (including its main country of operation) or, in the case of an investing company, details of its investing policy. If the admission is being sought as a result of a reverse takeover under AIM rule 14, this should be stated
- the number and type of securities in respect of which it seeks admission and detailing the number and type of securities to be held as treasury shares, including details of any restrictions as to transfer of the securities
- the capital to be raised on admission, if applicable, and its anticipated market capitalisation on admission
- the percentage of AIM securities not in public hands at admission (insofar as it is aware) and details of any other exchange or trading platform on which AIM securities (or any other securities of the company) are or will be admitted or traded as a result of an application or agreement of the applicant
- the full names and functions of its directors and proposed directors (underlining the first name by which each is known or including any other name by which each is known)
- insofar as is known to it, the full name of any significant shareholder (3%+), director or proposed director before and after admission, together with the percentage of each such person's interest (underlining the first name by which each is known or including any other name by which each is known in the case of individuals)
- the names of any persons who will be disclosed in the admission document as receiving fees (other than in the ordinary course of business) totalling £10,000 or more in the 12 months prior to admission or in relation to admission
- its anticipated accounting reference date, the date at which it has prepared the main financial information in its admission document and the dates by which it must publish its first three reports
- its expected admission date
- the name and address of its nominated adviser and broker.

At least three business days before the expected date of admission, an applicant must submit to the LSE a completed application form and an electronic version of its admission document. These must be accompanied by the nomad's declaration confirming the applicant's suitability for admission to AIM, as required by the AIM Rules for nomads.

Admission becomes effective only when the LSE issues a dealing notice to that effect. The LSE may make the admission of an applicant subject to a special condition.

2.3 AIM Rules and other Regulatory Requirements

Learning Objective

6.2.3 Know that AIM companies must comply with the AIM Rules for Companies and, when appropriate, the PR and DTR

AIM is renowned worldwide for its balanced approach to regulation which is uniquely suited to smaller companies. AIM rules are concise and principles based. They are divided into AIM rules for:

- companies
- nomads.

Because of the light-touch nature of the AIM regime, a significant emphasis is placed on the role of AIM nomads who are responsible for advising AIM companies on the interpretation of, and compliance with, the rules on an ongoing basis.

Additionally, a company seeking admission to AIM is subject to the requirements of the prospectus rules (discussed further below in Section 2.6 and in Chapter 5 of this workbook) and, on an ongoing basis, to certain provisions of the DTRs.

The rules on the disclosure of major interests in shares (provided in Chapter 5 of the DTRs, and detailed at Section 1.8.6 above) apply to those AIM companies which are incorporated under the Companies Act or which are incorporated and have their principal place of business in the UK. They do not apply to non-UK companies quoted on AIM, who are subject to their home state rules on vote-holder notifications.

2.4 Nominated Advisers (Nomads) and Brokers

Learning Objective

6.2.4 Know the requirement for AIM companies to appoint a nominated adviser and (nomad) a broker

Under the AIM Rules for Companies, an AIM company must retain the services of a nomad at all times. The nomad is responsible to the LSE for assessing the appropriateness of an applicant to the AIM, and for advising and guiding an AIM company on its responsibilities under the AIM Rules for Companies. The nomad must be approved by the LSE and included on the current nomad register maintained by the LSE.

In addition, an AIM company must at all times retain the services of a broker (which must be a securities house which is a member of the LSE) to support trading in the company's shares, and to assist in pricing and marketing in a flotation. If the company does not have a market maker registered for its shares, the broker must use its best endeavours to find matching business in the company's shares.

The nomad and the broker can be the same firm, providing that procedures are in place to manage conflicts of interest arising in the course of fundraising.

If an AIM company ceases to have a nomad, the LSE will suspend trading in its AIM securities. If within one month of that suspension the AIM company has failed to appoint a replacement nomad, its admission will be cancelled.

When a new nomad is appointed, the AIM company must notify the market of that fact, and the nomad itself must submit a new nomad's declaration to the LSE, pursuant to the AIM rules for nomads.

2.5 The Duties of the Nominated Adviser

Learning Objective

6.2.5 Know the duties of the nomad and that the nomad must comply with the AIM Rules for nomads

The main duties of the nomad are to confirm to the LSE that a company is appropriate for AIM, and to ensure it remains appropriate for AIM and is able to comply with the AIM rules on an ongoing basis.

These duties are broken down in the AIM rules for nomads into a number of different areas.

2.5.1 Eligibility

A firm seeking approval as a nomad must be, and continue to be, eligible to perform this function. In particular, it must:

- be a firm or company (individuals are not eligible)
- have practised corporate finance for at least the last two years
- have acted on at least three relevant transactions during that two-year period, and
- employ at least four qualified executives.

A qualified executive is:

- a full-time employee of the applicant
- someone who has acted in a corporate finance advisory role, which may include the regulation of corporate finance, for at least the last three years, and
- someone who has acted in a lead corporate finance role on at least three relevant transactions in that three-year period.

A proposed qualified executive must be able to demonstrate a sound understanding of the UK corporate finance market and AIM in particular.

Once approved as a nomad, the firm must continue to maintain its eligibility by maintaining sufficient qualified employees and continuing to act on relevant transactions.

2.5.2 Admission

On advising a company on seeking admission to AIM, the nomad must assess the appropriateness of that company for admission to AIM, using third-party resources as appropriate.

As part of this obligation, it is required to carry out extensive due diligence on the company (with reference to a prescriptive list of measures set out in the rules). It must also assess the company's board of directors and the suitability of the directors, and confirm that these directors understand their obligations under the AIM rules. They are required to oversee and have an active involvement in the preparation of the admission document or prospectus, and confirm to the LSE in writing the information provided in relation to AIM applicants.

2.5.3 Ongoing Obligations

The nomad must be available at all times to advise and guide the directors of its AIM clients about their obligations and to ensure compliance with the AIM rules, and must ensure that at least two members of staff are allocated to that company, of whom at least one is a qualified executive.

It must liaise with the LSE in any requests for information and inform the LSE as soon as practicable of any rule breach by its clients or itself.

It must review regularly the AIM company's financial trading performance and condition against any profit forecast, estimate or projection made by it, to evaluate whether an announcement is required. In this regard, it should review all announcements made by its clients in advance of their publication.

There is a general obligation to act with due skill and care at all times, as well as remaining independent and managing any conflicts of interest.

2.6 Prospectus Rules

Learning Objective

6.2.6 Understand when an AIM company will be required to issue a prospectus complying with the PRs

If a company proposes to seek admission to AIM in an offer for sale or subscription (ie, an offer which is not to qualified investors only) it must issue a prospectus (unless the issue falls within one of the prospectus rules exemptions). If it proposes to apply to AIM through an introduction, or placing, it will benefit from the exemption available in the prospectus rules, so that no prospectus is required. Instead, it is required to produce an admission document meeting the requirements of the AIM rules for companies, which prescribe an abbreviated form of the prospectus rules.

If a prospectus is required, this must be approved by the FCA before it is published. If an admission document is required, there is no requirement for approval either by the FCA or by the LSE; however, the company's nomad must approve its publication, and it must be made available both in hard copy and on the issuer's website.

A quoted applicant (already quoted for 18 months on an AIM-designated market) is not required to produce an admission document unless otherwise required by the PRs. Instead, it must submit its latest report and accounts, together with a detailed pre-admission announcement, to the LSE. An AIM-designated market is a market that AIM considers to have an acceptable standard of regulation, and includes the UK main market, the NYSE and the Johannesburg Stock Exchange (JSE), amongst others.

2.7 Disclosure Requirements around Price-Sensitive Information

Learning Objective

6.2.7   Know the requirement for the management and disclosure of price-sensitive information (AIM Rule 11)

AIM companies have the following ongoing obligations to:

- publish price-sensitive information without delay regarding their financial condition, sphere of activity and actual or expected performance
- disclose details of significant transactions
- seek shareholder approval for any transaction which qualifies as a reverse takeover
- ensure directors and applicable employees do not trade during a close period.

Within these requirements, the following specific rules apply.

The main requirement is that under AIM Rule 11, an AIM company must issue notification without delay of any new developments which are not public knowledge concerning a change in:

- its financial condition
- its sphere of activity
- the performance of its business
- its expectation of its performance

which, if made public, would be likely to lead to a substantial movement in the price of its AIM securities. The requirements of Rule 11 are in addition to any requirements regarding notification contained elsewhere in the rules.

An AIM company need not notify information about impending developments or matters in the course of negotiation and may give such information in confidence to:

- the AIM company's advisers and advisers of any other persons involved or who may be involved in the development or matter in question;
- persons with whom the AIM company is negotiating, or intends to negotiate, any commercial, financial or investment transaction (including prospective underwriters or placees of its securities);
- representatives of its employees or trades unions acting on their behalf;
- any government department, the BoE, the CMA or any other statutory or regulatory body or authority.

The AIM company must be satisfied that such recipients of information are aware that they must not trade in its AIM securities before the relevant information has been notified.

However, if the AIM company has reason to believe that a breach of such confidence has occurred or is likely to occur and, in either case, the matter is such that knowledge of it would be likely to lead to substantial movement in the price of its AIM securities, it must, without delay, issue at least a warning notification to the effect that it expects shortly to release information regarding such matter.

When such information has been made public, the AIM company must notify that information without delay. The information that is required by these rules must be notified by the AIM company no later than it is published elsewhere. An AIM company must retain a regulatory information service provider to ensure that information can be notified as and when required.

An AIM company must take reasonable care to ensure that any information it notifies is not misleading, false or deceptive and does not omit anything likely to affect the import of such information. It will be presumed that information notified to a regulatory information service is required by these rules or other legal or regulatory requirement, unless otherwise designated.

It should be noted that there is no requirement for an AIM company to maintain an insider list.

2.8 Summary of the Differences between Premium, Standard and AIM Listing

Learning Objective

6.1.3 Understand the key differences between premium listing and standard listing

	Premium Listing	Standard Listing	AIM Admission
Listing requirements			
Minimum market capitalisation on admission	£700,000 equity	£700,000 equity	No minimum
Three-year, revenue-earning track record	Yes	No	No
Working capital statement	Yes	Yes (but can be qualified)	Yes
Listing document	Prospectus	Prospectus	Prospectus/Admission Document
Minimum free float	25%	25%	No minimum
Pre-emption rights required	Yes	UK companies subject to CA2006 only	UK companies subject to CA2006 only
Requirement for sponsor for relevant transactions	Yes	No (unless migrating to Premium Listing)	Nomad (ongoing requirement)
Continuing obligations			
Restrictions on share dealing	Model Code	No restrictions	AIM Rule 21
Corporate governance	UK Corporate Governance Code	DTR 7.2	No official requirements
Shareholder approval for related party transactions	Yes (LR11)	No	No (notification under AIM Rule 13)
Shareholder approval for significant transactions	Yes (LR 10)	No	Yes (AIM Rule 14 – higher thresholds)
DTR application	Yes	Yes	No (except DTR5) (AIM rules apply)
Disclosure of inside information	Yes (DTR2)	Yes (DTR2)	Yes (AIM Rule 11)
Insider lists	Yes	No	No
Prospectus for secondary offerings	Yes (if > a 10% over rolling 12 months)	Yes (if > a 10% over rolling 12 months)	If required under prospectus rules

End of Chapter Questions

Think of an answer for each question and refer to the appropriate section for confirmation.

1. What are the role and duties of the FCA?
    Answer reference: Sections 1.1.1, 1.1.2

2. What are the key requirements for a premium listing?
    Answer reference: Section 1.1.3

3. What are the Disclosure and Transparency Rules?
    Answer reference: Sections 1.1.5

4. What is the difference between an RIE and a regulated market?
    Answer reference: Sections 1.2.1, 1.2.2

5. What is the purpose and status of the Listing Principles, and who do they apply to?
    Answer reference: Section 1.3

6. What are an issuer's obligations in terms of disclosing inside information?
    Answer reference: Section 1.5.2

7. When can a listed company delay the disclosure of inside information?
    Answer reference: Section 1.5.3

8. What is the purpose of an insider list, and who must maintain one?
    Answer reference: Section 1.5.6

9. What are the main duties of a sponsor?
    Answer reference: Section 1.2.6

10. What are the main methods for a company seeking a new listing for its shares?
    Answer reference: Section 1.7.1, 1.7.2

11. What are the trigger points for a person to notify a company of a substantial holding in that company?
    Answer reference: Section 1.8.1

12. What types of companies would consider admission to AIM?
    Answer reference: Section 2.1

13. What are the criteria for a company seeking admission to AIM?
    Answer reference: Section 2.2

14. What are the duties and purpose of a nomad?
    Answer reference: Section 2.4, 2.5

15. When is an AIM company required to produce a prospectus?
    Answer reference: Section 2.6

16. What are the main differences between premium listing, standard listing and AIM admission?
    Answer reference: Section 2.8

Glossary and Abbreviations

Aggregation

This is when multiple client orders are bulked together and processed as a single order. Customers must be notified of this procedure and its advantages and disadvantages.

Allocation

The division of a single aggregated order between two or more investors' accounts.

Alternative Trading System (ATS)

The term formerly used for a facility provided by authorised firms to allow for multilateral trading, by bringing together buyers and sellers of securities. ATSs were not exchanges. From 1 November 2007, ATSs were authorised as multilateral trading facilities, the term used under MiFID (see MTFs and MiFID).

American Depositary Receipt (ADR)

A negotiable instrument representing rights to a block of shares in (generally) a non-US company, traded on a US exchange; the ADR is an acknowledgement from a bank or trust company that the block of shares is held by it for the account of its client. ADRs are a common means for non-US companies to have their shares traded in the US.

Ancillary Services

Activities such as giving advice on MiFID instruments, which are passportable only if the firm is already passported in relation to a core investment service or activity (such as dealing), and if that firm is providing those services as ancillary services to that activity.

Appointed Representative

An appointed representative is an individual or an organisation which carries on certain regulated activities on behalf of an authorised firm under contract. The authorised person must have accepted responsibility in writing for the conduct of these regulated activities.

Approved Persons

Individuals who are approved by the FCA to undertake controlled functions. These individuals are required to comply with the FCA's Statements of Principle and Code of Practice for Approved Persons.

Authorisation

The FSMA requires firms to obtain authorisation prior to conducting investment business. Authorisation is gained by receiving one or more Part IV Permissions from the FCA.

Bank of England

The UK's central bank, which acts as the government's banker and determines interest rates via its Monetary Policy Committee (MPC) and is responsible for the stability of the financial system through the PRA.

Best Execution

Best execution requires that firms take into account not only price factors, but also such issues as other costs, speed, likelihood of execution and settlement, and all these in the light of the size and nature of the deal, in determining the means of obtaining the best outcome for a client when executing his deal.

BIS

UK Department for Business, Innovation and Skills. Government department responsible for trade, industry and business. Its wide range of responsibilities include competition, banking, insolvency, corporate governance and company law.

Bribery Act 2010

Law applicable to all commercial organisations, making it an offence to offer or take bribes or negligently prevent bribery. It will be a defence for a firm if it can demonstrate that it has adequate procedures to prevent such conduct by persons associated with it.

Capital Requirements Directive (CRD)

An EU directive setting out the financial rules for investment firms. The CRD came into force from 1 January 2007 (replacing the Capital Adequacy Directive (CAD)) and applies to banks, building societies and most investment firms. In the UK the CRD has been implemented by the FCA in its regulations through the General Prudential Sourcebook (GENPRU) and the Prudential Sourcebooks for Banks, Building Societies and Investment Firms (BIPRU). The aim of the CRD is to ensure that firms hold adequate financial resources and have adequate systems and controls to prudently manage the business and the associated risks.

Chinese Walls

Organisational barriers to the flow of information set up in large firms, to prevent the movement of confidential, sensitive information between departments and to manage any potential conflicts of interest.

Churning

Excessive trading by a broker in order to generate commission, regardless of the interests of the customer. It is also known as Switching.

Client

Individuals or firms that conduct business through an authorised person. Every client is either a customer (retail or professional) or an eligible counterparty (ECP).

Client Assets

Securities or other assets held by a firm on behalf of its clients. The assets have to be kept separate from the firm's own assets (segregated).

Code of Practice for Approved Persons

A code established by the FCA with regard to the behaviour of approved persons (see above). Compliance with the code is an indication of whether or not an approved person has complied with the Statements of Principle for Approved Persons.

Common-Platform Firm

Broadly, a firm which is subject to MiFID or the CRD and therefore subject to the common platform of organisational systems and controls.

Competition and Markets Authority (CMA)

Successor organisation to the UK Competition Commissioner, an independent body which carries out detailed investigations into mergers and acquisitions (and other anti-competitive situations), to establish whether they will have an adverse effect on competition within a particular UK market.

Conduct of Business (COBS) Rules

Rules made by the FCA under the Financial Services and Markets Act 2000 dealing mainly with the relationship between an authorised firm and its clients.

Contract for Difference (CFD)

An investment instrument consisting of a contract under which the parties hope to make a profit (or avoid a loss) by reference to movements in the price of an underlying asset. The underlying asset does not change hands.

Contracts of Insurance

Financial products specified by Part III of the Regulated Activities Order (RAO) 2001, with two subdivisions: general and long-term insurance contracts.

Controlled Functions

Certain roles within authorised firms for which the FCA requires the occupant to be approved (see Approved Persons).

Counterparty Risk Requirement (CRR)

Part of the financial resources requirement for authorised firms, requiring that timely provision is made in case of bad debts/non-deliveries.

CREST

See Euroclear UK & Ireland.

Criminal Justice Act 1993

A substantial Act which includes provisions relating to insider dealing, including a definition of that offence.

Customer Function

The controlled function conducted by persons who interact with a firm's customers, such as an investment manager or an investment adviser.

Debt Securities

Securities whereby the issuer acknowledges a loan made to it. The term includes instruments such as bonds, certificates of deposit (CDs) and commercial paper.

Dematerialised

The term used to describe stock which is held in electronic form rather than having ownership evidenced by way of paper certificates.

Depositary Receipts

Negotiable instruments evidencing rights over a block of shares which are held with a depositary – usually a bank or trust company. ADRs (see above) are a good example. Depositary receipts are specified investment instruments under the FSMA.

Designated Investment Business (DIB)

Some of the regulated activities are also designated investment business, giving rise to additional obligations under COBS. These include mainstream investment business, and exclude business such as deposit taking, mortgage business and funeral plans.

Designated Investment Exchange (DIE)

An overseas exchange designated by the FCA as meeting certain standards of investor protection in terms of such criteria as market efficiency, transparency and liquidity.

Designated Professional Body (DPB)

Professional bodies whose members are able to carry on limited financial services business without the need for authorisation from the FCA, providing that the limited financial services offered to clients are incidental to their main business. These are the professional bodies for lawyers, accountants, chartered surveyors, licensed conveyancers and actuaries.

Disclosure and Transparency Rules (DTRs)

The DTRs, in the FCA Handbook, implement the requirements of the Market Abuse and Transparency directives, and provides rules for the management and dissemination of information for listed companies, for the publication of financial statements, and for the disclosure of significant shareholdings.

Euroclear UK & Ireland

A recognised clearing house, Euroclear UK & Ireland is the organisation in the UK that facilitates the clearing and settlement of trades in UK and Irish company shares, particularly in dematerialised form. Prior to 1 July 2007, it was known as CREST.

European Economic Area (EEA)

The 28 member states of the European Union, plus Iceland, Liechtenstein and Norway.

European Securities and Markets Authority (ESMA)

The European body responsible for the regulation of investment firms and markets, and directly responsible for regulation of credit rating agencies.

European Supervisory Authorities (ESAs)

Pan-European financial services regulatory bodies, each with responsibility for a different financial sector, introduced in early 2011. The three ESAs are the European Securities and Markets Authority (ESMA), the European Banking Authority (EBA) and the European Insurance and Occupational Pensions Authority (EIOPA).

European Union (EU) Directives

Legislation issued by the European Union (EU) to its member states requiring them to enact and implement local legislation.

Exempt Persons

Firms or persons exempt from the requirement to be authorised to carry on regulated activities. The term includes bodies such as recognised investment exchanges (RIEs) and recognised clearing houses (RCHs).

FCA Handbook

The document containing the FCA rules, with which authorised firms must comply. The handbook is divided into a number of separate sourcebooks covering different subjects.

Financial Conduct Authority (FCA)

The regulatory body that from April 2013 is responsible for regulating conduct of business and markets and for authorising those firms not authorised by the PRA. In addition, under EU regulations, each member state must appoint a competent authority for the purpose of listing securities. The competent authority for listing in the UK is the FCA.

Financial Policy Committee (FPC)

New body within the Bank of England (BoE) which from 1 April 2013 is responsible for macro-prudential regulation.

Financial Resources Requirement (FRR)

The requirements as to the financial resources held by an FCA-authorised firm. The FRR is made up of primary and secondary requirements. The primary requirement addresses various standard sets of risks faced by a firm when undertaking business. The secondary requirement is set at the discretion of the FCA and covers its perception of the firm's additional risk.

Financial Services Act 2012

This Act created the FCA, the PRA and FPC to act as the new regulators.

Financial Services and Markets Act 2000 (FSMA)

The legislation that established the financial regulator (the FSA) and empowered it to regulate the financial services industry. The FSA was split in April 2013 – the FCA looks after conduct issues and the PRA looks after prudential issues.

Financial Services and Markets Tribunal

Established by the FSA as an independent body to hear appeals against FSA's (and now the FCA's) disciplinary decisions. It is run by the government's Ministry of Justice (formerly the Department of Constitutional Affairs). Abolished in April 2010 and replaced by the Tax and Chancery Chamber of the Upper Tribunal.

Financial Services Authority (FSA)

The agency created by the Financial Services and Markets Act 2000 to be the single financial regulator in the UK. Replaced by the FCA on 1 April 2013, with certain functions transferred to the PRA at the same time.

Fit and Proper

Under the FSMA, every firm conducting investment business must be fit and proper. The Act does not define the term; this is left to the FCA.

Forward Rate Agreement (FRA)

An agreement to pay or receive, on an agreed future date, an amount calculated by reference to the difference between a fixed interest rate agreed at the outset, and a reference interest rate actually prevailing on a given future date for a given period.

Future

A futures contract is a legally binding arrangement by which parties commit to buy/ sell a standard quantity and (if applicable) quality of an asset from/to another party on a specified date in the future, but at a price agreed today. Because the price is agreed at the outset, the seller is protected from a fall in the price of the underlying asset in the intervening time period (and vice versa).

Her Majesty's Revenue & Customs (HMRC)

The government department responsible for the administration and collection of tax in the UK, and the guidance notes on HM Treasury's rules for ISAs. HMRC is the result of the merger of two formerly separate departments, HM Customs & Excise and the Inland Revenue.

Her Majesty's Treasury (HMT)

The government department that is responsible for formulating and implementing the government's financial and economic policies. Among other things this means that it is responsible for financial services regulation in the UK. The FCA is accountable to HMT.

Home State

The term used for the EU country where a financial services firm conducting cross-border business is based.

Host State

The term used for an EU country in which a financial services firm is doing business but is not based.

ICAP Securities and Derivatives Exchange Ltd (ISDX)

ISDX plc is a recognised investment exchange in London. It operates a primary market for smaller companies seeking to raise capital and trade their shares (the ISDX Growth Market) and a regulated market for listed securities (ISDX main board), as well as an extensive secondary trading system in all London listed and AIM-traded shares.

Inside Information

Information relating to a security, or an issuer, which is not publicly known and which would affect the price of the security if it were made public.

Insider Dealing

One of several offences created under the Criminal Justice Act (CJA) 1993 which may be committed by an insider in possession of unpublished price-sensitive information if he attempts to deal in affected securities, encourages others to deal, or passes the information on.

Integration

The third stage of money laundering; integration is the stage at which the laundered funds appear to be of legitimate provenance.

InterContinental Exchange (ICE) Futures Europe

ICE Futures (formerly known as the International Petroleum Exchange (IPE)). One of six recognised investment exchanges, ICE deals in futures for energy products, such as crude oil and gas, and also in new instruments such as carbon emission allowances.

Joint Money Laundering Steering Group (JMLSG)

A group whose membership is made up of 17 trade bodies in the financial services industry. The JMLSG has published guidance notes which set out how firms should interpret and implement the money laundering regulations.

Know Your Client (KYC)

The Money Laundering Regulations 2007 and the FCA rules require firms to take sufficient steps, before taking on a client, to satisfy themselves as to the identity of that client.

Lamfalussy Process

The four-stage process for introducing and implementing European directives and regulations under the financial services action plan (FSAP).

Layering

The second stage of money laundering, in which money or assets are typically passed through a series of transactions to obscure their origin.

LCH.Clearnet

An independent clearing house which acts as central counterparty (CCP) for trades executed on Euronext.NYSE, LIFFE, the LME and ICE Futures, and for certain trades executed on the LSE. It is a recognised clearing house (RCH).

Listing Rules

Contained in the FCA Handbook, the Listing Rules provide rules for the London Stock Exchange (LSE) main market and other listed companies including criteria for listing, processes, documentation and continuing obligations. The listing rules are based on principles which take into account the interests of listed entities, maintenance of investor protection and the need to protect the reputation of the market.

London International Financial Futures Exchange (LIFFE)

A recognised investment exchange for futures and traded options, the largest derivatives exchange in the UK.

London Metal Exchange (LME)

The market for trading contracts in base metals and some plastics.

London Stock Exchange (LSE)

The dominant UK market for trading in securities, especially shares and bonds. The LSE is a recognised investment exchange (RIE).

Market Abuse

A set of offences introduced under S.118 FSMA, judged on what a regular user would view as a failure to observe required market standards. The offences include abuse of information, misleading the market, and distortion of the market.

Market Maker

A firm which quotes bid and offer prices for a named list of securities in the market. Such a firm is normally under an obligation to make a price in any security for which it is market maker, at all times.

Markets in Financial Instruments Directive (MiFID)

An EU directive which replaced the Investment Services Directive (ISD) on 1 November 2007. It allows firms authorised in one member state to offer/provide financial services to customers in another member state, subject to some restrictions.

Misleading Statement

The term used for false, misleading or incomplete information given about an investment, in order to (or with the effect of) affecting its value – a criminal act under S.397 of the FSMA and a potential form of market abuse.

Model Code

This sets out standards of conduct for directors of a listed company, adherence to which should avoid their falling foul of insider dealing legislation. For example, it stipulates that a company director should not deal in his company's shares without permission, and may only do so at certain times.

Money Laundering

The process whereby criminals attempt to conceal the true origins of the proceeds of their criminal activities, and to give them the appearance of legitimacy by introducing them into the mainstream financial system.

Money Laundering Regulations 2007

The regulations under which authorised firms, and some other businesses, are required to comply with certain administrative obligations in order to prevent money laundering. The obligations include record-keeping, identification of clients, appointment of a nominated officer to receive suspicion reports, and staff training. Failure to comply may result in a fine and/or imprisonment.

Money Laundering Reporting Officer (MLRO)

A senior employee who is responsible for assessing internal money laundering suspicion reports, and if these appear justified, reporting those suspicions to NCA.

Multilateral Trading Facilities (MTFs)

A system operated by authorised firms which brings together multiple buyers and sellers of securities, but which is not an exchange. Prior to 1 November 2007 (when MiFID provisions came into force), most MTFs were operated as alternative trading systems (ATSs). See above for MiFID and ATSs.

National Crime Agency (NCA)

The law enforcement agency to which suspicions of money laundering must be reported by a firm's money laundering reporting officer (MLRO).

Nominated Adviser (Nomad)

A firm which has been approved by the London Stock Exchange (LSE) as a nominated adviser for AIM companies and whose name has been placed on the register of nomads, published by the LSE. The nomad is responsible for advising companies on admission to AIM, and on a continuing basis once they are admitted. As such, nomads take responsibility for ensuring companies are, and remain, suitable for admission to the AIM, and comply with its rules.

Nominated Officer

A term for the officer who is required to receive a firm's internal suspicion reports under the Proceeds of Crime Act 2002 (POCA), the Terrorism Act and the Money Laundering Regulations; in practice, usually the same individual as the MLRO.

Nominee

The party which, under a legal arrangement, holds assets in its own name on behalf of the true beneficial owner.

Option

An option gives the holder the right (but not the obligation) to buy or sell a fixed quantity of an underlying asset on, or before, a specified date in the future. There are two basic types of option – puts and calls. The holder of a call option has the right to buy the underlying asset at a given price. The holder of a put option has the right to sell the underlying asset at a given price.

Panel on Takeovers and Mergers (PTM)

The Panel on Takeovers and Mergers (PTM) is a regulatory body located in London, charged with the administration of the City Code on Takeovers and Mergers. Its role is to ensure that all shareholders are treated fairly during takeover bids. The PTM's authority is derived from the Companies Act 2006.

Part 4A Permission

The specific activity which an authorised firm is permitted to carry on. It is so called because Part 4A permissions are granted by the Financial Conduct Authority (FCA) and/or the Prudential Regulation Authority (PRA) under Part 4A of the Financial Services and Markets Act (FSMA 2000).

Passporting

The method by which firms authorised in one EU member state are – under MiFID – permitted to carry on regulated financial services activities in another EU state without the need to become fully authorised in that other state.

Placement

The first stage of money laundering in which money is introduced into the financial system.

Pre-emption Rights

Under the Companies Act 2006, shareholders in public companies must be provided with pre-emption rights, which are the right for existing shareholders to be offered, in preference to any new shareholders, any new shares issued for cash by a company. Effectively, this is a right of first refusal, designed to protect the interest of shareholders in their company.

Premium Listing

One of the two listing options for companies on the London Stock Exchange (LSE) main market, with criteria and continuing obligations which are super-equivalent to those of the relevant European Union (EU) Directives. The other option is standard listing.

Prescribed Market

A multilateral trading facility (MTF) which is operated by a UK Recognised Investment Exchange (RIE), including AIM and ISDX Growth Market.

Principles for Businesses

11 key principles established by the Financial Conduct Authority (FCA) which must be observed by authorised firms. These principles are detailed in the FCA's Handbook.

Proceeds of Crime Act 2002 (POCA)

Legislation which contains, among other things, anti-money laundering provisions. This includes the offences of assisting money laundering, tipping-off and failing to report suspicions of money laundering.

Prohibition Order

An order which may be exercised by the Financial Conduct Authority (FCA) under powers given to it under Section 56 of the Financial Services and Markets Act (FSMA). Such an order prohibits the individual in connection with whom it is granted from carrying out particular controlled functions on the grounds that he is not fit and proper.

Prospectus Rules (PR)

Contained in the Financial Conduct Authority (FCA) Handbook, the PRs implement the Prospectus Directive and provides the rules as to when a prospectus is required, its contents and format, and the process for its approval by the FCA.

Prudential Regulation Authority (PRA)

Subsidiary of the Bank of England (BoE) which, since 1 April 2013, is responsible for prudential regulation for systemically important firms.

Qualified Investor (QI)

Investing institutions, large companies and self-certified small and medium enterprises and individuals. Offering shares to qualified investors only, or to limited numbers of qualified investors, may provide an exemption from the requirement to publish a prospectus under the Prospectus Rules (PRs).

Recognised Clearing House (RCH)

A term used to denote those clearing houses recognised by the Bank of England (BoE) as providing appropriate standards of protection in the provision of clearing and settlement facilities to certain markets. There are currently four organisations granted this status.

Recognised Investment Exchange (RIE)

A term used to denote those UK exchanges which operate markets in investments, meeting certain standards set by the Financial Conduct Authority (FCA). There are currently six exchanges granted this status.

Recognised Overseas Investment Exchange (ROIE)

An overseas exchange offering membership or providing facilities within the UK, and having been recognised by the Financial Conduct Authority (FCA) as meeting appropriate standards of investor protection. There are currently nine ROIEs.

Regular User

A hypothetical person regularly using a particular market. It is through the eyes of the regular user that behaviour is assessed for determining whether it meets the standards required under the legacy offences of the market abuse regime.

Regulated Activities

Activities for which a firm requires authorisation from the Financial Conduct Authority (FCA), unless it is exempt from the need for authorisation. Regulated activities are defined in relation both to the activities themselves, and to the investments to which they relate.

Regulated Activities Order 2001 (as amended)

The statutory instrument which defines the range of regulated activities.

Regulated Market

A market which is designated as a regulated market in that it meets the required regulatory standards to be awarded this status, and operated by a RIE.

Regulatory Decisions Committee (RDC)

A committee of the Financial Conduct Authority (FCA) which is responsible for disciplinary decisions.

Regulatory Information Service (RIS)

Companies subject to the Disclosure and Transparency Rules (DTRs), the Listing Rules (LRs) City Code and/or the AIM Rules are required, in a range of circumstances, to make announcements to the market. These announcements must be made via a regulated information service. Companies making announcements can choose from one of eight providers who have been approved by the FCA to act as an RIS.

Scheme of Arrangement

A Companies Act procedure whereby a company seeks shareholder and court approval for its reorganisation or reconstruction.

Sell Out

Under S.985 of the Companies Act 2006 minority shareholders' interests are protected: they have the right to insist that a successful bidder buys them out within three months of the end of their bid.

Significant Influence Functions (SIFs)

Certain functions carried out by directors and other senior personnel. In the approved persons' regime, these comprise the governing functions, the required controlled functions, the systems and control functions and the significant management functions.

Squeeze-Out

Under the Companies Act 2006, where a purchaser has made a takeover offer for a company and acquired 90% of the shares to which his offer relates, he can compulsorily acquire the remaining shares at the same price as the main takeover offer.

Stabilisation

The activity of supporting the price of a new issue of securities or bonds in order to minimise the volatility that can sometimes arise with new issues.

Stakeholder Pensions

Introduced in 2001 as a low-cost pension scheme. A stakeholder pension scheme is an example of a packaged product.

Standard Listing

One of the two listing options for companies on the London Stock Exchange (LSE) main market, with EU-minimum levels of regulation in terms of listing criteria and continuing obligations. The other option is premium listing.

Statements of Principle for Approved Persons

A set of principles established by the FCA with which approved persons are required to comply at all times.

Stock Exchange Trading Service (SETS)

The LSE's electronic order book system for UK blue chip securities.

Threshold Conditions

The conditions which a firm must meet before the FCA will authorise it.

Tipping-Off

An offence established under various pieces of anti-money laundering and terrorist financing legislation. It involves disclosing the fact that an investigation is, or is likely to be, under way, if that disclosure may imperil any such investigation.

Training and Competence Sourcebook

Part of the business standards block of the Financial Conduct Authority (FCA) Handbook which sets out FCA's requirements in connection with all staff (but especially in connection with people employed in controlled functions). The sourcebook includes commitments which firms must make in connection with training and competence, including with regard to staff training, maintenance of competence, supervision and record keeping.

Trustee

A person or organisation who is the legal owner of assets held in trust for someone else. The trustee is responsible for safeguarding the assets, complying with the trust deed and (if the trust is a unit trust) overseeing the activities of the unit trust's manager.

UK Corporate Governance Code (the Code)

A set of principles of good corporate governance providing a code of best practice aimed at companies with a premium listing on the London Stock Exchange (LSE). It is overseen by the Financial Reporting Council (FRC) and its importance derives from the FCA's LRs which require that premium listed companies disclose how they have complied with the code, and explain where they have not applied the code – in what the code refers to as comply or explain. The code adopts a principles-based approach in the sense that it provides general guidelines of best practice.

Upper Tribunal

Tribunal hearing appeals against decisions of the Financial Conduct Authority (FCA). Replaced the Financial Services and Markets Tribunal, which was abolished in April 2010.

Warrant

An investment instrument giving the holder the right to buy a set number of the underlying equities at a predetermined price on specified dates, or at any time, up to the end of a predetermined time period. Warrants are usually issued by companies or by securities houses.

Whistleblowing

The term used when an individual raises concerns over potential wrongdoing. The Public Interest Disclosure Act (PIDA) 1998 provides some statutory protections for whistleblowers.

ABI
Association of British Insurers

ACCA
Association of Chartered Certified Accountants

ADR
American Depositary Receipt

AGM
Annual General Meeting

AIM
Alternative Investment Market

AML
Anti-Money Laundering

AMPs
Accepted Market Practices

APER
Statements of Principle and Code of Practice for Approved Persons

APR
Approved Persons Regime

ARROW
Advanced, Risk-Responsive Operating Framework

ASX
Australian Securities Exchange

ATS
Alternative Trading Systems

AUT
Authorised Unit Trust

AUTH
Authorisation Sourcebook

BBA
British Bankers' Association

BCD

Banking Consolidation Directive

BIPRU

The Prudential Handbook for banks, building societies and investment firms

BIS

(Department for) Business, Innovation and Skills

BoE

Bank of England

BMSA

Business Model and Strategy Analysis

CAD

Capital Adequacy Directive

CASS

Client Assets Sourcebook

CCD

Concentration with a community dimension

CCP

Central Counterparty

CD

Certificates of Deposit

CEBS

Committee of European Banking Supervisors

CEIC

Closed-Ended Investment Company

CESR

Committee of European Securities Regulators (replaced by ESMA in 2011)

CFD

Contract for Difference

CJA

Criminal Justice Act

CIS

Collective Investment Scheme

CMA

Competition and Markets Authority

CML

Council of Mortgage Lenders

COB

Conduct of Business

COBS

The Conduct of Business Sourcebook (replaced COB on 1 November 2007)

COMP

The Compensation Sourcebook

COND

Threshold Conditions

CP

Consultation Paper

CPS

Crown Prosecution Service

CRA

Credit Rating Agencies Regulation

CRD

Capital Requirements Directive

CRO

Chief Risk Officer

CRR

Counterparty Risk Requirement

CTA

Counter-Terrorism Act 2008

DEPP

Decisions Procedure and Penalties Manual

DG Comp
Directorate General for Competition

DIB
Designated Investment Business

DIE
Designated Investment Exchange

DOIE
Designated Overseas Investment Exchange

DMD
Distance Marketing Directive

DMO
Debt Management Office

DPA
Data Protection Act

DPB
Designated Professional Body

DTCC
Depository Trust & Clearing Corporation

DTR
Disclosure and Transparency Rules

EAMP
Emission Allowance Market Participants

EBA
European Banking Authority

EBC
European Banking Committee

EC
European Commission

ECB
European Central Bank

ECMR
European Community Merger Regulation

ECOFIN
European Council of Financial Ministers

ECP
Eligible Counterparty

EDX
Equities Derivatives Exchange

EEA
European Economic Area

EFCC
European Financial Conglomerates Committee

EG
Enforcement Guide

EGM
External General Meeting

EIB
European Investment Bank

EIOPA
European Insurance and Occupational Pensions Authority

EIOPC
European Insurance and Occupational Pensions Committee

EMIR
European Market Infrastructure Regulation

ESA
European Supervisory Authority

ESC
European Securities Committee

ESMA

European Securities and Markets Authority

ESRB

European Systemic Risk Board

ETF

Exchange-Traded Fund

EU

European Union

FATF

Financial Action Task Force

FCA

Financial Conduct Authority

FIT

Fit and Proper Test for Approved Persons

FOS

Financial Ombudsman Service

FPC

Financial Policy Committee

FPO

Financial Promotion Order

FRA

Forward Rate Agreement

FRC

Financial Reporting Council

FRR

Financial Resources Requirement

FSA

Financial Services Authority

FSF

Firm Systematic Framework

FSAP

Financial Services Action Plan

FSMA

Financial Services and Markets Act (2000)

FX

Foreign Exchange

GDR

Global Depository Receipts

GENPRU

The General Prudential Sourcebook

GM

General Meeting

HGS

High Growth Segment

HMRC

Her Majesty's Revenue & Customs

HMT

Her Majesty's Treasury

ICAEW

Institute of Chartered Accountants of England and Wales

ICE

InterContinental Exchange

ICVC

Investment Company with Variable Capital

IMF

International Monetary Fund

IPE

International Petroleum Exchange

IPO

Initial Public Offering

IPRU
Interim Prudential Sourcebooks

ISA
Individual Savings Account

ISD
Investment Services Directive

ISDX
ICAP Securities and Derivatives Exchange

JMLSG
Joint Money Laundering Steering Group

JSE
Johannesburg Stock Exchange

KYC
Know Your Client

LCH
London Clearing House

LIBOR
London InterBank Offered Rate

LIFFE
London International Financial Futures and Options Exchange

LME
London Metal Exchange

LR
Listing Rules

LSE
London Stock Exchange

MAD
Market Abuse Directive

MAR
Market Conduct Sourcebook

MiFID
Markets in Financial Instruments Directive

MiFIR
Markets in Financial Instruments Regulation

ML
Money Laundering

MLRO
Money Laundering Reporting Officer

MPC
Monetary Policy Committee

MTF
Multilateral Trading Facility

NS&I
National Savings & Investment

NASDAQ
National Association of Securities Dealers Automated Quotations

NCA
National Crime Agency

NED
Non-Executive Director

NO
Nominated Officer

NOMAD
Nominated Advisers

NYSE
New York Stock Exchange

OEIC
Open-Ended Investment Company

OFT
Office of Fair Trading

OTC
Over-the-Counter

OTF
Organised Trading Facility

PCBS
Parliamentary Commission on Banking Standards

PDMR
Persons Discharging Managerial Responsibility

PERG
Perimeter Guidance

PIDA
Public Interest Disclosure Act (1998)

PLC
Public Limited Company

POCA
Proceeds of Crime Act (2002)

PPF
Pension Protection Fund

PR
Prospectus Rules

PRA
Prudential Regulatory Authority

PRIIP
Packaged Retail and Insurance-based Investment Product

PRIN
Principles for Businesses

PTM
Panel on Takeovers and Mergers

QI
Qualified Investor

RAO
Regulated Activities Order

RCH
Recognised Clearing House

RDC
Regulatory Decisions Committee

RICS
Royal Institution of Chartered Surveyors

RIE
Recognised Investment Exchange

RIS
Regulatory Information Service

ROCH
Recognised Overseas Clearing House

ROIE
Recognised Overseas Investment Exchange

SEF
Social Entrepreneurship Fund

SFO
Serious Fraud Office

SIF
Significant Influence Function

SIPP
Self-Invested Personal Pensions

SMR
Senior Managers Regime

SOCPA

Serious and Organised Crime Police Act 2005

SOP
Statements of Principle

SRA
Sector Risk Assessment

SRO
Self-Regulatory Organisation

SRU
Special Resolution Unit

STOR
Suspicious Transaction and Order Report

SUP
Supervision Sourcebook

SYSC
Senior Management Arrangements, Systems and
Controls Sourcebook

TA
Terrorism Act

TC
Training and Competence Sourcebook

TCF
Treating Customers Fairly

TVR
Total Voting Rights

UCITS
Units in Collective Investment Undertakings

UKCGC
UK Corporate Governance Code

UKLA
United Kingdom Listing Authority

UN
United Nations

VC
Venture Capital

Multiple Choice Questions

The following questions have been compiled to reflect as closely as possible the standard that you will experience in your examination. Please note, however, they are not actual exam questions.

1. Which of the following is one of the FCA's statutory objectives?

    A. To ensure retail clients are not over-charged for financial products
    B. To prevent authorised firms from going into default
    C. To secure the appropriate degree of protection for consumers
    D. To ensure authorised firms have adequate financial resources

2. Which of the following is TRUE of the market abuse regime under the FSMA?

    A. Market abuse is a criminal act
    B. The FCA is not permitted to impose a fine on offenders
    C. The FCA can withdraw approval or authorisation from offenders
    D. Offenders can be fined up to a maximum of £100,000

3. In order to be considered inside information, the relevant information must be:

    A. Price-sensitive
    B. Open-ended
    C. Recently obtained
    D. Non-regulated

4. Which of the following is TRUE in relation to the rules on personal account dealing?

    A. Transactions carried out by an investment manager under a fully discretionary management service are exempt
    B. All personal account dealings must be approved by the firm's compliance officer
    C. Financial analysts are not permitted to undertake personal account transactions in listed companies
    D. Transactions in UK-authorised OEICs and unit trusts are caught by the personal account dealing rules

5. Which of the following is one of the general principles governing the conduct of takeover activity in the UK?

    A. Having an open and co-operative relationship with the regulator
    B. Managing conflicts of interest
    C. Avoiding false markets
    D. Maintaining high standards of management and control

6. Under which of the following circumstances is an announcement generally required in relation to a potential takeover?

    A. A 10% stake in a target company has been disclosed

    B. A mandatory bid under Rule 7 has been triggered

    C. There has been a 5% increase in the share price of a company during a single week

    D. There is rumour and price speculation surrounding a possible bid

7. Which of the following is eligible for approval as a nominated advisor?

    A. An approved person providing corporate finance advice

    B. Any FCA-regulated firm that is authorised to provide corporate finance advice

    C. A firm that has practised corporate finance for two years and has four qualified executives

    D. A firm that has practiced corporate finance for three years and has three qualified executives

8. In which of the following circumstances does the Takeover Code not apply?

    A. An offer for a private company established in Guernsey that was listed until three years ago

    B. An offer for a UK-registered and UK-managed company traded on AIM

    C. An offer for a UK company conducted by way of a scheme of arrangement

    D. An offer for an open-ended investment company incorporated in the UK

9. Which of the following statements is TRUE?

    A. The DTRS contain elements which are historically required by MiFID and MiFID II from 2015, and therefore apply to issuers on prescribed markets, as well as regulated markets

    B. The DTRs contain elements which are, since 2005, required by the Market Abuse Directive and therefore apply to issuers on prescribed markets, as well as regulated markets

    C. The DTRs contain elements which are required by both MiFID II and the Prospectus Directive and therefore apply to issuers on prescribed markets, as well as regulated markets

    D. The DTRs contain elements which are required by both the AIFMD and the Collateral Directive and therefore apply to issuers on prescribed markets, as well as regulated markets

10. The maximum penalty for an individual in breach of the Bribery Act 2010 is:

    A. Ten years' imprisonment and/or an unlimited fine

    B. Seven years' imprisonment and/or an unlimited fine

    C. Two years' imprisonment and/or an unlimited fine

    D. Fourteen years' imprisonment and/or an unlimited fine

11. An individual has acquired inside information and has encouraged a friend to deal in the affected securities. Which of the following statements is therefore TRUE?

    A. The individual will only have committed an offence if the friend actually deals in the securities

    B. The individual has committed an offence

    C. Only the friend will be guilty of an offence

    D. The deal will be automatically void

12. Which of the following is an offence under the Proceeds of Crime Act 2002?

    A. Failure to disclose suspicions of money laundering

    B. Acting on insider information

    C. Encouraging someone else to deal on inside information

    D. Failure to undertake appropriate know your customer checks for new clients

13. Which of the following is a MiFID core activity?

    A. Services in relation to underwriting

    B. Foreign exchange services

    C. Receipt and transmission of orders

    D. Safe keeping and administration of financial instruments for the accounts of clients

14. Which one of the following types of investment is defined as a specified investment under the Regulated Activities Order?

    A. NS&I certificates

    B. Building Society bank accounts

    C. Commodity futures for commercial purposes

    D. OEIC shares

15. Which of the following groups of persons is generally not deemed to be acting in concert under the Takeover Code?

    A. A company, together with its directors

    B. A company, together with its corporate finance advisers

    C. A company, together with its market makers

    D. A company, together with its pension fund

16. Which of the following is TRUE of the client order handling requirements?

    A. Client orders can be delayed to allow bulk dealing

    B. Executed client orders are required to be allocated by the close of business

    C. Executed orders are required to be promptly and accurately recorded and allocated

    D. Clients will only be informed of difficulty in carrying out their orders when they have not been completed by the close of business

17. Which of the following BEST describes a squeeze-out as defined in Section 979 of the Companies Act 2006?

    A. The purchase of minority shareholdings by a successful bidder, within three months of their bid going unconditional

    B. If a successful bidder has acquired at least 90% of a company, he may automatically purchase the remaining shares

    C. If a bidder secures at least 75% of the voting shares in a company, he can compulsorily purchase all of the remaining shares

    D. The agreement at a general meeting to allow the compulsory purchase of minority shareholdings

18. MiFID firms may accept payments or non-monetary benefits from a third party only if:

    A. The client is a professional client

    B. The amount is below that specified in the firm's conflicts of interest policy

    C. The payment is recorded and details provided to the client on request

    D. The payment enhances the quality or service and is disclosed to the client

19. Which of the following is a required function for all authorised firms under the Approved Persons regime?

    A. Partner function

    B. Non-executive director function

    C. Customer function

    D. Compliance oversight function

20. What is an alternative method to a rights issue for a listed company to raise new capital?

    A. Introduction

    B. Bonus issue

    C. Capitalisation issue

    D. Placing

21. In which of the following circumstances does a firm have to comply with the suitability rules?

    A. If its recommendation is to increase a regular premium to an existing life assurance contract

    B. If its recommendation is for a client to undertake a pension transfer

    C. If the firm is acting as an investment manager for a retail client and recommends a particular specified investment

    D. If the client is permanently resident outside the EEA

22. Which of the following is TRUE in relation to reporting a suspicious transaction and the MLRO?

    A. The MLRO is responsible for disclosing suspicious transactions to the NCA

    B. The MLRO must always make the customer aware that the transaction is suspicious before making any report

    C. Freezing the funds from a suspicious transaction negates any requirement to report

    D. Authorised firms need only appoint an MLRO when they deal for/on behalf of retail clients

23. The Management and Control principle of business requires firms to have adequate systems in place specifically relating to:

    A. Customer fairness

    B. Cash flow resources

    C. Risk management

    D. Staff training

24. Which of the following is NOT one of the disciplinary powers of the FCA?

    A. Issuing a public statement in the form of a final notice

    B. Withdrawing or amending the permissions of an authorised firm

    C. Imposition of a fine, without limit

    D. Imposing a custodial sentence of up to two years

25. During a takeover bid, which of the following transactions in offeree securities must be disclosed?

    A. The acquisition of the offeree's non-convertible debt securities by the offeror

    B. All dealings in offeree shares undertaken by the offeror company

    C. All dealings in offeree shares undertaken by existing shareholders of the offeree

    D. All dealings in the shares of a cash offeror by existing shareholders of the offeror

26. Which of the following is TRUE in relation to the SYSC rules on disclosing conflicts of interest?

    A. Disclosure must be in the format of a formal letter to clients

    B. Firms are permitted to delay disclosing any conflicts to clients while they undertake business/ carry out transactions on their behalf

    C. Firms need not disclose such conflicts to professional clients

    D. Disclosure to the client should be seen as the last resort by the firm in managing such a conflict

27. Which of the following should a firm do to manage conflicts of interest?

    A. Decline to act for a client in a specific transaction unless they acknowledge the potential issues that may arise from carrying out their transaction

    B. Verbally advise the client of the conflict of interest

    C. Locate its investment banking and investment management divisions in separate buildings

    D. Implement an information barrier between different business units

28. Which of the following is exempt from the Financial Promotion rules?

    A. The promotion to a professional client of a packaged product

    B. The promotion of non-MiFID business to a retail client

    C. The promotion of packaged products to a UK-domiciled retail client

    D. Communications by a company to its shareholders

29. Which of the following provisions of COBS does NOT apply to a non-MiFID firm carrying on corporate finance business?

    A. Client categorisation

    B. Inducements

    C. Personal account dealing

    D. Providing product information

30. Which of the following is a statutory right for shareholders under the Companies Act 2006?

    A. Companies must hold AGMs, but the gap between them can be up to 18 months

    B. A general meeting which is not an AGM can be called by a shareholder with 3% of voting rights in a company

    C. Ordinary resolutions require at least 70% approval of votes cast to be approved

    D. A special resolution requiring at least 75% of votes cast is required to waive pre-emption rights

31. To whom should a firm's MLRO report suspicious activity?

    A. HMT

    B. FCA

    C. SFO

    D. NCA

32. Which of the following is a requirement for admission of a company to AIM?

    A. At least 10% of the issued share capital must be available to the public

    B. It must publish a prospectus

    C. It must appoint an NO

    D. The expected market value of its securities must be at least £500,000

33. Which of the following is TRUE in relation to a company seeking a listing of its shares on the main market of the LSE?

    A. All companies must appoint a sponsor, which must be a member firm of the LSE

    B. Only premium issuers need appoint a sponsor, which must be a firm approved by the FCA

    C. Both premium and standard issuers must appoint a sponsor, which must be a firm approved by the FCA

    D. Only premium issuers need appoint a sponsor, which must be a member firm of the LSE

34. What is the FCA's general approach to the supervision of authorised firms?

    A. Principles-based

    B. Detailed rules-based

    C. Outcomes-focused

    D. Prescriptive and directional

35. A firm identifies a conflict of interest whilst carrying out a transaction on behalf of a client. Which of the following actions should the firm undertake?

    A. Disclose the nature of the conflict to the client after completing the transaction

    B. Provide a verbal disclosure to the client of the nature of the conflict

    C. Disclosure the nature and source of the conflict to the client prior to carrying out the transaction

    D. Document the conflict, but do not disclose the conflict to the client

36. Which of the following is NOT TRUE of the Takeover Panel's role?

    A. It regulates the conduct of public takeovers in the UK

    B. It provides advice and guidance to advisers and principals in public takeovers in the UK

    C. Its role has a statutory basis, provided in the Companies Act 2006

    D. It has the power to fine and censure parties who breach the City Code

37. Who is responsible for approving a prospectus produced by an AIM company?

    A. The LSE

    B. The FCA

    C. The sponsor

    D. The company's leading bankers

38. Which of the following is TRUE in respect of the UK Corporate Governance Code?

    A. All companies listed on AIM and the main market are legally required to comply with it

    B. The Code is a set of rules that all UK-registered companies with a premium listing in the UK must comply with

    C. The Code must be complied with by all UK financial services companies

    D. The Code is a guide to good practice and applies to all companies with a premium listing of equity shares in the UK

39. Which of the following is a requirement for a company seeking admission to the Official List?

    A. The expected market value of its shares must be at least £200,000

    B. Its securities must be admitted to trading on a recognised investment exchange

    C. It must have made profit for at least three years

    D. At least 10% of its shares must be available for purchase by the public

40. Which of the following is TRUE in relation to a scheme of arrangement?

    A. Prior approval is not required from the Takeover Panel when used for a mandatory bid

    B. Shareholders vote on the exchange of their shares in the company for cash or shares in the offeror company

    C. The Takeover Code on takeovers does not apply

    D. The FCA must approve the use, and terms, of the scheme of arrangement

41. The FCA's best execution rules apply:

    A. When a firm owes contractual or agency obligations to its clients

    B. When a firm trades as principal

    C. To operators of collective investment schemes in respect of unit purchases in that scheme

    D. To professional clients unless they choose to opt out

42. To be considered market abuse under FSMA 2000, a behaviour:

    A. Is considered unacceptable by an institutional investor

    B. Is likely to distort the market

    C. Constitutes a breach of the Criminal Justice Act 1993

    D. Constitutes a breach of the Money Laundering Regulations 2007

43. The HGS is a new segment of the main market, designed to assist mid-sized European and UK companies that require access to capital and a public platform to continue their growth. Which of the following statements is true?

    A. The HGS and AIM markets are both non-EU regulated markets but sit within the UK's listing regime

    B. The HGS market has EU-regulated market status but sits outside the UK's listing regime

    C. The HGS market has UK-regulated market status and sits within the UK's listing regime

    D. The HGS market is for the equity and bond segments of UK and wider EEA trading businesses

44. Which of the following statements is TRUE in relation to regulated markets, RIEs and MTFs?

    A. An RIE may operate a regulated market and/or an MTF

    B. RIEs, MTFs and regulated markets are all exempt from the requirement to be authorised by the FCA

    C. A regulated market may operate an MTF

    D. Both regulated markets and MTFs can only be operated by an RIE

45. Which of the following is NOT a required part of a prospectus?

    A. Directors' recommendation to shareholders

    B. Summary

    C. Registration document

    D. Securities note

46. Which of the following instruments are caught under the insider dealing legislation?

    A. Corporate debentures

    B. Commodities

    C. Foreign exchange

    D. Shares in OEICs

47. Which of the following are NOT financial instruments covered by MiFID?

    A. Contracts for difference

    B. Foreign exchange

    C. Units in collective investment schemes

    D. Credit derivatives

48. In a hostile bid, what is the MAXIMUM time permitted by the City Code between the formal offer being posted to shareholders and the first response from the offeree company's directors?

    A. 7 days

    B. 14 days

    C. 28 days

    D. 39 days

49. In which of the following circumstances is a prospectus required for a company looking to list on the LSE?

    A. Bonus or capitalisation issue

    B. Issue of non-transferable securities

    C. Shares offered for sale by an OEIC

    D. Rights issue with a value of £100 million

50. Which of the following must be directly authorised under the FSMA to carry on regulated activities?

    A. Recognised investment exchange

    B. Hedge fund manager

    C. Recognised clearing house

    D. Appointed representative

51. Which of the following of the FCA's powers derive from the FSMA?

    A. Setting remunerations levels and structures for all staff working in authorised firms

    B. Supervision of authorised firms

    C. Regulating firms' recruitment policy

    D. Setting disciplinary procedures for all staff employed at authorised firms

1.　　　C　　　　　Chapter 1, Section 2.1

The FCA does not operate a no-fail regime for authorised firms, therefore option B is incorrect. The FCA does not regulate pricing and does not specify the cost/charges that authorised firms can charge on financial products, therefore option A is incorrect. The FCA does specify the amount of financial resource firms must have, but this is not one their statutory objectives, therefore option D is incorrect.

The correct answer is option C. One of the FCA's statutory objectives is to ensure that there is appropriate protection for consumers; one example of this is the client money rules where cash managed/held by a firm is held in client money bank accounts and not in the name of the firm.

2.　　　C　　　　　Chapter 1, Sections 7.1–7.7

Option C is correct. The offence of market abuse is civil rather than criminal, whereas insider dealing is a criminal offence. The FCA may impose an unlimited fine. It may also withdraw approval/authorisation of a person within the regulated sector found guilty of market abuse.

3.　　　A　　　　　Chapter 1, Section 5.1

Inside information relates to securities, and is specific/precise, not publicly available and price-sensitive.

4.　　　A　　　　　Chapter 2, Section 6.2

All authorised firms must have arrangements in place to prevent their employees, who are relevant persons, and who are involved in activities that could lead to conflicts of interest or who could have access to inside information, from entering into inappropriate transactions.

There some exception to the rules, notably transactions carried out under a discretionary management service and transactions in units/shares of certain classes of funds where the relevant person is not involved in the management of the fund.

5.　　　C　　　　　Chapter 4, Section 2.3

The Takeover Code has six general principles governing the conduct of takeover bids in the UK. General Principle # 4 is:

False markets must not be created in the securities of the offeree company, of the offeror company or of any other company concerned by the bid in such a way that the rise or fall of the prices of the securities becomes artificial and the normal functioning of the markets is distorted.

6.　　　D　　　　　Chapter 4, Section 2.5.2

The most important rules governing the pre-bid environment relate to the secrecy of negotiations. The Panel is concerned to prevent leaks about potential bids, which could result in the development of a false market in the securities of both the bidder and target companies. An announcement will generally be required in the following circumstances:

A firm intention to make an offer has been reached.

There is untoward movement in the target's share price, for example, a movement of 10% since the start of bid talks, or 5% in the course of a single day.

A mandatory bid under Rule 9 has been triggered (ie, a 30% interest in a company has been acquired or a controlling holding consolidated).

There is rumour and speculation surrounding a possible offer. However, an announcement is only required if there is substance to the rumour; it is not required in response to unsubstantiated gossip.

Talks are extended beyond a small number of parties (so that a leak becomes more likely).

7. C Chapter 6, Section 2.5.1

An entity seeking approval as a nominated adviser (nomad) must be a firm or company which has practised corporate finance for at least two years, acted in a lead corporate finance role on at least three relevant transactions in that two-year period and which employs at least four qualified executives. The LSE, not the FCA, grants approval for nomad status.

8. D Chapter 4, Section 2.2.1

Option D is correct because the Takeover Code does not apply to offers for OEICs. It applies to all offers (ie, offers and potential offers, however implemented) for all companies, which are registered in the UK, Channel Islands or Isle of Man and which have securities trading on a UK-regulated market. It also applies to unlisted public companies (including AIM companies) which are both registered and have their central place of management in the UK, Channel Islands or Isle of Man. Additionally, the Takeover Code applies to offers for UK/CI/IoM-registered and managed private companies which have, in the past ten years, had their shares traded on an exchange or have offered listed shares to the public.

9. B Chapter 6, Section 1.1.2

Under the DTR, any listed company (both premium and standard listed) has a continuing obligation to disclose to the market details of any new major or significant developments in its activities which are not in the public domain but which would, if known, significantly affect its share price (ie, inside information). Such information may not be disclosed solely to all or a section of its shareholders but must be disclosed to the market as a whole.

These disclosures must be made through a RIS, and it may not be used for any non-regulatory disclosures.

If the company has a legitimate reason for delaying the disclosure of inside information (for example, matters in the course of negotiation), it must ensure that this information is kept secure and avoid leaks. It may not avoid or delay the disclosure of inside information solely to avoid or delay a negative impact on its share price.

10. A Chapter 1, Section 4.6

The maximum penalty for an individual in breach of the Bribery Act is ten years and an unlimited fine. The principal money laundering offences are regarded as more serious and attract a maximum sentence of up to 14 years.

11. B Chapter 1, Sections 5.2

A person commits an offence under the insider dealing legislation if he encourages someone else to deal in price-affected securities when in possession of inside information.

12.   **A**   **Chapter 1, Section 4.2**

The offences under POCA 2002 are: concealing; arrangement; acquisition; use and possession; failing to disclose; and tipping off. Detailed provisions, including the know your customer requirements, are contained in the Money Laundering Regulations.

Depending on the offence, an individual found guilty under POCA can be sentenced to jail for up to 14 years and/or face an unlimited financial fine.

13.   **C**   **Chapter 1, Section 8.2.3**

The correct option is C – the receipt and transmission of orders. All the other options are classified as MiFID ancillary services.

14.   **D**   **Chapter 1, Section 1.5**

Commodity futures for commercial purposes, NS&I products and building society bank accounts are not included in the RAO list of specified investments. Therefore, option D is correct because OEIC shares are specified as investments covered by the RAO.

15.   **C**   **Chapter 4, Section 2.4.1**

There are a number of relationships which give rise to a presumption of acting in concert. However, a company is generally not presumed to be acting in concert with its market makers.

16.   **C**   **Chapter 2, Section 7.4**

Firms must apply procedures and arrangements which provide for the prompt, fair and expeditious execution of client orders, relative to the other orders or trading interests of the firm. In particular, these should allow comparable client orders to be executed in the order in which they are received.

17.   **B**   **Chapter 1, Section 3.2.1**

Sections 979–985 of the Companies Act 2006 provides:

A. Sell-out rights – if a bidder has acquired 90% of the shares in a company in the course of a takeover offer, the minority shareholders have the right to require that the bidder acquires their shares within three months of the end of the bid.

B. Squeeze-out rights – if a bidder has acquired 90% of the voting rights to which his offer related, during the course of a takeover, he has the right to acquire the remaining minority shareholding, within three months of the end of the offer.

18.   **D**   **Chapter 2, Section 2.2**

The rules on inducements apply to both retail and professional clients, and apply regardless of a firm's conflicts of interest policy.

- For a third-party payment to be acceptable it must satisfy all of the following criteria:
- Be disclosed to the client prior to the provision of the service.
- Enhance the quality of the service that the firm is providing to the client.
- Not impair compliance with the firm's duty to act in the best interest of the client.

19. **D** **Chapter 1, Section 2.6.1**

The correct answer is D as there is a requirement for all firms to appoint someone to the compliance and oversight function.

Options A (partner function) and B (non-executive director) are governing functions. Option C is a customer-dealing function.

20. **D** **Chapter 6, Section 1.7**

In a bonus issue and a capitalisation issue no new funds are raised by the company. In an introduction, company shares are introduced to a market to allow its shareholders to trade in those shares and therefore no new capital is raised for the company. A placing involves offering new shares to institutional shareholders, in exchange for new capital for the issuer.

21. **B** **Chapter 2, Section 7.2**

Option B is correct; the other options are all specifically exempt from the requirement to assess suitability.

22. **A** **Chapter 1, Section 4.4**

Although the MLRO/NO is responsible for reporting suspicious transactions, they need only be sent to NCA. Employees within a firm who identify a suspicious transaction should report this to the firm's MLRO/NO, although this may, in some firms, be the same individual as the compliance officer.

Firms are required to appoint an MLRO/NO and have adequate processes and procedures to monitor and report suspicious transactions of all clients – both professional and retail.

23. **C** **Chapter 1, Section 2.2**

The third principle requires firms to have adequate risk management systems.

24. **D** **Chapter 1, Section 2.9**

The RDC may publish final notices on the FCA's website, and may withdraw or amend the permissions of an authorised firm, as well as imposing fines with no limit. However, it may not impose custodial sentences, which is a power of the courts in relation to criminal offences.

25. **B** **Chapter 4, Section 2.10**

Once a company is in an offer period (ie, once the existence of bid talks has been disclosed to the market) the disclosure requirements of the Takeover Code apply. These require disclosure of holdings in equity and securities convertible into equity, both of the offeree and of a paper offeror (ie, an offeror whose offer is in shares rather than in cash).

A shareholder in either company is required to disclose the existence of a 1% interest in the offeree/paper offeror at the outset, and then any acquisitions or disposals of interests, however small, throughout the offer period.

During the offer period, both the offeror and offeree must disclose any dealings as principal by themselves or their concert parties in the shares of the other.

26. **D** **Chapter 2, Section 5.3.2**

If the arrangements that a firm puts in place to manage potential conflicts of interest are insufficient to ensure, with reasonable confidence, that the risk of damage to the interests of a client can be prevented, the firm must clearly disclose the general nature and/or source of conflicts of interest to the client before undertaking business for/on behalf of them.

Disclosure must be made in a durable medium and include sufficient detail, taking into account the nature of the client, to enable that client to take an informed decision with respect to the service in the context of which the conflict of interest arises.

While disclosure of specific conflicts of interest is required under SYSC 10.1.8, an over-reliance on disclosure without adequate consideration to how conflicts may appropriately be managed is not permitted.

Therefore, the disclosure of a conflict of interest should be undertaken as a last resort, if its internal controls (managing conflicts) do not manage the risk of material damage to the client's best interests.

27. **D** **Chapter 2, Section 5.5**

In order for a firm to manage its conflicts in an appropriate manner, it must consider and implement, where appropriate, a number of options including information barriers (eg, Chinese walls) between different business units and departments, appropriate reporting lines, remuneration structures, segregation of duties and a policy of independence.

28. **D** **Chapter 2, Section 3.1.5**

The financial promotions rules are disapplied in some cases, notably certain communications. One such exemption is a communication by a company to its shareholders and its creditors. Others include communications made by a government, bank or financial market, and promotions made only to investment professionals.

All the other options are covered by the financial promotion rules.

29. **D** **Chapter 2, Section 1.2**

COBS 18.3 provides a list of provisions which generally apply to non-MiFID firms carrying on corporate finance business. These include client categorisation, inducements and personal account dealing but not providing product information.

30. **D** **Chapter 1, Section 3.6**

An AGM must be held no later than 15 months from the previous AGM.

Under Section 303 of the Companies Act, shareholders representing 5% or more of the voting rights in a company may convene a general meeting.

An ordinary resolution (to approve mostly routine business, such as the payment of a dividend) can be passed by a simple majority (ie, more than 50% of votes cast in favour).

A special resolution (for non-routine business, such as the disapplication of pre-emption rights or a change of name) requires 75% of votes cast to be passed.

31.   D   Chapter 1, Section 4.4

A firm's MLRO must report any suspicious activity to the NCA.

32.   C   Chapter 6, Section 2.4

A company seeking admission to AIM must appoint an NO and retain their services while admitted to AIM.

However, there are no minimum requirements for free float or market value. As AIM is not a regulated market (it is an exchange-regulated market) the company is only required to publish a prospectus if it is offering shares to a wide number of non-qualified investors (more than 100 in any EU member state). Otherwise, it can publish an admission document.

33.   B   Chapter 6, Section 1.6

Any company applying for a premium listing of its securities on the LSE main market must appoint a sponsor. There is no requirement for the sponsor to be an LSE member firm, but it must be a firm approved as a sponsor by the FCA. Additionally the company must appoint a sponsor to advise it on certain transactions, such as those requiring the production of a prospectus or Class 1 circular. Companies with a standard listing need only appoint a sponsor when applying to migrate up to premium listing.

34.   C   Chapter 1, Section 2.4.2

Following the review of its operations, the FCA has changed its focus on supervision to an outcomes-based risk-based approach to supervision. This means that it focuses its resources on mitigating those risks which pose a threat to the achievement of its single strategic and three operational objectives and that it has regard to the efficient and economic use of its resources.

35.   C   Chapter 2, Section 5.3.2

If a firm's arrangements to manage potential conflicts of interest are insufficient to ensure, with reasonable confidence, that the risk of damage to the interests of a client can be prevented, the firm must clearly disclose the general nature and source of conflict to the client before undertaking business for/on behalf of them.

Disclosure must be made in a durable medium, which is defined as paper or any instrument which enables the recipient to store information addressed personally to them in a way accessible for future reference for a period of time adequate for the purposes of the information. Therefore a verbal notification is not allowed.

36.   D   Chapter 4, Section 1.1.1

The Takeover Panel is an independent body whose function is to issue the City Code and to supervise and regulate takeovers and other matters to which the Code applies in accordance with the rules set out therein. It operates in close collaboration with the FCA. Its statutory status and powers are provided in the Companies Act 2006. It has the power to censure (publicly or privately) parties who breach the Code, but does not have the power to impose fines.

37. **B** **Chapter 5, Section 1.3.2**

All UK prospectuses are approved by the FCA, irrespective of where the issuer's securities are traded.

38. **D** **Chapter 3, Sections 1.1 and 1.2**

The UK Corporate Governance Code applies to all companies (both UK and non-UK) with a premium listing on the LSE main market. This therefore excludes those companies traded on AIM. The Code is seen as best practice to be applied on a comply or explain basis and is neither law nor a set of rules.

39. **B** **Chapter 6, Section 1.4**

For a company to be admitted to the Official List, the expected market value of its securities must be at least £700,000 for shares and £200,000 for debt securities. Its securities must also be admitted to trading on an RIE; its securities must be freely transferable and free from any lien; it must have adequate free float, ie, at least 25% of its shares must be available for public purchase; and it must have a three-year revenue-earning track record. There is no requirement for the company to have made profits during this time.

40. **B** **Chapter 4, Section 2.17**

A scheme of arrangement is an alternative method of launching a takeover bid that is commonly used for an agreed recommended offer. In a contractual offer, shareholders agree to sell their shares to the offeror. By contrast, under a scheme of agreement, shareholders must vote on the proposed transaction, including the exchange of their shares for some form of consideration.

The Takeover Code applies to any change of control however implemented, whether it is a contractual offer or a scheme of arrangement. A scheme will generally not be permitted for a mandatory offer.

41. **A** **Chapter 2, Section 7.3**

Option B is incorrect as the rules only apply to retail and professional clients; a firm trading as principal will normally be classified as an ECP, and the rules do not apply. C is incorrect because CIS operators are exempt from the best execution rules. D is also incorrect because retail and professional clients cannot opt out of the best execution rules.

The best execution rules under COBS require firms to execute orders on the terms that are most favourable to their client. Broadly, they apply if a firm owes contractual or agency obligations to its client and is acting on behalf of that client.

42. **B** **Chapter 1, Section 7.1**

The definition of market abuse behaviour includes the requirement that it must be likely to distort the market in the investment.

43. **B** **Chapter 6, Section 1.3.3**

The HGS market has UK regulated market status, and sits within the UK's Listing Regime.

44. **A** **Chapter 1, Section 1.2.6, Chapter 6, Section 1.2.2**

An RIE is an investment exchange that meets the standards required for exemption from the requirement for authorisation. An RIE operates one or more markets, which may include a regulated market and/or an MTF. A regulated market is one which meets the standards to be designated regulated market. An MTF may be operated by an RIE or may be operated by an authorised firm which is not an RIE.

45. **A** **Chapter 5, Section 1.3.3**

A prospectus must include the following: a summary, a registration document and a securities note. In practice these may be approved as three separate documents, or they may be combined and approved as a single document.

46. **A** **Chapter 1, Section 5.2.1**

Debt securities are caught under the insider dealing legislation; however, the other three options are not.

47. **B** **Chapter 1, Section 8.2.5**

A wide range of financial instruments are covered by MiFID. However, foreign exchange (except where related to the provision of an investment activity or service) and bank accounts are not covered.

48. **B** **Chapter 4, Section 2.16**

In a hostile bid, the offeree company's directors must post defence documents to all their shareholders by day 14. These include the directors' response to the offer, recommending shareholders to reject the offer.

49. **D** **Chapter 5, Section 1.1**

A prospectus is required when a company a) offers transferable securities to the public, or b) seeks admission for transferable securities to a regulated market in the UK. The main market of the LSE is a regulated market.

Exemptions are available. In particular, an exemption is available if the issue relates to less than 10% of the company's issued share capital in any rolling 12-month period, if the capital to be raised is under €2.5 million or if the offer is a bonus issue or relates to shares issued under an employee share scheme. The nature of the regulated market issuer is irrelevant; the Prospectus Rules exemptions for regulated market issuers apply equally to premium and standard issuers.

50. **B** **Chapter 1, Section 1.7**

A hedge fund manager needs to be authorised when it undertakes the activity of portfolio management. The others are exempt from the FSMA requirements when carrying on specific regulated activities. For instance, an appointed representative (or tied agent) will have a contract with an authorised firm, which allows them to carry on regulated activities, with the authorised firm accepting responsibility for the appointed representative's conduct in respect of the regulated activities undertaken.

51.   **B**   **Chapter 1, Section 1.2.2**

The FCA's powers, derived from FSMA, allow it to make rules. These fall under the headings of authorisation, supervision, discipline and enforcement, including the power to supervise authorised firms.

Syllabus Learning Map

Syllabus Unit/ Element		Chapter/ Section
Element 1	**The Regulatory Environment in the UK**	**Chapter 1**
1.1	**The Regulatory Infrastructure** On completion the candidate should:	
1.1.1	*understand* the European context of financial services regulation (ie, the role of European institutions, in particular the European Securities and Markets Authority (ESMA), and regulations/directives)	1.1
1.1.2	*know* the regulatory infrastructure generated by the Financial Services and Markets Act 2000 (FSMA 2000) and the Financial Services Act 2012 and the status and relationship between Her Majesty's Treasury (HM Treasury), the Bank of England (BoE), the Financial Policy Committee (FPC), the Prudential Regulation Authority (PRA) and the Financial Conduct Authority (FCA) and between the FCA and the Recognised Investment Exchanges (RIE), Recognised Overseas Investment Exchanges (ROIE), Designated Investment Exchanges (DIE), Recognised Clearing Houses (RCH), Designated Professional Bodies (DPB), regulated markets and Multilateral Trading Facilities (MTF)	1.2
1.1.3	*understand* the implications of the general prohibition (FSMA 2000 C.8, Part 2, S.19) • the general prohibition offences • enforceability of agreements entered into with an unauthorised person	1.3
1.1.4	*know* what regulated activities (FSMA 2000 Part II, Regulated Activities Order (RAO) 2001) constitute designated investment business in the UK	1.4
1.1.5	*know* which designated investments are covered by the Regulated Activities Order (RAO) 2001 (as amended)	1.5
1.1.6	*know* what are excluded activities in relation to designated investment business in the UK (PERG 2.8)	1.6
1.1.7	*know* who constitute exempt persons in relation to designated investment business in the UK (PERG 2.10)	1.7
1.2	**The Roles of the FCA and PRA** On completion the candidate should:	
1.2.1	*know* the FCA's general duties (Financial Services Act 2012 c. 21, Part 2, Section 6, 1B) and the PRA's general objective (Financial Services Act 2012 c. 21, Part 2, S.6, 2B)	2
1.2.2	*Know* the eight regulatory principles to be applied by both the FCA and PRA (Financial Services Act 2012 c. 21, Part 2, S.6, 3B)	2
1.2.3	*know* the powers of the FCA and the PRA with regard to rule making in respect of their powers regarding: • authorisation • supervision • enforcement • sanctions • disciplinary action	2

Syllabus Unit/ Element		Chapter/ Section
1.2.4	*understand* the importance of the Principles for Businesses (PRIN 1.1.2, 1.1.7, 2.1.1)	2.2
1.2.5	*understand* the approach of the FCA to supervision and the role of risk based supervision (SUP 1A.3)	2.4, 2.5
1.2.6	*know* the senior management responsibilities: • purpose (SYSC 1.2.1, 1.2.1A) • apportionment of responsibilities (SYSC 2.1.1) • recording the apportionment (SYSC 2.2.1) • systems and controls (SYSC 3.1.1) • compliance (SYSC 6.1.1–5), internal audit (SYSC 6.2.1, 6.2.1A) and risk functions (SYSC 7.1.2/3/5)	2.5
1.2.7	• *know* the Statements of Principle and Code of Practice for Approved Persons (APER 1.1A.1 1.2.3, 1.2.3A 2.1A,2 2.1B.2 3.1.1A, 3.1.1B-3.1.7A, 3.1.7B, 4.1-4.7)	2.3
1.2.8	*understand* the FCA's controlled functions (SUP 10A.4): • the five functional areas and the main roles within each • the four areas of significant influence functions (SUP 10A.5.1, 10A.6.1, 10A.7.1, 10A.8.1, 10A.9.1/2, 10A.10.1/3) • the requirement for FCA approval prior to appointment • the on-going requirement to be fit and proper • the consequences of a qualified versus 'clean' withdrawal on termination of employment (SUP 10A.12)	2.6
1.2.9	*understand* the obligations to notify the FCA (SUP 15.3)	2.6
1.2.10	*understand* the criteria applied to ensure approved persons are fit and proper to conduct investment business, with retail and professional clients (FIT 1.3, 2.1, 2.2 & 2.3)	2.7
1.2.11	*understand* the new Accountability Regime ('Senior Managers Regime') regime for banks – Senior Managers, Certificate Regime and Conduct Rules	2.8
1.2.12	*know how* the Senior Managers Regime applies to individuals, including approval by the PRA/FCA, 'fit and proper' certificates and the notification of breaches of the Conduct Rules	2.8
1.2.13	*know* the FCA's powers to require information (FSMA 2000 C.8, Part 11, S.165) and its investigatory powers (Enforcement Guide (EG) 3)	2.9
1.2.14	*know* the role, scope and consequences of the Regulatory Decisions Committee's (RDC) responsibility for decision making and its interaction with the FCA's Enforcement and Financial Crime Division (DEPP 1.2, 3.1–3.4, 4.1)	2.10

Syllabus Unit/ Element		Chapter/ Section
1.2.15	*know* the FCA's disciplinary powers with respect to (DEPP 2.2, 2.3, DEPP 2 Annex 1G, 2G, DEPP 5.1, EG 7.1-7.5, EG 7.10-7.19, EG 8, EG 9.3-9.18, EG 9.25-9.28, EG11): • authorised firms • approved persons/individuals subject to the new Accountability Regime for Banks (Senior Managers Regime, Certificate Regime & Conduct Rules) • other persons directly or indirectly involved	2.10
1.2.16	*know* the role of the Tax and Chancery Chamber of the Upper Tribunal	2.11
1.3	**Company Law** On completion the candidate should:	
1.3.1	*know* the provisions contained in the Companies Act 2006 relating to Schemes of Arrangement and reconstruction (s.895-904, 907, 912, 922)	3.1
1.3.2	*know* the provisions contained in the Companies Act 2006 relating to 'squeeze out' and 'sell out' (s.974–985)	3.2
1.3.3	*know* the provisions contained in the Companies Act 2006 relating to the reduction of share capital (s.641)	3.3
1.3.4	*know* the provisions contained in the Companies Act 2006 relating to pre-emption rights (CA85 s.89 and CA06 s.561, 565–566, 568)	3.2
1.3.5	*know* the provisions contained in the Companies Act 2006 relating to investigations by inspectors (s.1035–1039)	3.4
1.3.6	*know* the provisions contained in the Companies Act 2006 relating to financial assistance for the acquisition of a public company's own shares (s.678–680)	3.5
1.3.7	*know* the main statutory rights of shareholders in the Companies Act 2006 (s.303–306, 314–315, 338–340, 994–998)	3.6
1.3.8	*know* the provisions contained in the Companies Act 2006 relating to company meetings (s.284, 303–305, 307–310, 318–319)	3.6
1.3.9	*know* the provisions contained in the Companies Act 2006 relating to notices by a company requiring information about interests in its shares (S.793–795)	3.7
1.3.10	*know* the provisions contained in the Companies Act 2006 relating to requirements to be a public company (s.90, 92, 94)	3.8
1.3.11	*know* the provisions contained in the Companies Act 2006 relating to restrictions on public offers by a private company (s.755, 760)	3.8
1.3.12	*know* the duties of directors, in particular in relation to conflicts of interest (s.170–175)	3.9
1.3.13	*understand* the relevance of local law when dealing with companies established outside the UK	3.10

Syllabus Unit/ Element		Chapter/ Section
1.4	**Money Laundering, Counter Terrorism and Bribery** On completion the candidate should:	
1.4.1	*know* that the UK legislation on money laundering and counter terrorism funding can be found in the Proceeds of Crime Act (POCA) 2002, the current Money Laundering Regulations 2007, Terrorism Act 2000, Counter Terrorism Act 2008 (s.7) and that the guidance to these provisions can be found in the Joint Money Laundering Steering Group (JMLSG) Guidance Notes	4.1
1.4.2	*understand* the terms 'money laundering', 'criminal conduct' and 'criminal property' and the application of money laundering to all crimes (POCA 2002 s.340)	4.1
1.4.3	*know* the obligations placed on senior management in relation to anti-money laundering regulation, including the obligation to arrange regular money laundering training for individuals	4.3
1.4.4	*understand* the main offences set out in POCA 2002, Part 7 s.327, 328, 329, 330, 333 (assistance, ie, concealing, arrangements, acquisition, use and possession; failure to report; tipping off)	4.2
1.4.5	*understand* the implications of Part 7 regarding the objective test in relation to reporting suspicious transactions	4.2
1.4.6	*understand* that appropriate disclosure (internal for staff and to the National Crime Agency (NCA) for the firm) is a defence	4.2
1.4.7	*know* the maximum penalties for committing the offences set out in POCA 2002	4.2
1.4.8	*understand*: • the necessity to obtain documentation proving identity and to record the Know Your Customer (KYC) process • the necessity to verify identity and the existence and nature of the entity • the types of documents that would be appropriate and the consequences of failure to obtain such KYC documentation	4.3
1.4.9	*understand* the requirement to identify both source of funds and source of wealth	4.3
1.4.10	*understand* the importance of being able to recognise a suspicious transaction and the requirement for staff to report to the Money Laundering Reporting Officer (MLRO) and for the firm to report to the National Crime Agency (NCA)	4.4
1.4.11	*understand* the difference between laundering the proceeds of crime and the financing of terrorist acts	4.5
1.4.12	*understand* the purpose of Her Majesty's Treasury's (HM Treasury) sanctions list	4.5
1.4.13	*understand* the main offences set out in the Bribery Act 2010 and the penalties for committing the offences set out in that Act	4.6

Syllabus Unit/ Element		Chapter/ Section
1.5	**Insider Dealing** On completion the candidate should:	
1.5.1	*understand* the meaning of the terms 'inside information' and 'insider' (Criminal Justice Act 1993 (CJA 1993) s.52/56/57/58)	5.1
1.5.2	*understand* the offences described in the Criminal Justice Act 1993 and the securities to which it applies (CJA 1993 s.54, Schedule 2)	5.2
1.5.3	*know* the penalties for the criminal offence of insider dealing (CJA 1993 s.61(1))	5.2
1.5.4	*know* the general and special defences available with regard to insider dealing (CJA 1993 s. 53 and Schedule 1 paragraphs 1-5)	5.3
1.6	**1.6 The Financial Services Act 2012 Part 7** On completion the candidate should:	
1.6.1	*know* the purpose, provisions, offences and defences of the Financial Services Act 2012 Part 7 in relation to misleading statements and impressions	6.1, 7.2
1.7	**Market Abuse** On completion the candidate should:	
1.7.1	*know* the statutory offences of market abuse (FSMA 2000, C.8 Part 8, s. 118(2)-(8) , s.123(1))	7.1
1.7.2	*know* the due diligence defence (FSMA 2000, C.8 Part 8 s.123(2))	7.3
1.7.3	*know* the penalties for market abuse	7.3
1.7.4	*understand* the enforcement regime for market abuse (Market Conduct (MAR) 1.1.4-1.1.6, 1.2.20-1.2.21)	7.3
1.7.5	*know* 'statutory exceptions': Takeover Code, FCA Rules, buy-back and price stabilisation	7.7
1.7.6	*know* the status of the FCA's Code of Market Conduct (MAR 1)	7.6
1.7.7	*understand* when price stabilisation is used (MAR 2.1.5)	7.7
1.7.8	*know* the obligation to report suspicious transactions (SUP 15.10)	7.8
1.8	**Markets in Financial Instruments Directive (MiFID)** On completion the candidate should:	
1.8.1	*know* the purpose and scope of MiFID including: • the concept of passporting within the EEA • the categories of MiFID financial instruments • the responsibilities of the home and host state regulators	8

Syllabus Unit/ Element		Chapter/ Section
Element 2	**FCA Conduct of Business Sourcebook**	**Chapter 2**
2.1	**The Application and General Provisions of the FCA's Conduct of Business Sourcebook to Corporate Finance Business** On completion the candidate should:	
2.1.1	*know* the application of COBS to corporate finance business (COBS 1.1 (and Annex 1), COBS 18.3)	1.1
2.2	**Rules Applying to all Firms Conducting Designated Investment Business** On completion the candidate should:	
2.2.1	*know* the requirement for a firm to act honestly, fairly and professionally in accordance with the best interests of its client (COBS 2.1)	2.1
2.2.2	*know* the application and purpose of the rule on prohibition of inducements (COBS 2.3.1–2.3.9)	2.2
2.2.3	*know* the rules, guidance and evidential provisions regarding reliance on others (COBS 2.4.4–2.4.10)	2.3
2.3	**The Financial Promotion Rules** On completion the candidate should:	
2.3.1	*know* the application of the rules on communication to clients, including financial promotions and the firm's responsibilities for appointed representatives (COBS 4.1)	3.1
2.3.2	*know* the implications of FSMA 2000, C.8, Part 2, s.21, the purpose of the financial promotion rules and the relationship with Principles 6 and 7 (PRIN 2.1.1)	3.1
2.3.3	*know* the rule on fair, clear and not misleading communications and the guidance on fair, clear and not misleading financial promotions (COBS 4.2)	3.1
2.3.4	*know* the rule on identifying promotions as such (COBS 4.3)	3.1
2.3.5	*know* the main exemptions to the financial promotion rules in the Financial Promotions Order	3.1
2.3.6	*know* the general rule in connection with communicating with retail clients (COBS 4.5); the rules on past, simulated past and future performance (COBS 4.6); and the rule on financial promotions containing offers or invitations (COBS 4.7)	3.2
2.3.7	*know* the rules on unwritten promotions; the restriction on cold calling (COBS 4.8); and the rule in relation to financial promotions for overseas persons (COBS 4.9)	3.2
2.3.8	*know* the requirement for approving financial promotions and the circumstances in which it is permissible to rely on another firm's confirmation of compliance (COBS 4.10)	3.2

Syllabus Unit/ Element		Chapter/ Section
2.4	**Client Categorisation** On completion the candidate should:	
2.4.1	*understand* client status (PRIN 1.2.1–1.2.3, Glossary, COBS 3) in particular: • the application of the rules on client categorisation (COBS 3.1) • the definition of 'client' (COBS 3.2) • the nature of a corporate finance contact and a venture capital contact (COBS 3.2.1, 3.2.2) • the definitions of retail client (COBS 3.4); professional client (COBS 3.5) and eligible counterparty (COBS 3.6)	4.1
2.4.2	*understand* client status (PRIN 1.2.1–1.2.3, Glossary, COBS 3) in particular: • when a person is acting as agent for another person (COBS 2.4.1–2.4.3) • the rule on classifying elective professional clients (COBS 3.5.3– 3.5.9) • the rule on elective eligible counterparties (COBS 3.6.4– 3.6.6) • when it is necessary to provide clients with a higher level of protection (COBS 3.7) • the requirement to provide notifications of client categorisation (COBS 3.3)	4.2
2.4.3	*know* the procedures and record-keeping requirements in relation to client categorisation (COBS 3.8)	4.3
2.5	**Conflicts of Interest (SYSC 10, PRIN 2.1)** On completion the candidate should:	
2.5.1	*understand* the concept of conflicts of interest and the application and purpose of the rules and procedures on conflicts of interest (SYSC 10.1)	5.1
2.5.2	*understand* the circumstances in which conflicts of interest can arise and types of conflicts particularly relevant to corporate finance (SYSC 10.1.3–10.1.5, 10.1.13–10.1.15)	5.2
2.5.3	*know* the rules on managing, disclosing and recording conflicts of interest (SYSC 10.1.6–10.1.9)	5.3
2.5.4	*understand* the rule that requires a conflicts policy and the contents of the policy (SYSC 10.1.10–10.1.12)	5.4
2.5.5	*understand* how to manage conflicts of interest to ensure the fair treatment of clients (SYSC 10.2) including for example information barriers	5.5
2.5.6	*understand* the rules on managing conflicts of interest in the context of investment research and research recommendations (COBS 12.1, 12.3.1–4, 12.4.1)	5.6
2.6	**Personal Account Dealing (COBS 11.7)** On completion the candidate should:	
2.6.1	*understand* the application and purpose of the personal account dealing rules and the restrictions on personal account dealing (COBS 11.7.1– 11.7.3)	6.1

Syllabus Unit/ Element		Chapter/ Section
2.6.2	*know* the arrangements required to comply with the personal account dealing rules including the notification requirements and exceptions regarding personal account dealing (COBS 11.7.4– 11.7.7)	6.2
2.7	**Advising and Dealing (COBS 9 & COBS 11)** On completion the candidate should:	
2.7.1	*understand* the requirement to provide suitable advice (COBS 9.2.1– 9.2.7)	7
2.7.2	*understand* the requirement to provide best execution (COBS 11.1.6, 11.2.1, 11.2.6–11.2.7) and the rules on client order handling (COBS 11.3.1–11.3.6)	7.3, 7.4

Element 3	Corporate Governance and Business Ethics	Chapter 3
3.1	**The UK Corporate Governance Code** On completion the candidate should:	
3.1.1	*understand* the main principles of the UK Corporate Governance Code relating to: • leadership • effectiveness • accountability • remuneration • relation with shareholders	1
3.1.2	*understand* the 'comply or explain' approach to corporate governance	1.2
3.2	**The UK Stewardship Code** On completion, the candidate should:	
3.2.1	*understand* the principles of the UK Stewardship Code	1.3
3.3	**Chartered Institute for Securities and Investment's Code of Conduct** On completion the candidate should:	
3.3.1	*know* the Chartered Institute for Securities & Investment's Code of Conduct	2
3.3.2	*be able* to apply the Code of Conduct to the provision of corporate finance advice	2

Element 4	Takeovers and Mergers	Chapter 4
4.1	**Relevant Bodies** On completion the candidate should:	
4.1.1	*understand* the role of the Panel on Takeovers and Mergers (the Takeover Panel or PTM) in takeovers and mergers	1.1
4.1.2	*understand* the role of the UK and EU competition authorities and the Pensions Regulator in respect of takeovers and mergers	1.2

Syllabus Unit/ Element		Chapter/ Section
4.2	**The Takeover Code** On completion the candidate should:	
4.2.1	*understand* the legal nature and purpose of the Takeover Code (Section 2 of the Introduction)	2.1
4.2.2	*understand* the duty to consult the Takeover Panel (s.6(b) of the Introduction)	2.1, 2.2
4.2.3	*know* the companies, transactions and persons subject to the Takeover Code (Section 3 of the Introduction)	2.2
4.2.4	*know* the six general principles	2.3
4.2.5	*know* the definitions of 'acting in concert', 'dealings', 'interests in securities' and 'relevant securities'	2.4
4.2.6	*know* Rules 2, 7.1, 17.1 – Announcements	2.5
4.2.7	*know* Rule 3 – Independent Advice	2.6
4.2.8	*know* Rule 4 – Prohibited Dealings	2.7
4.2.9	*know* Rule 5 – Timing Restrictions on Acquisitions	2.8
4.2.10	*know* Rules 6, 11 – Minimum Level and Nature of Consideration to be Offered	2.9
4.2.11	*know* Rules 8, 24.4, 25.4 – Disclosure of Dealings and Interests	2.10
4.2.12	*know* Rules 9, 37 and Appendix 1 – The Mandatory Offer, Redemption or Purchase by a Company of its Own Securities and 'Whitewashes'	2.11
4.2.13	*know* Rule 13 – Conditions and Pre-Conditions	2.12
4.2.14	*know* Rules 19, 20 – Information	2.13
4.2.15	*know* Rule 21 – Restrictions on Frustrating Action	2.14
4.2.16	*know* Rule 28 – Profit Forecasts and Quantified Financial Benefits Statements	2.15
4.2.17	*know* Rules 31–35 – Timing and Revision	2.16
4.2.18	*know* Appendix 7 – Schemes of Arrangement	2.17

Element 5	Prospectuses	Chapter 5
5.1	**Prospectus Rules** On completion the candidate should:	
5.1.1	*understand* when a prospectus approved by the FCA in accordance with the Prospectus Rules (PR) will be required	1.1
5.1.2	*know* which offers to the public are exempt and when an admission of shares to a regulated market is exempt (PR 1.2)	1.1
5.1.3	*understand* the interaction between the Prospectus Rules and the Financial Promotion regime (COBS 4)	1.2

Syllabus Unit/ Element		Chapter/ Section
5.1.4	*understand* the requirement to prepare, have approved (PR 3.1.7–3.1.8) and publish (PR 3.1.10) a prospectus (PR 3.1.1, 3.1.3)	1.3

Element 6	Equity Capital Markets	Chapter 6
6.1	**Regulation of UK Equity Capital Markets** On completion the candidate should:	
6.1.1	*understand* the FCA's role as the competent authority in the UK in the form of the United Kingdom Listing Authority (UKLA) and the purpose of the listing rules (LR) and the disclosure transparency rules (DTR)	1.1
6.1.2	*understand* the differences between a regulated market, a Recognised Investment Exchange (RIE) and a Regulated Market and a Multilateral Trading Facility (MTF)	1.2
6.1.3	*understand* the key differences between premium listing and standard listing	1.1, 2.8
6.1.4	*know* the requirements to be admitted to the High Growth Segment (HGS)	1.3
6.1.5	*understand* the Listing Principles (LR 7) including the guidance on Listing Principle 2 with regards to procedures, systems and controls. (LR 7.2.2)	1.3
6.1.6	*understand* the key requirements for listing (LR 2.2)	1.4
6.1.7	*understand* an issuer's obligation to disclose inside information (DTR 2.2)	1.5
6.1.8	*understand* when an issuer may delay the public disclosure of inside information (DTR 2.5)	1.5
6.1.9	*understand* how an issuer must control access to inside information including the requirement to draw up insider lists (DTR 2.6, 2.8)	1.5
6.1.10	*understand*: • the requirement for a company with a premium listing to appoint a sponsor (LR 8.2) • the role of a sponsor generally • the role of a sponsor on a transaction (LR 8.3, 8.4)	1.6
6.1.11	*understand* the main methods of bringing shares to listing and the differences between them, eg, introduction, offer for sale, offer for subscription, placing, rights issue, open offer and vendor consideration placing	1.7
6.1.12	*understand* the vote holder and issuer notification rules (DTR 5)	1.8
6.1.13	*understand* the class tests for proposed transactions entered into by companies with a premium listing (LR 10.2.2, 10.2.3)	1.9
6.2	**The rules specific to the Alternative Investment Market (AIM)** On completion the candidate should:	
6.2.1	*understand* the status of AIM as an 'exchange-regulated market' and a prescribed market	2.1
6.2.2	*know* the criteria for admission to AIM	2.2

Syllabus Unit/ Element		Chapter/ Section
6.2.3	*know* that AIM companies must comply with the AIM Rules for Companies and, when appropriate, the PR and DTR	2.3
6.2.4	*know* the requirement for AIM companies to appoint a nominated adviser (nomad) and a broker	2.4
6.2.5	*know* the duties of the nomad and that the nomad must comply with the AIM Rules for nomads	2.5
6.2.6	*understand* when an AIM company will be required to issue a prospectus complying with the PRs	2.6
6.2.7	*know* the requirement for the management and disclosure of price sensitive information (Rule 11)	2.7

Examination Specification

Each examination paper is constructed from a specification that determines the weightings that will be given to each unit. The specification is given below.

It is important to note that the numbers quoted may vary slightly from examination to examination as there is some flexibility to ensure that each examination has a consistent level of difficulty. However, the number of questions tested in each unit should not change by more than 2.

Element number	Element	Questions
1	The Regulatory Environment in the UK	20
2	FCA Conduct of Business Sourcebook	10
3	Corporate Governance and Business Ethics	2
4	Takeovers and Mergers	8
5	Prospectuses	3
6	Equity Capital Markets	7
Total		**50**

Assessment Structure

A one-hour examination, consisting of 50 multiple-choice questions.

Candidates sitting the exam by Computer Based Testing will have, in addition, up to 10% additional questions as trial questions that will not be separately identified and do not contribute to the result. Candidates will be given proportionately more time to complete the test.

CISI Associate (ACSI) Membership can work for you...

Studying for a CISI qualification is hard work and we're sure you're putting in plenty of hours, but don't lose sight of your goal!

This is just the first step in your career; there is much more to achieve!

The securities and investments industry attracts ambitious and driven individuals. You're probably one yourself and that's great, but on the other hand you're almost certainly surrounded by lots of other people with similar ambitions.

So how can you stay one step ahead during these uncertain times?

Entry Criteria:
Pass in either:
- Investment Operations Certificate (IOC), IFQ, ICWIM, Capital Markets in, eg, Securities, Derivatives, Advanced Certificates; or
- one CISI Diploma/Masters in Wealth Management paper

Joining Fee: £25 or free if applying via prefilled application form   **Annual Subscription (pro rata):** £125

Using your new CISI qualification* to become an Associate (ACSI) member of the Chartered Institute for Securities & Investment could well be the next important career move you make this year, and help you maintain your competence.

Join our global network of over 40,000 financial services professionals and start enjoying both the professional and personal benefits that CISI membership offers. Once you become a member you can use the prestigious ACSI designation after your name and even work towards becoming personally chartered.

* ie, Investment Operations Certificate (IOC), IFQ, ICWIM, Capital Markets

Benefits in Summary...
- Use of the CISI CPD Scheme
- Unlimited free CPD seminars, webcasts, podcasts and online training tools
- Highly recognised designatory letters
- Unlimited free attendance at CISI Professional Forums
- CISI publications including *S&I Review* and *Change – The Regulatory Update*
- 20% discount on all CISI conferences and training courses
- Invitation to CISI Annual Lecture
- Select Benefits – our exclusive personal benefits portfolio

The ACSI designation will provide you with access to a range of member benefits, including Professional Refresher where there are currently over 60 modules available on subjects including Behavioural Finance, Cybercrime and Conduct Risk. CISI TV is also available to members, allowing you to catch up on the latest CISI events, whilst earning valuable CPD hours.

Plus many other networking opportunities which could be invaluable for your career.

Professional Refresher

Self-testing elearning modules to refresh your knowledge, meet regulatory and firm requirements, and earn CPD hours.

Professional Refresher is a training solution to help you remain up-to-date with industry developments, maintain regulatory compliance and demonstrate continuing learning.

This popular online learning tool allows self-administered refresher testing on a variety of topics, including the latest regulatory changes.

There are currently over 60 modules available which address UK and international issues. Modules are reviewed by practitioners frequently and new topics are added to the suite on a regular basis.

Benefits to firms:
- Learning and tests can form part of business T&C programme
- Learning and tests kept up-to-date and accurate by the CISI
- Relevant and useful – devised by industry practitioners
- Access to individual results available as part of management overview facility, 'Super User'
- Records of staff training can be produced for internal use and external audits
- Cost-effective – no additional charge for CISI members
- Available to non-members

Benefits to individuals:
- Comprehensive selection of topics across industry sectors
- Modules are frequently reviewed and updated by industry experts
- New topics introduced regularly
- Free for members
- Successfully passed modules are recorded in your CPD log as Active Learning
- Counts as structured learning for RDR purposes
- On completion of a module, a certificate can be printed out for your own records

The full suite of Professional Refresher modules is free to CISI members or £250 for non-members. Modules are also available individually. To view a full list of Professional Refresher modules visit:

cisi.org/refresher

If you or your firm would like to find out more contact our Client Relationship Management team:

+ 44 20 7645 0670
crm@cisi.org

For more information on our elearning products, contact our Customer Support Centre on +44 20 7645 0777, or visit our website at cisi.org/study

Feedback to the CISI

Have you found this workbook to be a valuable aid to your studies? We would like your views, so please email us at learningresources@cisi.org with any thoughts, ideas or comments.

Accredited Training Partners

Support for examination students studying for the Chartered Institute for Securities & Investment (CISI) Qualifications is provided by several Accredited Training Partners (ATPs), including Fitch Learning and BPP. The CISI's ATPs offer a range of face-to-face training courses, distance learning programmes, their own learning resources and study packs which have been accredited by the CISI. The CISI works in close collaboration with its ATPs to ensure they are kept informed of changes to CISI examinations so they can build them into their own courses and study packs.

CISI Workbook Specialists Wanted

Workbook Authors

Experienced freelance authors with finance experience, and who have published work in their area of specialism, are sought. Responsibilities include:

- Updating workbooks in line with new syllabuses and any industry developments
- Ensuring that the syllabus is fully covered

Workbook Reviewers

Individuals with a high-level knowledge of the subject area are sought. Responsibilities include:

- Highlighting any inconsistencies against the syllabus
- Assessing the author's interpretation of the workbook

Workbook Technical Reviewers

Technical reviewers provide a detailed review of the workbook and bring the review comments to the panel. Responsibilities include:

- Cross-checking the workbook against the syllabus
- Ensuring sufficient coverage of each learning objective

Workbook Proofreaders

Proofreaders are needed to proof workbooks both grammatically and also in terms of the format and layout. Responsibilities include:

- Checking for spelling and grammar mistakes
- Checking for formatting inconsistencies

If you are interested in becoming a CISI external specialist call:
+44 20 7645 0609

or email:
externalspecialists@cisi.org

For bookings, orders, membership and general enquiries please contact our Customer Support Centre on +44 20 7645 0777, or visit our website at cisi.org